The Art of Modern

Custom
Knifemaking

100 Custom Knife Related
Projects In the Making

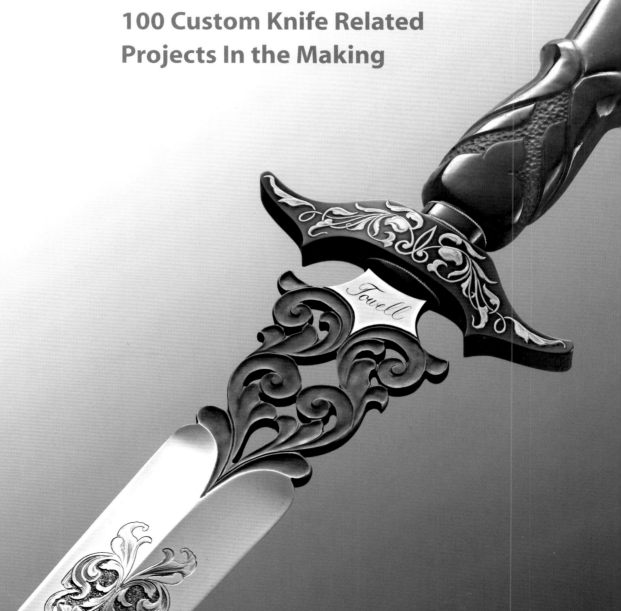

The Art of Modern

Custom Knifemaking

100 Custom Knife Related Projects In the Making

Dr. David Darom

Series producer
Paolo Saviolo

Biography Editor
Dennis Greenbaum

Photography
Jim (Coop) Cooper, SharpByCoop.com
Eric Eggly, PointSeven Studios, Inc.
Tomo Hasegawa, Francesco Pachì, Dr. Fred Carter,
Dewald Reiners, Alain Miville-Deschênes, Chris
Marchetti, Dennis Greenbaum, Mitch Lum, Oleg
Yermolaiov, Mike Draper, Kim Aaron Green, Avi Mor,
Johan Pretorius, Angela Ellard, Loretta Jakubiec,
Hilton Purvis, Lynda Horn, Helmut Kempe, Brady
Whitcomb, Owen Wood, Sue Broadwell, Phil Roach,
Kim Davis, Jim Weyer, Dave Thurber, Nir Darom
and Dr. David Darom

CHARTWELL
BOOKS, INC.

All texts were written by the artists and edited by
Dr. David Darom

Photography:
The photographers whose work is depicted throughout this book hold the copyrights to the images they created.
They authorized the author to digitally manipulate the original backgrounds, creating new ones for the book.

Digital image processing: Dr. David Darom and Nir Darom
Book Design: Nomi Morag, Jerusalem, Israel
Copyeditor: Evelyn Katrak, Jerusalem, Israel
Indigo proofs: Panorama Ltd., Jerusalem, Israel. info@panorama.co.il
Color conversions: Ya'acov Laloum, Jerusalem, Israel

Each knifemaker is granted the use of parts or all of the material in their section for their own needs, providing
this book is quoted as their source.

© 2006 White Star S.p.A.
Via Candido Sassone, 22/24
13100 Vercelli, Italy
www.whitestar.it

This edition published in 2008 by
CHARTWELL BOOKS, INC.
A division of BOOK SALES, INC.
114 Northfield Avenue
Edison, New Jersey 08837
USA

ISBN 13: 978-0-7858-2359-9
ISBN 10: 0-7858-2359-X
REPRINTS:
1 2 3 4 5 6   12 11 10 09 08
Printed in China

Front cover:
Buster Warenski, "Fire and Ice", 1995

The third knife in Warenski's Legacy Series, was designed with rubies and diamonds, hence its name, "Fire and Ice". The 8"
(203 mm) blade is made of work-hardened 18k gold. The handle is rutilated quartz crystal with light reflecting golden rutile
crystals. All the fittings and the sheath are 18k gold sculpted and engraved. In all, 28 ounces of 18k gold, 22 rubies (4.25
carats) and 75 diamonds (7 carats). The red gouache-type enameling adds the final "blaze" to the "fire". Engraving by Julie
Warenski. Overall length 13" (330 mm).
In memory of Buster Warenski, a wonderful man and a great knifemaker (1942-2005).

Back cover:
A selection of finished art knives that are shown in-the-making on various sections throughout the book.

Title page, from the left:
"September 11, 2001, WTC Knives", 2005
Steve Johnson's "Survival" Knife, 2005
Blade made of case hardened steel from a fallen World Trade Center "I" beam and marked "ONE OF SEVEN". Hilt
and oval inlay (marked "09-11-01") made of bronze from the Sphere situated in the World Trade Center Plaza.
Handle is sambar stag. Overall length 9 1/4" (235 mm).
Dietmar Kressler's "Survival" Knife, 2005
Blade made of Damascus combined with WTC "I" beam steal. An oval billet, set into the choil, is marked "WTC"
on one side and 09-11-01 on the other. Handle slabs are legal elephant ivory. Overall length 9 1/4" (235 mm).
Ron Lake's Folder, 2005
Fallen Bronze from the WTC Plaza Sphere was used for the handle, set with small "I" beam shaped bits of steel,
cut from larger pieces. 8 notches cut into the pivot pin represent the 7 towers that collapsed and the Sphere.
Overall length 6 5/8" (168 mm). From the collection of Louis De Santis, USA

First published in a limited edition of 1500 copies, June 2006

Table of Contents

Preface

Opposite from the top:
The Art of Modern Custom Knifemaking
Two examples of exquisite custom knife artistry from the collection of Ed Wormser, USA.
"Semi-Skinner", 2001
Made by Bob Loveless (USA) and beautifully engraved by Manrico Torcoli. Overall length 8" (203 mm).
"Tail-Lock Interframe", 1990
Made by Ron Lake (USA). Engraving and scrimshaw flawlessly executed by Francesco Amatori. Overall length 7" (178 mm).

This is the third in what has become a series of high-quality books on the wondrous art of custom knifemaking. Talk about this book began late one night in a hotel room, across the street from the Cobb Galleria in Atlanta, Georgia, the long-time location of the world famous Blade Show. We were there for the 2004 show, and soon after we had arrived we began talking about the possibility of producing a world-class book, that would offer a closer look at what goes into the making of a custom knife. Not intended as a "how-to book", this book was conceived instead as a way of providing a brief but comprehensive glimpse into the art of knifemaking, in the hope that the reader might come away with a much greater appreciation for the skill and artistry required to make the "oldest tool in the world".

When this book was no more than just an idea, David was still deeply involved in the production of his second knife book, Art and Design in Modern Custom Fixed-Blade Knives. It was not due to be released until the spring of the following year and he still had a lot of work ahead of him. And yet here we were already talking about concepts for a third book. When one takes into consideration the huge number of participants, the thousands of photographs that need to be examined, edited and retouched, each with their own explanatory caption; and all the articles, which further help to educate and intrigue the reader - these books are a huge undertaking. Just the number of man-hours required to establish and maintain contact with all the participants and coordinate all the necessary correspondence can prove to be a formidable task.

Our responsibilities were split, with David bearing the brunt of the burden by handling all the creative aspects and overseeing production and quality control, and Dennis being charged with contacting most North American knifemakers, working out arrangements with all the participants and being responsible for a portion of the text.

On the left:
Creating a Book, 2005
The setup where three books on the world of custom knives and knifemaking were created. Dr. David Darom with his G5 Apple Macintosh, and its superb 23" Apple Flat Panel monitor, a Nikon Super CoolScan 5000 true 4000 dpi negative and transparency scanner, a flatbed scanner, the Epson Archival 2100 high quality printer and the combined fax, copy machine and laser printer.

Opposite:
Shane Taylor, USA
Born in 1962, in Montana, Shane started experimenting with Damascus at the age of 23 and has been hooked ever since. An ABS Mastersmith, specializing in Mosaic Damascus folders and bowies, he is also one of the founders of the Montana Knifemakers Association. www.taylorknives.com
"Reign of Evil", 2005
This double-action folding knife is the third in Shane Taylor's "Good Vs. Evil" series. The story of this knife is evil reaching its zenith. There are four Mosaic Damascus demons in the blade, and another Mosaic demon (on the handle) is encircled with flames made of carved mammoth ivory and gold. This is considered a double window frame, with the Mosaic underneath ivory, which is inlaid under the steel of the handle. The entire piece is nitre-blued and inlaid with 24k gold. The thumb stud is a carved, gold inlaid hand. The back bar features a very intricate gold inlaid design, both inside and out. Overall length 10 1/2" (267 mm).

Most of the pictures shown in this book were photographed by the makers themselves, documenting steps involved in the process of making the knife for their section. This also includes most of the pictures of their finished knives as well as of the related artwork! The level of photography achieved was possible in most cases only after many hours of coaching and guiding by David, by phone and by email, not to mention the industriousness and enthusiasm on the part of the makers.

From the moment of the book's inception, David and Dennis spent countless hours of exciting communication with makers around the world, and then David devoted over 2,000 hours of his time working on the computer - the amount of time required to create this one-of-a-kind encyclopedic volume, with over 1,500 original never-before-published photographs. The texts, comments and picture captions were written by the makers (nearly 80,000 words) and kept, wherever possible, in their own words, allowing them to relate to the reader on a more personal level.

In addition to featuring those knifemakers who are more established and renowned for their work, we hoped this book would also provide a venue for new and up-and-coming knifemakers. We feel we have achieved a good balance of the two. These knifemakers were spread out over all parts of the globe. And just as diverse as their locales around the world are their techniques.

As you look through the following pages you will find no two methods exactly alike! Indeed, if there is one thing plainly evident throughout this book, when it comes to making a knife, there is clearly more than one way to "skin a cat".

We would like to thank the many friends who helped us along the road up to the moment this enormous project was completed. Our deepest thanks go to world-class knife collectors Don Guild (Hawaii), Dr. Larry Marton (USA), Ed Wormser (USA) and Yehoshua Greenfeld (Israel), who shared with us valuable knowledge and advice. Special thanks are due to Mrs. Nomi Morag (Israel) for her painstakingly accurate and highly professional work in designing the book and putting together the thousands of pictures, captions and texts into one magnificent volume. To Nir Darom (Israel) and his wife Naomi for their valuable contribution and professional advice regarding digital manipulation of the images for the book. To Paolo Saviolo (Italy), the true gentleman and connoisseur of the arts, who has now, after publishing and distributing this third book in the series, become like family to us all. Many thanks are due to Jeff Velasco (Brazil), for his great help in presenting the exciting sections of four Brazilian knifemakers, to Hilton Purvis (South Africa) for coordinating and helping out with the sections of the South African knifemakers and to Nestor Benitez (Argentina) for coordinating and sending the material for the Argentinean knifemakers sections.

To our wives, Tehiya Darom and Michelle Greenbaum, who were behind us all the way and were our best critics. And of course our undying gratitude goes out to those knifemakers, from all parts of the globe, who are always a source of admiration and inspiration.

Opposite, from left:

Owen Wood and Amayak Stepanyan
"Collaboration knives"
Detail of bolsters on a small folding dagger made by Owen Wood and engraved in an Art Deco theme by Amayak Stepanyan.

"Two Warnecliff Folders", 2005
Made by Owen Wood, the blades are a composite of Explosion pattern Damascus and dramatic angled layers of nickel and 1095. One with stainless scales engraved in deep relief with Art Nouveau ribbons and scrolls by Amayak Stepanyan. The other with Mother-of-Pearl and Black-lip pearl scales and 18k gold bolsters engraved in Art Deco style by Amayak. Gold screws and bale. Blade lengths are 2" (50 mm) and 2 5/16 " (60 mm).

"Three Folding Daggers", 2005
Made by Owen Wood. Composite blades with a fine "herringbone" center panel, wrapped with tight Explosion pattern Damascus and Black-lip pearl scales. The front and rear bolsters in steel and in 18k gold, dramatically engraved in deep relief by Amayak Stepanyan, in his favorite Art Deco themes. Blade lengths are 3" (75 mm) and 3 5/32" (80 mm).

Dr. David Darom
June 2006

Dennis Greenbaum

Opposite, from the top:
The 2005 Chicago Custom Knife Show
In its second year, this show has become one of the top knife shows in the USA. Over one hundred of the world's best knife makers from 5 continents take part in this event that is promoted by Ed and Cathy Wormser. www.chicagocustomknifes how.com
The 2005 Art Knife Invitational (AKI)
The Art Knife Invitational, a biannual show held in San Diego (California), is totally unlike any knife show in the world. Attended by an invitation only audience, it is host to 25 of the world's most respected knife makers. They display between four and eight knives each to a select group of collectors, who drop bid cards in boxes adjacent to each knife. The bidding/buying is complete in less than one day. The show is promoted by Phil Lobred. www.sanfranciscokni ves.com

A look at Custom Knife Purveyors and Knife Shows

By Neil Ostroff, USA
Purveyor of quality handmade custom knives
www.TrueNorthKnives.com

Purveyor: Commercial supplier of goods: a person or company supplying goods.
Microsoft® Encarta® Reference Library 2005. © 1993-2004 Microsoft Corporation. All rights reserved.

I was into knives long before I opened my business. Like many others I started off collecting cheaper factory-made folding pocket knives - Case, Schrade and Buck - and gradually moved up to Spyderco, William Henry Knives and Chris Reeve knives. Inevitably, as I got older and had the means, I moved into the incredible world of custom handmade knives.

When I decided to make the jump from collector to purveyor, I made it a point to attend as many knife shows as possible in order to broaden my knowledge of the business. In this way, I came to meet and get to know the makers. This helped me determine the direction my business should take.

In the knife business, I have found a culture where tolerance and mutual respect play a major role in the ongoing success of this wonderful industry of ours. In my prior experience in other businesses, it was quite unusual to find competitors who so generously shared information, such as a knifemaker who will show another how to make a knife a bit better without feeling that there is a risk to his or her own livelihood. They do so in order to preserve the integrity and continued growth of the industry and to provide the youth with some help in achieving their goals.

Some say there are now too many knife shows, some say not enough. I know of so many knife buyers and collectors who live in remote areas and would give anything to have the opportunity to attend a knife show. Unfortunately, in many cases, they cannot. This is one of many areas where an Internet Purveyor provides an invaluable service.

A successful knife show is one that meets certain criteria. The promoter must provide a first-rate venue for the show. Once found, this venue should not be changed unless absolutely necessary. People are creatures of habit and feel comfortable going back to the same

Art Knife Invitational, 2005
Six magnificent custom made art-knife treasures that changed hands at this prestigious one day invitational only show, held in San Diego every other year. 120 one-of-a-kind art knives were made especially for this event by the 25 members of this elite group of custom knifemakers.
"Zipper Bladelock" and *"Leverlock"* by Michael Walker (USA).
"Folding Dagger" and *"Engraved Interframe Folding Dagger"* by John W. Smith (USA).
"Folding Dagger" and *"Folding Gold Dagger"* by Henry H. Frank (USA).

place where they have had success or a pleasant experience before. The show location, usually a hotel, should be one that is easily accessible for knifemakers and buyers alike. The room that will hold the knife show should have proper lighting and be spacious. The promoter ought to aggressively advertise the show in order to attract the buyers - not only from the area in proximity to the show, but nationally and internationally. In addition, the promoter must gather a solid line-up of highly sought after knifemakers for these customers to buy from. Both of these goals must be achieved in order to have a successful show, one that makers and buyers will be eager to return to year after year.

There are knife purveyors who depend solely on knife shows to do business. This requires traveling across the country with inventory in hand and setting up a table at Custom Knife shows to display and sell their knives. Hard work, indeed. Often we find purveyors who combine both the Internet and knife shows in order to vend their wares.

In my capacity as an "Internet-based" purveyor, I cater to a vast international audience of collectors and enthusiasts. With the technology available today to well-informed Internet merchants, much data can be gathered in terms of the buying patterns of customer based on demographics, shifting trends and clients habits. Sustained contact with the customers through Internet-based channels, like email and discussion forums, also proves to be very valuable.

Finally, the Internet website must be properly maintained and always up-to-date in terms of available inventory. Digital images should be clear and give a comprehensive description of each item listed. We are asking a client to purchase a knife that he or she cannot touch or feel. For this reason as much information as possible must be made available to the prospective buyer.

A knife purveyor's website is a "virtual store". Notwithstanding the product, any brick-and-mortar retail store must have a proper, well-displayed inventory ready for the customer to buy. A retail Internet website is no different.

Exotic Knife Handle Materials

By Dennis Greenbaum, USA

I love to see a knife with a handle made from one of my favorite woods such as a highly figured Snakewood, a wonderful burled Redwood, or perhaps Desert Ironwood with especially deep and clear chatoyant effect. Something about the way it looks when the metal is juxtaposed with the rich, warm colors of a rare, exotic wood, never fails to stir something deep within me.

On the other hand, I must admit that I also love the look of "presentation-grade" Mother-of-Pearl, when set against nitre-blued Damascus bolsters and blade. The visual contrast between the pearl and the blue steel can be quite stunning. But then again, when I think about some of the exquisitely carved ivory handles I've seen...ahhh, it just doesn't get any better.

So many incredible choices... When they are all so very beautiful, which material or combination of materials to use for the next knife is a question that always presents an interesting conundrum for the knifemaker. The list of possible materials is nearly endless. To try and enumerate all of them, especially in an article of this length, would be difficult if not impossible. I have my own personal favorites, and most of them fall into the category known as "exotic materials."

Certainly one of the most fascinating aspects of modern knifemaking is the extraordinary variety of materials that are used in the construction of knife handles. For centuries knifemakers inherently used those materials that were indigenous to their area. But now, particularly with the help of the Internet and overnight, worldwide shipping, we have access to just about any material our heart desires. If it's attractive and relatively durable, knifemakers will find a way of incorporating these materials into a knife; as the entire handle or a set of "scales", or as an added, decorative element.

Often rare and exotic, the materials used for knife handles can come from all parts of the globe. Black-lip Mother-of-Pearl from Tahiti, Snakewood from South America, Stag from India, Desert Ironwood from Mexico and mammoth ivory from Siberia and Alaska, are but a few of the many breathtaking materialsthat can now be imported from the far corners of the earth.

Treasures from the Deep

Nature provides us with a host of marvelous resources many of which, over the past couple of thousand years, have proved to be more than suitable for knife handle components. Some of the most exciting of these resources come to us from the warmer waters of the world. For example, since man first began making knives, various species of mollusk have long been utilized because of the wonderful, decorative qualities of the linings of their shells. Attracted to the iridescent parts of these shells, with their shimmering, rainbow-like surfaces, knifemakers are always on the lookout for the most beautiful (and most valuable) samples of Black-lip, Gold-lip, or the somewhat more traditional (but no less exciting) White-lip Mother-of-Pearl. These treasures from the water are so exotic and "otherworldly" in appearance that they are constantly sought after by the world's leading knifemakers, who in turn always seem to find more and more creative ways to best show off these wonders from the deep.

Also prized, is another type of mollusk, Abalone. There are a number of varieties, among them Paua, or Awabi, or Red Abalone, all of which are renowned for their dazzling array of color - greens, blues, pinks, and shades of violet and purple. Mostly used on small folding knives or incorporated for embellishment as inlays, Abalone is difficult to find in large pieces. So over the years methods have been developed to composite smaller pieces in such a way as to make them look very much like a larger piece of natural, "traditional" abalone. With these "mosaic" laminates, knifemakers are able to access the beautiful colors of Abalone, but in sections sizable enough to be used on larger knife handles.

Yet another "gift from the sea", and one of my personal favorites, is coral. Like so much of nature's most colorful assets, this treasure is found in warmer climates and comes to us in a number of exciting varieties such as Apple Coral, Tiger Coral or Blue Coral. With its vivid colors and sometimes dramatic patterns, coral can make quite a striking addition to the handle of a knife. Like Mother-of-Pearl, coral is most often only available in pieces 2 1/2"- 4 1/2" in length and so, typically, it is used on smaller knives, and often as an inlay.

Opposite, from the left:

Exotic Wood Handles
Larry Fuegen, "Gentleman's Bowie", *2004*, with a hand carved Desert Ironwood handle.
Edmund Davidson, "Loveless Design Big Bear", 2005, with stabilized maple burl handle.
Steve R. Johnson, "Loveless-style Wilderness", 2004, with a Desert Ironwood handle.
Steve R. Johnson, "Cottontail", 2004, with Snakewood handle slabs.
Edmund Davidson, "Max's Fancy Hunter", 2005, with stabilized California buckeye for the handle.

With the growing number of knifemakers and the rapidly increasing interest in "art" knives and "gents" knives (sometimes referred to as "pocket jewelry"), it is becoming more difficult than ever to find the most breathtaking examples of Mother-of Pearl, Abalone, and coral. And as is the case with any diminishing resource, especially one that is in great demand, it's no wonder that the cost of such treasures is constantly on the rise.

Ivory

Among today's knifemakers and knife collectors, one of the "hottest" and most sought after types of exotic handle material is ivory, in all its forms. "True" ivory comes from elephants and mammoths; however, the term is generally applied to the tusks of other mammals as well.

Easy to carve and finish to a lustrous shine, elephant ivory is prized for its cream-like color and unique grain pattern. For the experienced knifemaker it is relatively easy to work, and it is favored by scrimshaw artists. Well aware of the long-standing ban on elephant ivory, knifemakers are always careful to purchase "pre-ban" ivory, which is typically at least 25 years of age and has been well documented.

The mammoth is the direct ancestor of the elephant, and the ancient ivory of the mammoth is every bit as beautiful. Given that fact, in recent years it has become "open season" on the mammoth, and its ivory has pretty much taken the place of the world's demand for elephant ivory. Mammoth ivory is anywhere from 5,000 to 40,000 years old, and its condition, color and usefulness are greatly dependent on its age, how long it was frozen and in which region, the sex of the mammoth, whether or not it was in actual contact with the soil, the type of soil, and how much it has oxidized over the years. The surface of the outer bark, or "bark ivory", can have a wide range of color, from brown, black and tan, to the highly prized blues.

Ancient walrus ivory is another type of fossil ivory, and it is even more rare than mammoth. It too can be gorgeous, and it is often found interlaced with colors of grey, black, brownish-black, bluish-black and even orange. Neither mammoth ivory nor ancient walrus tusk can be replenished and they are therefore, both quite expensive. Incorporating either material into the handle of a knife will always inherently raise the value of the knife.

Opposite:
Francesco Pachì, Italy
Natural Materials for Handles
Seven beautiful folding knives made by one gifted knife artist, displaying his use of premium quality natural materials for handle slabs. Turtle shell, coral, Gold-lip pearl, Black-lip pearl, Pink pearl and the classic Mother-of-Pearl, all harmonious in color and texture with the design and materials used in each knife.

Rare Woods

There are some folks who feel that wood has no place being part of a "high-end" knife. That has always struck me as a strange notion. Perhaps wood is perceived as too commonplace, too ordinary. But while the finest examples of such materials as pearl or ivory can be very, very expensive (and worth every penny) the simple fact is that certain wonderfully figured exotic woods are often more difficult to find than the aforementioned exotic materials, and they can be quite pricey in their own right.

Even if he or she were to find a good source for exotic woods, a knifemaker can pick through piece after piece of a particular unique wood and still not be lucky enough to locate just the right sort of figure or color. For example, a gorgeous exotic wood such as Snakewood, with its distinctive, dramatic stripes (for which the wood is so aptly named), can be very difficult to find in perfect or near perfect form. When it's less than perfect Snakewood can be only so-so. But when it's right, it is downright stunning. A very hard and dense wood, Snakewood is especially well suited for knife handles. And when the figure is just right, there are few materials that can match Snakewood for its drama. Once popular with 17th and 18th-Century furniture makers, Snakewood is extremely expensive and is probably one of the most expensive hardwoods in the world.

Long prized for its intense black color, ebony is another exotic wood that has been used for knife handles for thousands of years. Very dense, strong and hard, Gaboon ebony is often jet-black in color; it carves beautifully and can be turned very nicely on a lathe. Because of its density, it is notoriously tough on cutting tools. Ebony is often used for an entire handle, but because of its color, it also makes an absolutely wonderful accent material. Like other exotic hardwoods, ebony is very expensive, but it always adds value and beauty to a knife.

Desert Ironwood, truly one of my favorites, has been in such great demand for so long, it is becoming harder to find. And although not technically classified as such, it is considered by some to be an endangered species. Found only along the boundaries of the Sonora Desert, the finest and rarest examples of Ironwood have a unique quality known as chatoyance ("Tiger's Eye" effect). As it is moved about, the wood changes color and appearance, and when it's finished properly the end result can be breathtaking.

When I consider these materials and some of the numerous wonderful knife handle materials not covered in this article, I can't help but think how many of them are, in their own right, absolute natural works of art. Wood, ivory, pearl, horn, stone, fossilized dinosaur, amber, metal, or synthetic... the list goes on and on. The materials available to the modern knifemaker are limited only by the imagination. And it's more apparent than ever that the imagination of today's knifemaker knows no limits.

Opposite from the left:

Metallic Knife Handles
George Dailey, "Small Gent's Folder", 2001, with scales, screws, bail and Tiffany set thumbknob in 18k gold.
Wolfgang Loerchner / Ron Lake Collaboration, 2001, with carved stainless steel handle and Damascus inlays.
Wolfgang Loerchner, "Wings", 2001, with very deeply cut file work on a 416 stainless steel handle.
Joe Kious, "Model 11", 1995, The entire knife is made from Devon Thomas stainless "Ladder" pattern Damascus. The handle is fluted with files then etched.

Working Warthog Tusks into Knife Handles

By Mike Skellern, South Africa

Warthog tusks have recently become popular handle material for knives and other tools. This is partly due to the legal aspects of using other ivories and partly due to the inherent beauty and stability of the tusk ivory of the African wild pig (*Phacochoerus aethiopicus*).

The most suitable material comes from the lower tusks of the mature boar, which should be 12" (305 mm) or longer and possess sufficient solid ivory of workable size.

The individual tusks are well curved, so the handle slabs are cut from either side of the main curve, as this is the straightest section. These "slabs" are not identical and this usually adds appeal and interest to the two opposite sides of the knife. The figure, color and pattern of the tusks make each piece fairly unique. The manner of use and the depth of sculpting account for much variation in the resulting knife handles. The tusk can be left *au natural*, well fissured and colored, or it can be worked down to uniform ivory, which in turn enables carving or scrimshaw as appealing embellishments. The tusks are quite often deeply colored, especially if they have been in contact with soil or muddy water or could have absorbed minerals, as happens with the fossil mammoth and other ivories. Although very stable, they do eventually succumb to cracking if exposed for too long to the African sun. Excessive heat that builds up during the working process can also cause cracks, color changes or warping of the tusk material.

The tip and the hollow base of the tusk are usually cut off, leaving a solid central portion long enough to fit the handles. Because the tusks are twisted as well as curved, each side of this remaining piece should be flattened to fit the contours of the knife. This is usually done by pushing each side of the tusk onto a flat grinder until the desired handle size is reached. This is the first and most important step in achieving the desired end result. The surface color and texture may be a very thin layer and must be dealt with carefully to achieve the final texture in the completed handle.

"I nearly always finish natural materials planned to be handles slightly raised in relation to the bolsters, to allow for slight climatic

Opposite, from the top:

Warthog Tusk Knife Handles

Mike Skellern names his knife models after various dog breeds.

"Wolfhound", 2005

Liner lock with warthog tusk handle and a double edged ATS-34 blade. The frame and bolsters are anodised titanium. Originally designed as a "tactical" folder, the knife has lent itself to "dressing up". Overall length 8" (205 mm).

"Wolfhound" with Aikutchi Style Blade, 2005

Blade and bolters made of hardened and tempered, stainless Damasteel. Handle is warthog tusk finished for the scrimshaw of a scorpion by Toi Skellern. Overall length 8" (205 mm). Fom the collection of Manfred Koch, Italy.

Two "Mastiff" Folders, 2005

These two liner locking folding knives have Damasteel blades, hardened to 59 Rc and titanium frames and bolsters. The fours handle slabs used for these two knives were made from a single warthog tusk. Overall length 7 5/16" (185 mm).

changes in dimensions. I cover the bolsters with two layers of tape and finish the tusks to match that level initially. It is convenient to shape or round the handles to their final contours at this stage. I start with a belt grinder, then a flat grinder, shape files, sandpaper and eventually polishing on the buff. This is the second tricky part, one too many file-swipes can cut through the pattern/color you have been working hours to achieve. Work at this stage must be slow and careful, remembering that the final polishing will also remove some of the surface characteristics. If one has a very old tusk in which some minor and non-structural cracks are discovered, they can be infiltrated with cyanoacrylate, which can be finished off inconspicuously. The maker should always make a potential customer aware of such issues with bone, fossil ivory or other natural handle materials. If handle screws are to be used, I store the polished handles in an airtight packet while finishing off the rest of the knife. When using rivets, the handles are taped up in-situ".*

Unfortunately, not all of the handles-to-be end up on masterpieces. Some end up in the "miscellaneous" box along the way, resulting from what knifemakers call, the "turn-out" factor that is always present when working with natural materials.

Investment Cast Knives

By Dr. Fred Carter

Opposite, from the top:

Investment Cast Knives
Designed and made by Dr. Fred Carter
"Interframe Hunter", with a 3" (76 mm) blade, overall length 7 1/4" (184 mm).
"Double Ground Boot Dagger", with a 4 1/2" (114 mm) blade, overall length 8 3/4" (222 mm).
"Large Fighter", with a 6 1/2" (165 mm) blade, overall length 11 3/4" (298 mm).
"Single Sided Hunter", shown from both sides with a 4 1/8" (105 mm) blade. Overall length 9" (228 mm).

Investment casting is a common practice in many industries today; parts for pistols, rifles and aerospace utilize this method of production. The casting process involves the replication of a wax model, which is encased in ceramic to make a mold and then filled with molten metal. David Boye pioneered the use of 440C in the construction of knives in the mid 1980s, coining the term "Dendritic 440C steel". The 440C when melted and cooled develops a carbide pattern that resembles a branching tree, or what is called a dendritic pattern. These branching carbides are very hard and give a long-lasting and aggressive cutting edge to the blade.

The process starts with an injection mold that carries the imprint of the knife. The mold is clamped together and hot wax is forced into the mold, filling the empty cavity. The mold is taken apart, then the wax model is removed and attached to a central wax core, forming a tree-like structure that holds many replicas of the part to be cast. The wax tree is dipped alternately into a thin ceramic clay slurry and fine sand many times until the walls are built up to the desired thickness. These ceramic molds are dried and the wax is melted out. Prior to filling, the ceramic molds are fired at a high temperature, which makes them very hard and solid. The metal is heated by induction well beyond the melting point. The induction heating process is accomplished in a non-melting container by surrounding the metal with coils of heavy wire through which a high-frequency alternating current is passed. This high-frequency current induces currents in the metal, which due to the resistance of current flow, causes the metal to heat. Induction heating is rapid, with the metal becoming a white-hot liquid in only minutes.

The ceramic molds are heated to a very high temperature and the white-hot metal is poured into the red-hot molds filling the knife shaped cavities. Upon cooling, the ceramic is removed - not an easy process, as it is very hard material - and the individual knives are cut away from the core. The knives are annealed, reground and heat-treated to an extreme hardness. The handles or inlays are fitted, and the knife is given its final finish. The end result is an economical, hard-working field knife with exceptional cutting ability.

1

2

3

1 The linen micarta master model of an interframe hunter was hollow ground and the handle inlay area cut out on the pantograph.

2 Two-piece injection mold with pins for holes in the handle. When the pins are removed the wax model will have the handle holes and thong holes in place.

3 An open injection mold showing both halves and the finished wax knife model just after being injected.

4 Wax knife model ready to mount on central tree core. Note the central sprue for injecting the hot metal. The back sprue ensures complete filling of the mold.

5 Wax models on "trees" ready to be coated with ceramic and sand. The trees are dipped in a ceramic slurry and then several times into sand, building up the wall thickness.

6 Ceramic clay and sand on the wax models, ready to be fired. Note the thickness of the ceramic coating. Even with this thickness the molds often break when being filled with liquid metal.

4

5

6

7 Ceramic molds being fired prior to being filled with metal. The wax is burned out and the ceramic clay is converted into hard ceramic.

8 Bars of steel in the induction melting pot. These bars melt almost instantly when the current is applied.

9 Slag being skimmed from molten metal to ensure only clean metal is poured into the molds.

10 Molten metal being poured into the hot molds, a hot, dirty and dangerous job.

11 Master model, wax model and rough metal knife blank on mold.

12 Rough ground knives ready for heat treatment and handle inlay.

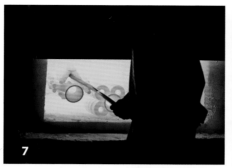

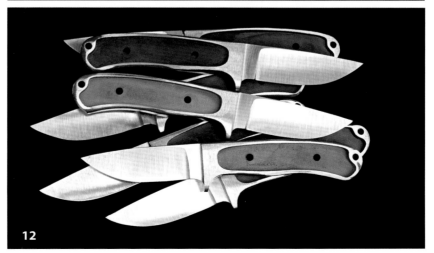

Charles Kain
ckain1406@sbcglobal.net

Charles Kain
The Story of the Jinn Trilogy

By Dr. David Darom

Charles Kain was born in 1963, in Indiana, USA. He acquired his early interest and skills in mechanism design when playing in his grandfather's garage and helping him with his car repair work. In his early teens, while walking through a local gun and knife show, Charles spotted a Damascus dagger with a fluted grip. He had never actually seen such a beautiful weapon, and that moment stayed with him all through his high school and college days, waiting for the right time to emerge as a driving focus for the rest of his life. During his college years, majoring in English and Computer Science, he apprenticed under a clockmaker, fascinated by the intricate workings of clocks, both modern and antique. He then accepted a job as clockmaker and later purchased the clock shop and began running it as an independent business. Gradually he put together enough equipment to start forging Damascus and making knives. His wife, Janet, was incredibly supportive and even bought him an anvil for his birthday and hammers and tongs for Christmas.

Knifemaking became serious for Charles in 1998, when he made his first art knives and began exhibiting at knife shows, uncovering a passion for creating that had not existed before. His artistic explorations led him into the realm of myth, searching and developing some of the many mythologies of the world in his DarkLight Art Knives. *"In forging these myths into the metals of my art I hope to develop, and illustrate, a better understanding of the myth's nature, origins and creators. Each DarkLight is unique and focuses specifically on the myth that it is to explore. My greatest desire is to continue designing that which has never before been seen, artistically as well as mechanically.*

Opposite, from the left:
Awakening, 2005
Lockback design folding knife with Twisted Mosaic blade, Chaos pattern Mosaic bolsters and Nick Smolen Firestorm center grips and Twist Damascus spacer. Lockbar & eye Inlays of Gibeon Meteorite, Mokume Gane, Black & Gold-Lip Pearl, abalone in the eye. Closed length 5 3/8" (136 mm), open 9 3/4" (248 mm).

Ascension, 2005
Linerlock design folding knife with Multi-bar Twist Damascus blades of 1984, 15N20, nickel and cable Damascus, eyes of Twisted Damascus and grips of mild steel. Inlays are Gibeon Meteorite, Mokume Gane, Mosaic Damascus and abalone. Closed length 8 1/4" (210 mm), with both blades open 17 1/2" (444 mm).

The Jinn Trilogy

The Jinni are a race of beings, created before man from a smokeless flame and banished from Earth for crimes against their creator. Like man, individual Jinn can be good, bad or indifferent and like man the Jinni hold powers that sometimes tempt them into

behaviors that are harmful to others. This Trilogy of knives focuses on a single aspect of the Jinn myth, that of summoning an Afreet, an evil Jinn, and the consequences of that act. The story of the Jinn Trilogy is told here in Charles' own words.

Knife 1, "Awakening", Summoned & Bound

"The Trilogy begins with Awakening, the summoning and binding of an Afreet. Here the Mage summons a dark Jinn and uses his magic to bind the Afreet's power to his will. Awakening's left side portrays the Mage, in Mokume Gane, summoning the Afreet; the filework along the spine illustrates the simple repeated incantation used. The Jinn is illustrated in Meteorite and Mother-of-Pearl; a being of great power and otherworldly origin. The knife's right side depicts the Mage binding the Afreet to a contract; constraining and confining its power.

Knife 2, "Ascension", Struggle for Mastery

"Second in the Trilogy is Ascension, illustrating the struggle between summoner and summoned. As the conflict deepens the Mage finds himself beset by the unexpected. Each time the Jinn is ordered to perform, the resulting outcome is not quite what the summoner wanted. Ascension boasts two blades, one Mage, one Afreet. The blades are balanced; but a careful examination will show that the Mage blade is slightly lesser. Both blades carry eyes; the Jinn eye glares in fiery anger, the Mage eye gleams dully with resigned determination. In his heart the summoner begins to learn the fate to which he has consigned himself. Ascension's plates have a worn patina, as the two combatants have tired themselves to near exhaustion".

Knife 3, "Apex", Conquest & Punishment

"In this final chapter of the Trilogy, the Mage is defeated. Trapped in the Jinn's endless devices of scheming evil, the Mage is unable to protect himself, much less attempt control of the Afreet. Here the Jinn is everywhere; it surrounds the Mage and holds him in check with just the barest effort. The filework on the spine shows a subtle reworking of the original summoning incantation; a reshaping of the Mage's magic to create a clockwork prison of power to entrap and make helpless the one-time summoner. The blade is a Gordian Knot pattern of Twisted and Cable Damascus - Jinn and Mage joined inextricably together.

Opposite:

Apex, 2005

A button-lock geared automatic design using a geared mechanism to regulate the opening of the blade. The gears, made of brass and steel, serve to slow the blade and create a more controlled function.
Gordian Knot style Twisted Damascus blade of 1084, 15N20, nickel and cable Damascus. Twist Damascus eye, grips of mild steel, spacer made of Gordian Knot Damascus and the inlays are of Monianalusta Meteorite, Mokume Gane, Black-Lip Pearl and abalone. Closed length 6" (152 mm), open 10 1/4" (260 mm).

Superlative Photography

Eric R. Eggly of PointSeven Studios
By Dr. David Darom

Eric Eggly
eric@pointsevenstudios.com

Opposite:
Eric Eggly, 2005
The man behind the camera.

Many in the knifemaking community know Eric as a knife photographer. What many may not know is that he has been creating images for the advertising industry for the past 23 years. Eric started his career in advertising in the Detroit market, initially assisting many well-known photographers in the area until eventually shooting full-time for his own commercial photography studio.

His clients include Ford Motor Company, General Motors, Chrysler, Audi, VW, FTD, Dana Corp, the Detroit Red Wings, TRW, Libbey Glass, Owens Illinois, Owens Corning Wacker Chemical Corp. and numerous others. He creates images for annual reports, catalogs, billboards, magazines, brochures, and corporate communications, dealing primarily with advertising agencies, corporations, public relations firms and design firms.

This illustrious career in the world of professional photography has allowed him to bring 23 years of experience, talent and knowledge to the knifemaking community. Investing hugely in technology and using only the best of available equipment, he creates the images his clients in the advertising industry expect from him just as well as the images that those in the knifemaking community have come know.

Knife photography accounts for only a small percentage of Eric's business, but his admiration for those in the knifemaking industry far surpasses the economic benefits. "It is one of the most unique forms of art I have ever seen or have had the experience of photographing and the makers are some of the most dynamic and creative people I've had the privilege of being associated with".

His 4,700-square-feet studio is located in northwestern Ohio. Shooting with several different camera formats, Eric prefers using his Hasselblad V series cameras along with a full contingent of lenses and accessories, Profoto strobes and FJ Westcott light modifiers. He uses PhaseOne digital backs with his Hasselblad cameras including at this time an H25 and a P45. These digital backs will produce an 8-bit picture file that is 112 MB in size, or a 16-bit file that

Opposite page and above:

The Photographic Art of Eric Eggly, 2005

These images of knives by Joe Kious (opposite) and Buster Warenski (above) are examples of Eric's final art work created through his extraordinary photography. These are the images that the knifemakers receive from him. For the illustrations in my books on the world of custom knives, Eric kindly gave me the permission to digitally manipulate his images and display them on plain backgrounds, combining at times, several knife images on one page. Some of the knives Eric has photographed are also displayed throughout the introduction sections of this book.

is 224 MB. All his computer work is done on Apple Macintosh computers, of which he has many, using the latest version of Adobe Photoshop (CS2) along with several plug-ins that make his life easier. After many years of working on Adobe Photoshop, way back from the days of version 2.0, Eric can be considered an expert user. Color correction and final image manipulation is done on a Dual Processor G5 2GHz, with an Apple 23" Flat Panel monitor. He also uses a ColorVision Spyder for monitor calibration on all the monitors used in the studio, including the laptops.

Hoping to be part of the knife community for many years to come, Eric feels very gratified to be able to create images for other artists and help them sell their fantastic creations. *"I have a simple goal of continuing to fine-hone my craft and evolve as an artist myself, continuously learning and striving for excellence".*

Making Fixed-Blades

Gaétan Beauchamp

Todd Begg

David Brodziak

William Burger

Ruben Calo

Don Cowles

Audra Draper

Heather & Kevin Harvey

Thomas Haslinger

Robert Hensarling

Michael Jankowsky

Steve R. Johnson

Avraham Koraty

Mardi Meshejian

Tracy Mickley

Alain Miville-Deschênes

Antonio Montejano Nieto

Dusty Moulton

Hidetoshi Nakayama

Francesco Pachì

Rik Palm

Bertie Rietveld

Ariel Salaverria

Joe Szilaski

Michael A. Tyre

Michael Vagnino

Stephen Vanderkolff

Gustavo C. Vilar

Ricardo Vilar

Rudi Zirlin

Opposite, from the left:
"Knives In-The-Making", 2005
Five of the many fixed-blade knives shown while being made, in the pages of the following sections. Michael Tyre's *"Damascus Southwestern Bowie"*; Michael Andersson's *"Mimer"*; Tom Ferry and David Broadwell's collaboration *"The Base of the Mountain"*; David Brodziak and Carol Ann O'Connor's collaboration *"Medieval Dragon Dagger"* and Alain Miville-Deschênes' *"Minotaur".*

Gaétan Beauchamp
"Drop Point Knife with Indian-Head Scrimshaw", 2005

Gaétan, born in 1957, lives in the city of Stoneham, a fifteen minute drive north of Québec, his home nestled in a picturesque valley with the Huron River in his backyard. Stoneham is home to people who are proud of their native, french roots. The area has a distinct European flavor and is alive with activity in summer and winter. Ski resorts, as well the heritage museum sites, attract tourists from all around the world. Québec city is well known as being the cradle of French civilization in North America. Maintaining their heritage has not been without its problems or rewards. The struggle to preserve their culture and identity is evident in the determination and individuality of French craftsmen such as Gaétan Beauchamp. As a result of these qualities, their work stands out. They are independent in terms of ideas and designs. Seeming to thrive on challenges, they are eager to learn new skills and to produce a better product, as it was for Gaétan. A talented artist, he has gained international fame for his award winning knives and scrimshaw.

125, de la Riviere
Stoneham, Québec, Canada G0A 4P0
Phone: (418) 848-1914
Fax: (418) 848-6859
email: knive@gbeauchamp.ca
Site: www.gbeauchamp.ca

"Drop Point Knife with False Edge", 2005 Water-buffalo handle, 416 SS bolsters, "Fire Ball" pattern Devin Thomas Stainless Damascus blade. Indian-head scrimshaw by the maker. Overall length 9" (225 mm).

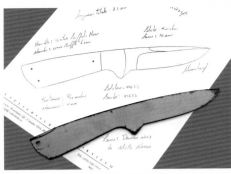

1 All projects begin on paper. This is the only way to make dreams come true. Measurements and sizes are important so Gaétan always create a template and then draw it onto the steel bar.

4 The blade is held firmly on the magnetic table. Gaétan finds it important to wear a good respirator preferring the full-face type so he doesn't have to wear safety glasses.

8 Grinding the blade begins with a 60 grit ceramic belt. Then, it is replaced with a 120 grit belt, 220 and 400 grit. The last two are aluminum belts.

12 Heat treating the blade leaves it with a surface layer of dark scale which has to be removed. This is a long process starting with a 220 grit sand paper, then 400 and 600.

2 Choosing the best materials is as important as the project itself. Here, buffalo horn was chosen for handle, stainless Damascus for blade and 416 stainless steel for bolsters.

3 After cutting the blade to shape from the Damascus bar, he like to get it perfectly flat. With some modifications, this old Model 612 Targa surface grinder does the job perfectly. The grinding wheel was changed to a 2X72 inch sand paper belt. The surface of the blade is made flat in one very fast and clean run. A dust collector behind the grinder keeps everything clean.

5 For his grinder, he built an adjustable flat table so that he can dove-tail the bolsters at 30 degrees as this particular angle gives the bolster a very nice look.

6 To create a perfect fit, the scales have to be shaped in the same angle as the bolsters. Gaétan always fits spacers between the tang and the handle material. Here he is using a red micarta spacer.

7 15 years ago Gaétan built this belt grinder with an 8" contact wheel and an idler wheel. Very basic but still working well. He shapes and grinds all his blades on this grinder.

9 When the bolsters are pinned to the blade, it is very important to shape them carefully before putting the handle on.

10 Both bolsters and scales have to be perfectly flat to fit on the blade. This is done on a self made flat surface connected to Gaétan's old grinder, making for a fast and accurate job.

11 A digital Paragon furnace is used for heat-treating. The blade is heated to 1975° and then quenched in oil. Then it is heated to 375° for 2 hours. The steel reaches a hardness of 58-60 Rc.

13 Gaétan uses a hand made AC-DC Electro Etch to add my name on the blade.

14 The bolsters are pinned on the anvil. A 7 degree counter-sink is used to enlarge the drill bit hole. with this angle, the pins won't show up on a mirror finish.

15 Water-buffalo horn from Asia is used for handle material. Gaétan buys the entire horn and cuts it into slabs. Then it is stabilized in order to avoiding shrinkage.

Gaétan Beauchamp
(continued)
"Indian-Head Scrimshaw", 2005

Through the use of various small jeweler's needles and other tools, scrimshaw consists of stippling (creating small dots or speckles) and scratching cuts and lines into the surface. Cuts and lines serve as receptacles for the paint that produces the finished image. Shadows are created by putting less pressure when cutting into the material, creating smaller dots. Different textures are created by controlling the distance between the dots.

16 Here are the materials needed to make a good knife: the blade, scales, bolsters and pins. All the rest is imagination, skill and dexterity.

17 Cyanoacrylate glue is used to glue the liners onto the scales. The glue comes in several forms, gel-type, medium thick and very thin. It is often used with an accelerator for faster drying.

18 For gluing the scales on the tang, Gaétan uses epoxy with a 8 hour drying time. To secure permanent bondage, the tang is sandblasted before applying the epoxy.

19 After pinning the scales on the tang, everything is held together overnight in vices.

20 Finishing the knife. After shaping the handle, a buffing wheel is used to get a nice mirror finish. It is essential to bring the handle to a mirror finish before beginning the scrimshaw.

21-24 Reverse scrimshaw, popularized by Beauchamp, is done on dark surfaces such as water-buffalo horn and other black backgrounds. In order to scrimshaw in white on a black background, the artist must think in inverse terms, much like working with the negative of a photograph. When working on a white background, one "plays" with the shadows to blacken the spaces. On black, one composes with the lighting to "bring out" the subject. Making a human face on a black background is always a challenge. A small mistake and the whole work has to be sanded off and started all over. One dot in the wrong place can change the whole physiology of a face...

25-26 *"My equipment consists of a monocular and small jeweler's needles sharpened to superfine points. I insert the needles into an Exacto knife handle. Using an assortment of needle sizes, I carefully scratch, stipple and cut the image into the handle surface using a series of small dots and lines, or a blend of both. I like to use oil paint which is waterproof when dry, will never fade and will remain there for ever. It is also easy so mix compared to ink"*. The finished scrimshaw is on the right.

Todd Begg
"Integral Predator", 2005

Born in Seattle, Washington, in 1971, Todd spent much of his younger years in the deep forests of the pacific northwest, camping, hunting and trapping. It was there that he developed an appreciation for fine knives. He tried making a few knives while still in high school, in metal shop classes, and realized that it was not just a passing hobby, he had found his passion. Later, while serving in the Army, he earned an associate degree in Machine Shop Technology, knowing that machining skills would help in his knife making abilities. After working in the aerospace industry for five years as a machinist, Todd went full time with his knife making in 2003. Influenced by the amazing grinding skills of Bob Lum and Bill Luckette and the Integral construction of Edmund Davidson and Ted Dowell's knives, Todd

developed what he calls his "In-line Handle" construction Integrals. *"I am blessed to have a family who is very supportive of my knife making occupation. I rely heavily on my wife, Tanya, who is also my business partner. Her support and efforts free me to focus on being creative".*

420 169th Street South
Spanaway, WA 98387, USA
Phone: (253) 531-2113
email: tntbegg@comcast.net
Site: http://www.beggknives.com

"Integral Predator", 2005 Made of D2 tool steel this knife is a full Integral with Todd's In-Line handle style. The handle is made of stabilized curly koa wood. Blade length is 6" (152 mm) and the overall length 11" (279 mm).

1 The raw matterials used to create this knife were stabilized curly koa wood and a bar of 3/8"x2" D-2 tool steel.

5 Machining the koa wood slab to fit the inlay pockets. The corner rounding end mill matches the radius of the end mill used to produce the corner radius in the handle pockets.

7 The blade is machined down to the proper thickness and the face of the guard is established. These areas are hand sanded to remove all tool marks before the blade bevels are ground.

10 The blade bevels are hollow-ground after heat treatment to give more control over the blade's shape and thickness.

2 Squaring up the ends of the steel on the Bridgeport mill.

3 Producing the handle pockets, making sure both sides are uniform in size and depth.

4 Machining one of Todd's trade-mark flutes along the handle spine. All of the tool marks are stoned out after machining is completed.

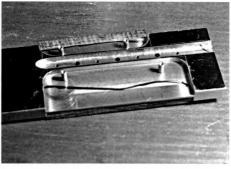

6 Fitting the inlays. Final fit is accomplished by hand and the steel threaded posts, used to attach the handle scales, are cut to size.

8 A 60° angle lathe tool (usually used for single point threading) is used in a shop-made horizontal-cut fly cutter to make the thumb serrations. Knife is held vertically in a fixture built specially for this purpose.

9 Profiling the knife after all of the machining is done. Approximately 12 hours of mill work has been completed before the standard "knife making" processes begins. An Integral needs many hours of work and has to be planned to the last detail before the knife is started. Todd's goal is to remove all clues of the knife's construction leaving no tool marks. *"I want a knife to look as if it was born and not built"*.

11 The koa wood inlays are rough radius-ground and the "bubble effect" of the handle inlays is starting to take place.

12 Final sanding of the inlays and satin finish of the blade is done at this time. Then the knife is sharpened and the logo is etched on the blade.

13 The knife is now ready for final finishing.

David Brodziak
"Medieval Dragon Dagger", 2005

David Brodziak was born in 1948, in South Wales, Australia. His family moved to Perth, Western Australia in 1958. He met and married Gail in 1972, then three years later moved to Albany on the southern coast of Western Australia and raised two sons. David started making knives in 1989 and became a full time maker in 1993. "I met Albany artist Carol Ann O'Connor in 1999 and we started to make a range of knives with medieval and fantasy themes. The combination of my knives and Carol's art was very successful right from its conception with several best art knife awards being won in the first year". The subject matter and method of application make these knives very unique. Together they have now produced close to ninety knives, which have sold to collectors in many different countries.

P.O. Box 1130
Albany 6330, Western Australia
Phone: (+61) 8 98 413314
Fax: (+61) 8 98 415065
email: brodziak@omninet.net.au
Site: www.brodziakcustomknives.com

"Medieval Dragon Dagger", 2005 Blade made of Odin's-Eye pattern Damasteel. Fittings are 416 stainless steel. Handle and scabbard are Lace Casuarina wood. The art work is acrylic coated with 20 layers of a two-part polymer protective finish. Overall length (in scabbard) 15 1/3" (389 mm).

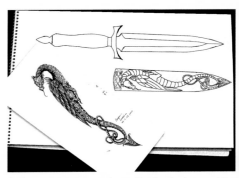

1 The customer requested a medieval style dagger with a dragon on the scabbard. A profile of the knife and intended artwork were submitted for his approval. With design and artwork approved, work on the knife could begin.

3 Using the design as a template, the blade's profile is drawn directly onto the billet then roughly cut with an angle grinder, leaving it about 1/8" oversize. The remaining material is removed with a course 40 grit finishing belt.

6 Turning the handle is done on a small lathe designed for turning pen blanks. David starts the turning process checking it with a callipers till the design shape is achieved. The handle is finished by sanding to 400 grit.

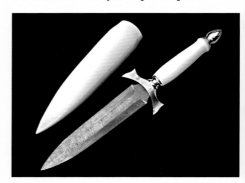

8 The handle and scabbard are painted with an ivory colored acrylic priming coat, which is the base for Carol Ann O'Connor to apply her art. The fittings are sent to our engraver and the blade is sent for heat treating.

2 A billet of Odin's-Eye pattern Damasteel was chosen by the client for the blade. Sections of 416 stainless cut from a bar will be used for the guard, ferule and pommel. David chose Lace Casuarina for the handle and scabbard.

4 The blade is a double hollow grind with a narrow island in the centre. Hand held over an 8 inch wheel it is roughly ground using a 40 grit belt then a 400 grit belt. It is finished by hand down to 2000 grit.

7 Turning the pommel starts with a block of 416 steel drilled and tapped on one end, then screwing and locking a 1/4" rod into it. With the block rotating at a high speed, an angle-grinder is used to shape and finish it.

9 "We have been working with Richard Chapman for eight years. With commissioned knives that are to be engraved, I send him the design and intended artwork. Here he used a floral scroll to tie in with the medieval design".

5 Milling the scabbard. "As I do not have a milling machine, I have learnt to use a good drill press to do most of my small milling jobs. The scabbard is made in two halves, having the blade profile drawn on each of them and then small amounts of wood removed from them with the milling bit. I keep checking the size of the pocket after each run, using the blade for size until a fairly snug fit is achieved".

10 Carol Ann O'Connor specialises in fantasy and medieval style paintings with some of her major works selling for many thousands of dollars. She enjoys painting on the knives, as her art becomes a tactile object that is intended to be handled rather that hung on a wall. Carol applies her art using very small brushes, building up the color with many coats and spending many hours on each knife design. Her work is protected with varnish.

William (Bill) Burger
"Swinburn", 2005

Bill Burger was born in 1935. At an early age he discovered a yearning to one day produce a knife that embodied practicality, comfort and pleasure for the user, and would also hopefully be admired as an art form to satisfy the connoisseur. It was not until he took the plunge and sought out the guidance of Owen Wood and Buzz Bezuidenhout that his dreams started to become a reality. The benchmark set by these experienced knifemakers became Bill's inspiration. *"In a world of mass production there appears to be a decline of appreciation for the true art form. Craftsmen, the dedicated 'soul' workers, are diminishing, masterpieces created by gifted men and women, producing articles of quality and individuality, are rare. Knifemakers are not there only to please customers, but have become dedicated*

artists in their own right, expressing their vision, and achieving personal satisfaction". His own appreciation for line and form, gathered from years of experience in his capacity as a professional photographer, aided him in producing knives that illustrate his distinctive personal style.

P.O. Box 515
Bethlehem, 9700 South Africa
Phone: (+27) 58 303 4830
email: scribble@iafrica.com

"Swinburn", 2005 A trout-and-fillet knife. The blade is "Bird's Eye" pattern Damascus, echoing the spot pattern on the brown trout. The Damascus pattern of the bolsters reflects the ripples formed on the surface of water. Handle is elephant ivory, scrimshawed by Bill's daughter, Sharon Burger. Overall length 8 5/8" (220 mm).

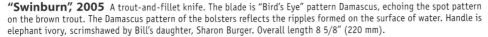

1 Bill begins by scribing the pattern onto the steel using a very fine dentist's drill ground to a fine point. He feels that one can work more accurately with fine lines.

5 The tang is tapered to the rear to 1 mm, beginning at the run-in of the cutting edge. Bill uses engineer's blue to facilitate a flat surface.

9 The bolster material is cut and clasped over the required area below the blade. 3 mm holes are drilled part of the way into the bolster, exactly 2 mm deep.

13 The bolsters are rounded on a flat disk grinder and later screwed in place on both sides of the blade.

2 The knife's profile is cut out on the band saw, as close as possible to the scribed line. Then, using a grinder, the excess is removed right up to the markings.

3 After punching the position of the holes in the bolster area and of the handle, these are drilled through using a 3 mm drill. In the handle area, these will mark the spots for the 7 mm holes drilled to lighten the tang.

4 After making sure that the material is perfectly flat, two grinding guide lines are scribed along the spine, set 0.3 mm apart from each other.

6 Rough finishing is done on the disc sander #6A.

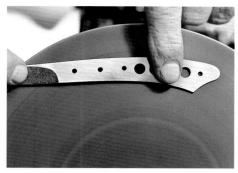

7 Grinding the blade begins with a 60 grit belt and is finished with 150 grit.

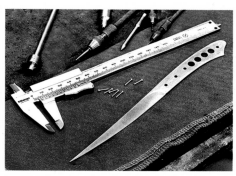

8 The ground blade finished off to a 150 grit.

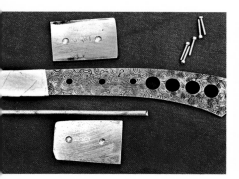

10 The blade, bolsters and brass rod.

11 A 3 mm brass rod is press-fit into the 3 mm holes in the blade, leaving 1.5 mm protruding. Then a 1.3 mm hole is drilled through the brass and the bolster, tapping the hole in the brass.

12 One bolster is placed over the blade, clipping it firmly over the brass studs. The bolster is removed after marking off its size and a recess line, 1 mm smaller, is drawn along its sides. It is finished to size with its counterpart.

14 The blade has the bolsters fitted on. The ivory slabs for the handle and scabbard are already rough-cut to shape.

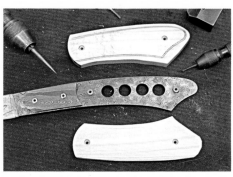

15 The handle material showing the recessed line before the beginning of the final shaping process.

Ruben Calo
"Persian Kard", 2005

Born in 1957, in Buenos Aires, Argentina, Ruben started collecting knives when he was a kid. Whether he was camping, fishing or hunting, knives had been with him at all times. He started making knives, totally self-taught, in 1989, when he was living in a small apartment and his largest tool was a hand drill. At the age of 36, he bought a new house with enough room to build his own shop, and has been making knives as a full time knifemaker ever since. Ruben creates his own designs, making each one of his knives a unique, one-of-a-kind piece. With his

vast experience in jewelry and engraving, his work caters to a select group that appreciate not only the knives and original designs, but also the careful attention to details in craftsmanship and exclusive materials used. the results of Ruben's workmanship are not only items of art but fully usable knives as well.

*Lavarden 142, Capital Federal
C1437FBD, Buenos Aires, Argentina
Phone: (+54) 011-4308 0896
email: ruben@calocustomknives.com.ar
Site: http://www.calocustomknives.com.ar*

"Persian Kard", 2005 The blade is made of SAE 9260 Swedish steel. file worked along the spine. Handle in axis deer stag, dyed and "aged", with nickel silver bolster and guard in simile gold. Pommel in chiseled nickel-silver with a Sterling silver sphere. Sheath in worked leather, with nickel-silver and Sterling silver fittings, chiseled with floral motives. Overall length 13 3/4" (350 mm).

1 Once the blade is ground, it is time to have it file worked. For this process, the blade is attached to a vise using a piece of leather to protect it while securing it in place. The type of file used depends on the desired results.

5 Ruben chooses a high quality piece of stag and cuts it to the desired size with a hacksaw. As the finished handle will be sanded, there's no need, at this stage, to protect it from any damage the vise might cause.

7 The first step in making the nickel-silver fittings is to bring them to the desired shape. After measuring the end section of the stag handle, Ruben uses a jewelry cube with different sized molds to create the rounded butt-cup.

10 With the nickel-silver pieces fixed to the working surface, it is possible to chisel the desired patterns into them. If a piece comes loose, it can be re-glued in place by heating some more sealing wax.

2 Ruben heat treats his knives himself, using an electronically regulated oven, which allows him to control all the variables for this process. This is the already pre-heated oven, ready to receive the blade.

3 Once the predetermined heating time in the oven is over, the blade is removed and placed in oil for quenching. This process needs to be repeated later at lower temperatures, to relieve stresses in the metal.

4 The blade, blackened by the heat treatment, is now held in the vise for polishing. This is done with sandpaper wrapped on a wooden cube. Polishing the sides and spine of the blade, achieves a hand rubbed satin finish.

6 With the piece of stag already roughly sanded, it is time to carve it, using a small round file. Once this process is finished, the stag handle will be ready to be dyed and get its final polishing.

8 Before chiseling begins, the already shaped pieces need to be annealed and filled with liquid sealing wax. This prevents them from cracking under the chisel and holds them firmly on the working surface.

9 "My workshop is located on the first floor of my house where I have plenty of natural light and fresh air. All my knives are completely hand made, following my own designs. The main steels I use are SAE 5160, SAE 9260, K110 and N678. For the handles I use stag and quality woods. For special projects I use mother of pearl, sterling silver, gold and precious stones. I also like to file-work my blades as I believe that gives each knife a special touch".

11 Once the parts are shaped and chiseled, they have to be soldered together to form the final pieces. To achieve this, they are placed on a refractory brick and heated with a torch until the added metal melts.

12 When a more complicated pattern is desired, it is drawn on the piece and a smaller chisel is used to follow the lines. This process is made entirely by hand and takes a lot of concentration and a very steady hand.

13 This is the shaped and worked leather for the sheath, as well as all of the nickel-silver fittings, already chiseled, polished and with a hint of a nice patina for an overall aged look.

Don Cowles
"Gemini", 2005

Don Cowles was born in California in 1941. He has lived all over the country, as well as in Venezuela, and currently resides in Royal Oak, Michigan. Don has had a lifelong fascination with knives, and made his first one in the Sixties. He made several more over the following years, but got serious about knifemaking when he purchased a Burr King grinder in 1994. In the decade of the 1990s, a group of knifemakers shared ideas and techniques over the internet in a forum called the "Knife List", hosted by Russ Kepler. Don acknowledges a great debt of gratitude to those participants, who included Bob Engnath, Wayne Goddard, Don Fogg, Howard

Clark, Ralph Turnbull, Scott Slobodian, and many others. Don pursued his own visions of personal cutlery, and a style evolved that is uniquely his own, in the form of small straight knives with clip pocket sheaths. Don is a member of the Miniature Knifemakers Society and contributes as moderator to online knife discussion forums.

1026 Lawndale Dr.
Royal Oak, MI 48067, USA
Phone: (248) 541-4619
email: don@cowlesknives.com
Site: http://www.cowlesknives.com

"Gemini", 2005 The 2 5/8" (67 mm) blade, made of Jerry Rados Turkish Twist carbon steel Damascus, has 14k gold accents and an A6 grade diamond set in 18k gold on the ricasso. Bolsters are 416 stainless steel, engraved by Jim Small. Exhibition grade Mother-of-Pearl scales with 14k gold pins. The ostrich lined sheath, lined with Ultrasuede, has a pocket clip and a rare earth magnet. Overall length 5 3/4" (146 mm).

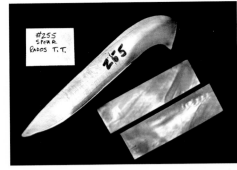

1 The design template was provided to Jerry Rados, who forged a Turkish Twist Damascus billet to the shape of the template, and surface ground it to a uniform thickness. Mother-of-Pearl was chosen for handle material.

5 Tapering of the tang is done entirely by hand, using a magnet and a pair of vise-grip pliers to hold the blade against the platen of the grinder, a slow and deliberate process.

9 The 416 SS bolsters are bandsawed, ground to size, and clamped to the blade one piece at a time. A temporary brass pin in the first hole keeps the bolster from shifting while drilling the second hole.

13 With the first side of the handle firmly attached, excess MOP is removed using a jeweler's saw and a bench pin. This is fussy work. Less fragile materials, such as wood, ivory and micarta, could have been cut on the bandsaw.

2 The design pattern for the knife was laid out on the billet in order to begin the process of grinding its accurate profile.

3 Don lays out the edges of both the blade and the tang using a height-gage and a surface plate.

4 Rough bevels are carefully ground up to the marked layout lines. Now, all the holes are drilled in the blank for the assembly of the bolsters and scales, as well as the holes in the blade itself where Don intends to do gold inlay.

6 More than one knife is usually being made at the same time in Don's shop. He stamps a unique number on each blade, keyed to a job sheet defining the material and the customer. This is essential information for heat treating.

7 Hollow grinding to about 400 grit. Again, this process is done by hand with careful and deliberate removal of small amounts of material on each pass. The progress of the grind is checked constantly.

8 The blade is heat treated in a furnace at 1525° F for 6-7 minutes, followed by quenching in warm oil and tempering at 400° F for one hour, leaving it covered with scale (right). The polished blade, inlaid with gold is on the left.

10 After the bolster's leading edges were shaped and finished with several grits on the belt grinder, the trailing edges need to be chamfered to the desired angle. This is done on the tilted table of a disk grinder.

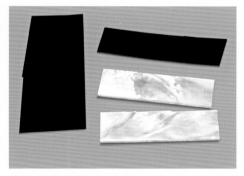

11 For this knife Don decided to have a contrasting black layer of fiber material under the Mother-of-Pearl scales. He epoxied the components together so he could treat them as a single unit when installing the scales on the knife.

12 With everything fitting up properly at this point, Don glues one side of the handle material to the tang, allowing it to set overnight. The components were wrapped in waxed paper, and clamped to prevent the parts from shifting.

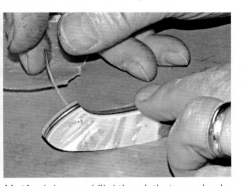

14 After holes were drilled through the tang and scales on both sides, the handle was rough-shaped on the belt grinder, and pins of 14k gold wire were inserted and glued in place.

15 The gold pins were trimmed as close to the surface of the pearl as possible, and final shaping of the handle begins, using the Burr King "Knifemaker attachment".

16 After shaping, the knife is placed in a swivel vise, and finely sanded and polished all the way through 2000 grit. Don uses a wood-backed pad of 50 durometer rubber on top of the sandpaper to provide a solid backing.

Audra Draper
"Gentle Jim", 2005

In 1969, in a small town in California, a young girl by the name of Audra Sharp was born. Three years later the family moved to another small town, in Riverton Wyoming. Divorced in 1992, Audra remarried in 1994 to Mike Draper. Together they have raised six children Jonathon, Rebecca, Elisabeth, Gregory, Christopher and Melissa. In 1992 Audra began working and apprenticing with Ed Fowler, American Bladesmith Society Master Bladesmith, and a local ranch owner in Riverton. In 1996 Audra received her Journeyman Smith rating and soon after the whole family moved to the country outside of Riverton where they built their workshop. In 2000, Audra Draper became the first woman to receive her Mastersmith rating from the American Bladesmith Society. Mike Draper began making knives full time in 2000 and the whole family got involved in the making and designing of knives.

"Draper Knives"
10 Creek Drive
Riverton, WY. 82501, USA
Phone: (307) 856-6807
Mobile: (307) 851-0426
email: adraper@wyoming.com
Site: www.DraperKnives.us

1 Beginning as a 37 layer stack of 15N20 and 1084 steel, the Damascus is forged and the hydraulic press used for the initial weld. Here, the #25 "little giant" trip hammer draws the billet, shaping of the knife.

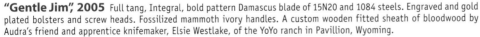

"Gentle Jim", 2005 Full tang, Integral, bold pattern Damascus blade of 15N20 and 1084 steels. Engraved and gold plated bolsters and screw heads. Fossilized mammoth ivory handles. A custom wooden fitted sheath of bloodwood by Audra's friend and apprentice knifemaker, Elsie Westlake, of the YoYo ranch in Pavillion, Wyoming.

7 After grinding the knife to shape, it is differentially hardened. Only the blade is hardened, avoiding the handle and other areas that will later be engraved. This is done with a torch.

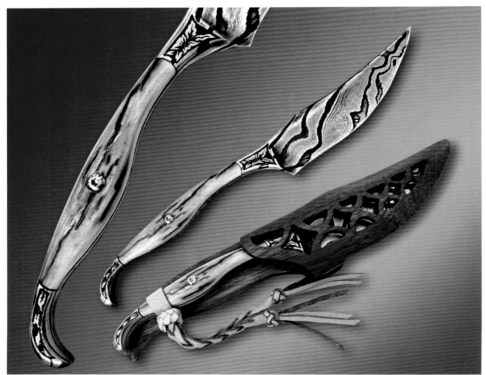

11 After the knife has been etched, everything has to be protected during the engraving so that the finished knife is not scratched accidently. Here the frame surrounding the main engraving is being engraved.

3 Holding the blade flat with the tongs, the belly of the blade is drawn out. As this occurs, the drop in the tip will rise up again.

4 Next, the curves of the handle are forged a little tighter, using the tip of the horn on the anvil.

2 While holding the handle of the knife with a pair of tongs, the tip is the first to begin taking shape dropping it down considerably.

5 While holding the tip of the knife with the tongs Audra can straighten the bow in the back of the knife by hitting the inner curves of the handle. She does this using the ball of the hammer.

6 After making sure that the blade is shaping out as planned, Audra makes certain that both blade and handle are straight and flat.

8 When the blade is brought to the proper temperature, the cutting edge is quickly quenched in heated oil. After the main heat is gone out of the blade the entire knife is quenched in the oil.

9 A piece of mammoth ivory is shaped to fit the handle. Screws as well as curved bolsters hold the handle in place. All of the finishing work on the ivory is done at this time. The ivory cannot be sanded after the knife is etched.

10 With the ivory polished to a finish, the areas to be engraved are painted off using several heavy coats of fingernail polish, protecting them during the etching process.

12 Still engraving. Between the handle and the screws, the engraving time on this knife was well over 8 hours.

13 Here is one of the screw heads after being engraved, transforming a regular torx screw head into a delicate flower.

14 The engraved areas on the bolsters and on the screw heads were all gold plated to give them a warmer look and to bring out the gold colors in the ivory.

Heather and Kevin Harvey (HEAVIN)
"Guardian" Knight's Sword, 2005

Kevin, born in Johannesburg, in 1970, began knifemaking at the age of 12 when his granddad took up the hobby. He qualified as a mechanical engineer in 1992. At the age of 21 he was the youngest member accepted into the Knifemakers' Guild of Southern Africa and became a Master Bladesmith with the American Bladesmith Society in 2003. He prefers making collectable art knives, Bowie knives and daggers using his own Damascus or that made by Heather. Heather was born in 1964, in Sharpeville, South Africa, and grew up in Rhodesia, now called Zimbabwe. She qualified as a farrier at the Montana State University, U.S.A in 1983. After this, she ran a successful horseshoeing business and then took up traditional blacksmithing when she developed an allergy to horses. She is South Africa's first qualified female farrier, blacksmith and bladesmith. Blacksmithing led to making Damascus steel and once she met Kevin, she learned to make knives. Heather enjoys forging Damascus, traditional African weapons and making forged period knives. Heather and Kevin often collaborate under the name of "Heavin" using the first and last three letters of each name.

Heavin Forge Knifemaking Studio and School
P.O. Box 768 Belfast 1100 South Africa
Phone: (+27) 13 253 0914
e-mail: heavin.knives@mweb.co.za
Site: www.africut.co.za

"Guardian" Knight's Sword, 2005 The blade is carbon steel "Heather's Feather" pattern Damascus. Guard and pommel sculpted from bronze. Pommel fitted with fine silver, amethyst crystal and damascus pierced plates. Grip material is hand fluted African blackwood root (Black Ivory) wrapped in fine silver wire. Overall mass is 3 pounds (1.4 kg). All engraving and stone setting by Kevin. Overall length 40 3/8" (1025 mm).

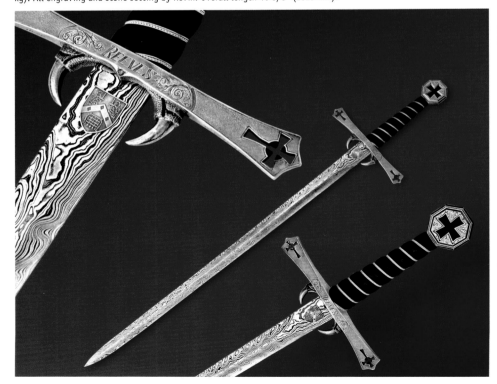

1 Heather begins by preparing, cutting and cleaning the raw material for the damascus billet from lengths of spring and tool steels. Five pieces of spring steel and four pieces of tool steel were cut to begin the layering process.

3 The "Iron Maiden", sixty pound, home made power hammer and Heather are best of friends. The heavy forging of the large billet is made easier using this powerful "striker".

6 A pattern called "Heather's Feather" is ground into the pre-formed blade using a four inch grinder. The grooves are cut in a third of the way on each side of the blade, fading out towards the spine and offset one side to the other.

7 Straightness is a constant challenge on such a long blade while forging out the bevels on the patterned pre-form. One strives for a diamond shaped cross section with the mid-rib running neatly down the center of the blade.

2 The billet is lengthened and cut almost in half with a hot cutting chisel and folded back onto itself by hand to double the layer count. The process of stretching and doubling was repeated five times to give 288 layers.

4 Heather uses a home made, self aspirated, gas forge at an elevation of above seven thousand feet where, supposedly, the low oxygen level in the atmosphere should not allow welding temperature to be reached easily.

5 The blade pre-form is forged to shape by hand, leaving it thicker and shorter than the final length. Safety equipment is always used whether forging or grinding. If you are wondering about the hair catching alight... well it has never yet happened, just remember not to use hair spray before forging!

8 Once the long and tiring job of bladesmithing is almost done, one needs to brush and clean the fire scale off the blade. Fire scale is very hard and if left on the blade, ruins grinding belts easily. The integral tang is held in a pair of box tongs selected from the "organized chaos" on the shelves behind. Up to this point Heather has enjoyed three full days of sweat. Both anvils in the workshop are over one hundred years old, the farthest one being a very unusual chain maker's anvil that has a small square tapered bick coming off of its far side. Heather collects anvils, which take up a bit more room than postage stamps. She gave an anvil to Kevin for his birthday a few years ago.

9 Final straightening during normalizing and before grinding, is easier done with four eyes, four hands, two brains and a shared passion for bladesmithing. Each Mastersmith have their specialties and preferred area of work but when their talents are combined to create a collaboration, the result is often something unique and special. Kevin and Heather feel privileged to be able to work together crafting the "antiques of the future", that hopefully will be enjoyed and cherished for generations to come.

10 The raw material of the bronze guard showing how a 50 mm diameter phosphor-bronze shaft has been cut to shape using a bandsaw.

11 The rough cut guard is smoothed and trued up with a roughing belt on a belt grinder, another home built machine. People seeing the completed sword wonder if the guard was cast, but instead it was carved by Kevin.

12 Knifemaking is everything from forging on a 100 pound power hammer to carving or engraving under a 25 power microscope. Here Kevin is carving eagle talons and will soon be engraving scroll work on the guard and pommel.

13 The pommel consists of two amethyst discs inlayed into a slice of phosphor bronze shafting. This is then covered by two pierced plates of damascus, from the same billet of steel as the blade and two plates of fine silver.

14 The grip is made of carved Black Ivory (African blackwood) root which Kevin dug out of the ground near the famous Kruger National Park. Fine silver wire is wrapped around the handle using four lengths of wire.

15 When the pommel is held up to the light, the amethyst crystals allow light to pass through, like a stained glass window effect. Each of the seven facets has the name of one of the seven Arch-angels engraved on it by Kevin.

16 Once Heather had finished doing her magic with the blade, it was Kevin's turn to prove his worth. The blade is carefully profiled and the bevels ground in. Symmetry is of highest importance.

17 Here the Harveys are using a custom built sword heat-treating tube furnace. Standing on a stool enables Kevin to lift out the long blade and quickly quench it in a deep tank of warm quenching oil.

18 Heat treating will almost always result in twists, warps and kinks on such a long blade. Repeated attempts at straightening at spring-tempering temperature for almost a day, succeeded in getting the sword blade "as straight as an arrow"!

19 Following the last grinding stage where the blade mass is reduced to the correct "feel", the blade is hand rubbed with emery paper up to 600 grit. This is where elbow grease is required!

20 After etching the blade to reveal its texture in ferric chloride and bring out the Damascus pattern, the high spots are hand polished to a brilliant lustre. More elbow grease! Now the sword is ready for final assembly.

21 The Reeves family of Benoni commissioned this sword in 1999 as a 21st birthday gift for their son, Mark, in 2006. The sword is to be a family heirloom and has space on the pommel for a further 13 generations names to be engraved. The amethyst is the birth stone for February, Mark's birth month. The Feather pattern Damascus blade and the carved talons were used to represent the African Fish Eagle that features on the new Reeves' family crest .

Thomas Haslinger
"The Golden Band", 2005

Born in Germany, in 1966, Thomas made his first knives in his early teens, a double-edged sword and a reproduction of a Buck folding hunter. A European-trained chef for over 2 decades, he has been making knives on a part-time basis since 1994 and in the year 2000 made the decision to become a full-time knifemaker. *"My knife art represents a distinctive style throughout, from exquisite one-of-a-kind art pieces to a daily used chef's knives. I strive on a fairly simplistic design approach and form, without compromising in function. The "Golden Band" project in these pages is one design that shows the distinct flow in my work. The concept of the knife with a finger as a handle and a gold band as a symbolic guard*

is unique, but represents daily life, in more than one way. Original drawings (dated 2001) of this piece where part of an evolution and a search for a combination of materials that would aim at keeping the knife graceful, yet functional."

*164 Fairview Dr. SE,
Calgary, Alberta, Canada T2H 1B3
Phone: (403) 253-9628
email: thomas@haslinger-knives.com
Site: http://www.haslinger-knives.com*

"The Golden Band", 2005 Devin Thomas Raindrop pattern Damascus blade steel. 10 grams of 14k gold, adorned by 8 fully cut diamonds make up the gold band. The handle is a carved mammoth ivory finger with horse hair and a nail in Mother-of-Pearl. Overall length 8 1/8" (206 mm).

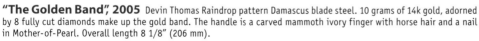

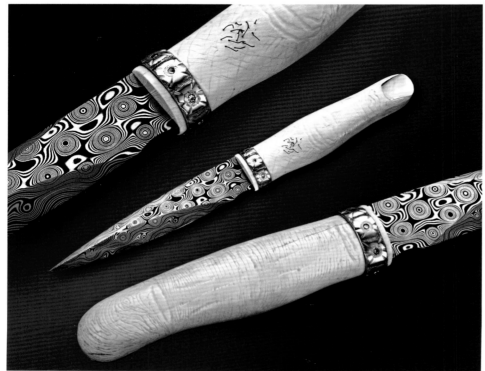

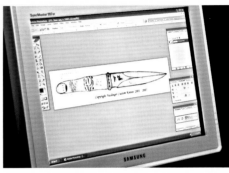

1 Designing and adjusting the original drawing in Adobe Photoshop. Haslinger finds this extremely helpful especially when communicating with customers.

5 Sanding to final shape on a slack belt to 240 grit which is followed by finer sanding to 600 grit.

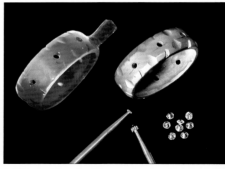

9 A wax model of the ring is made (on the left) and sent to be cast in 14k yellow gold. The cast gold ring (right), 8 full cut diamonds (total 0.25 carats) and the setting burrs used to set the diamonds in the ring.

13 The finger prints and fold lines are carved into the ivory. This is followed by polishing the finger joint areas with a rubberized medium.

2 Thomas Haslinger and one corner of his workshop.

3 The materials: Devin Thomas Raindrop pattern Stainless Damascus, mammoth ivory and the tools commonly used for laying out the design on steel.

4 Rough shaping the finger with various carving burrs using a Dremel hand piece.

6 Using a candle to cover the nail with soot and take a print for fitting the pearl into the nail cutout. Notice the brass bar on the candle, this enhances soot, but also keeps direct heat away from the ivory.

7 A premium quality Mother-of-Pearl slab with the "lifted" imprint from the nail. The pearl finger nail will be only 0.9 mm thick, convex shaped on the outside and concave on the inside.

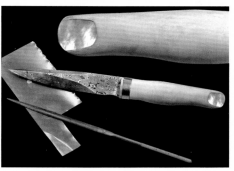

8 The finished nail is fitted in place. A brass shim-stock, used as a measuring tool, ensures that the sides are kept straight when fitting the ring on the knife.

10 A setting burr is employed to drill the seat to fit each individual diamond. After this the channel is cut for the girdle with a heart burr.

11 Texturing is added around the stones and on selected areas of the band for a stylized flower effect. Before final assembly, the ring will be slightly buffed and cleaned ultrasonically.

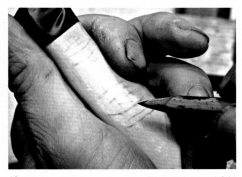

12 Marking the ivory where the finger prints and fold lines are running.

14 A light buffing removes the burrs raised from the cutting of the prints in the ivory.

15 Drilling the follicles for the hair using a 0.1 mm drill bit. Lacy, a quarter horse, was so kind to donate her hair for the next step.

16 In the last step, the hair is glued in the follicles. Now all that is left to do are the finishing touches, the cleaning and the sharpening.

Robert Hensarling
"Hensarling Hunter", 2005

Robert Hensarling, born in 1949, in Uvalde, Texas, is a Master Woodworker and a practicing blacksmith and bladesmith. For a quarter of a century, Robert has been producing museum quality sculpted rocking chairs, each taking up to eleven weeks to complete using the dense, burly, South Texas Mesquite treewood. He has been in over 20 television documentaries including HGTV's "Modern Masters" and "The Discovery Channel" because of his rocking chairs. Robert's Great Grandfather, Hiram Hensarling was a blacksmith in Texas during the late 1800's. Although being mostly self-taught, Robert credits his Dad, Bill Hensarling, for many of his abilities. Robert divides his time as needed between his crafts. In 1988 he fashioning railroad spikes

into letter openers and and fell in love with the anvil, forge, hammer, and the way steel moves. Fascinated with metallurgy, he constantly studies the properties of his favorite steels, 52100, and 5160.

South Texas Fine Woods, Inc.
4326 East Main
Uvalde, Texas 78801, USA
Phone: (830) 278-1832
email: Rhrocker@hilconet.com
Site: WWW.Mesquiterocker.com

"Hensarling Hunter", 2005 This is Robert's most popular knife. Usually forged from either 52100, or 5160 steel, which is carefully normalized, heat-treated, and tempered to give maximum performance. The guard and pins are nickel silver, with red spacers. The beautiful wood handle is select, premium, highly figured South Texas Mesquite, cut, milled, and processed by Robert. Overall length 9 1/2" (241 mm) and it comes with a custom sheath, also made by Robert.

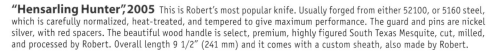

1 All designs start with simple drawings, on the floor, or anywhere space is available. Robert likes to gather all the various parts together before beginning the project.

3 After the basic blade shape is forged, Robert decides the type of tang he will forge. Here he is showing the amount of material that will be used for the tang.

6 After the basic grinding and drilling of the blade blank is done, it is carefully heat-treated in the forge, and quenched in an oil that is of proper consistency and temperature for the steel being heat-treated.

8 Finishing the shoulders of the blade to accept the guard, which is soldered on. Robert attaches a special fitting that allows him to make perfect grinds, for the guard. It is slow work, as the steel is hardened at this point.

2 The steel is carefully heated and forged out into a blade blank. Robert built this particular forge himself. It reaches welding temperature very quickly.

4 Part of the process of proper heat treatment, is the annealing of the steel, to make it softer. This is done to make it easier to grind, and drill. Here the blade is being placed in vermiculite to cool slowly and anneal.

5 The knife and tang are both forged on the anvil, and by using various air hammers and mechanical hammers. In this photo, Robert is drawing out the tang of the knife on his BLU air hammer. He also has four mechanical hammers, three of which are "Little Giant" power hammers. Anvils, vices, swedge blocks and cone mandrels are also used.

7 The knife is now further processed by grinding with various grits of sanding belts. Robert usually uses a convex grind as it is strong and holds an edge well.

9 The finishing technique involves the use of water stones instead of sandpaper. Starting with 180 grit, proceeding through several stone grits and finishing with 800. This process takes several hours per knife.

10 Stamping his name on a knife is Robert's way of guaranteeing that the work has been done in the most professional way he knows. "Many times I have gotten to this point, only to throw the blade away. It has to be perfect in every respect before my name goes on the blade, period".

Michael Jankowsky
"Making of an Integral Knife", 2005

Born in 1961, in Lübben/Spreewald, in the state of Brandenburg, Michael grew up close to the forest and game hunting, being the son of the forester Olgerd Igor Jankowsky. Soon, he began to collect knives and later finished his training as a cabinet-maker. Over the years, with his knife collection growing, he discovered an interest in knife making and in 1997, filed his first knife out a piece of ATS-34 steel. Today, Michael specializes in making Integral knives from PM-steel. *"The design of my knives is influenced greatly by my feelings. It is my very own distinctive handwriting. The results are handy Drop Point Knives or, at times, a nice Chute-Knife. Most of my knives are commissioned work, often embellished with exclusive engravings".* In 1999, Michael took part in the IMA-Munich, his first international professional knife show. In 2000 he became a member of the German Knife Makers Guild, DMG. In the IMA-Munich of 2001 Michael was awarded "Best Art Work" of the show for one of his knives.

Sonnenburger Str. 64
Berlin, 10437, Germany
Phone: (+49) 30 4497617
Fax: (+49) 30 4497617
email: micknives@gmx.de
Site: www.micknives.com

"UZ-1 Chute Knife", 2005 An Integral made of PM knife steel with a maroon linen micarta handle. Overall length 8" (205 mm).

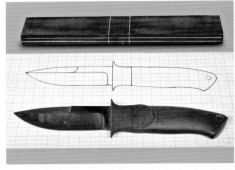

1 The first step in creating a true Integral custom knife is the making of a detailed drawing and a full size knife dummy. All the measurements are then transferred onto the blank.

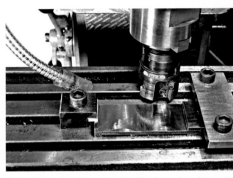

3 In the next milling cut, the blank receives its exact dimensions and a polished surface quality. After the milling process the steel is stress-relieve annealed, in order to eliminate a posterior shape distortion.

6 The outlines are being finalized, finger-cut as well as cutting-edge are being milled out.

8 Using a 36 grit abrasive belt, a coarse hollow grind is made. The flat back of the blade serves as a support plate and a guiding aid for the grinding process.

2 The machine work starts with the rough milling approaching close to the markings on the steel. The HSC-Co10 milling cutter used for this purpose requires a good cooling system.

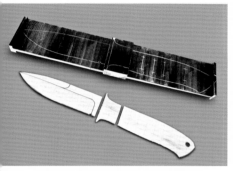

4 The outlines of the planned knife are being transferred via a cardboard pattern. It is very useful to brush on some waterproof ink to make the markings easier to see.

7 The knife's handle is being cut with a band-saw. The under surface of the handle end shows a small web, providing a stable support for the tapered tang.

3 After the hollow grind is equally done on both sides, the blade's back is finalized and the false edge is ground in. An even cut on both sides of the blade is crucial to eliminate any distortion during heat treatment.

5 The manually operated milling machine requires constant attention and concentration. In order to minimize both exertion and clamping, the milling is done slowly, in stages. Needless to say that a sharp milling cutter is crucial.

10 The fixing of all required bore-holes can also take place after the final grinding of the knife, but of course it is both easier and more precise to deal with the drilling after creating the outer contour of the knife. For PM knife steel, I use VHM-drills exclusively because these provide optimal results.

11 The grinding of the guard is a critical operation. A minor mistake at this stage can ruin the whole knife.

12 The machine grinding has progressed from 36 grit belts through 60, 120, 240, 360 and 600 grit. For sizes 360 to 600 and higher, special abrasive belts are used, giving a very smooth grind pattern.

13 The hollow ground blade and the guard are har polished using wet abrasive paper down to 1200 grit. Whi doing so, the abrasive paper is being pulled lengthwi until all traces of the grinding are eliminated.

14 The final polishing of the ricasso is being performed similar to the blade and guard. A homogeneous polishing pattern is achieved by moving the knife or grinding medium in one direction only.

15 During the last stage before hardening, the knife gets an overall polish with 1200 abrasive paper and diamond paste. Now it has its perfect finish! This is necessary in order to minimize grinding after the heat treatment.

16 Accurate heat treatment is crucial in order to obta a truly powerful custom made knife from high-alloy stee The hardening is completed in vacuum or an inert gas, th also prevents unwanted scaling of the knife.

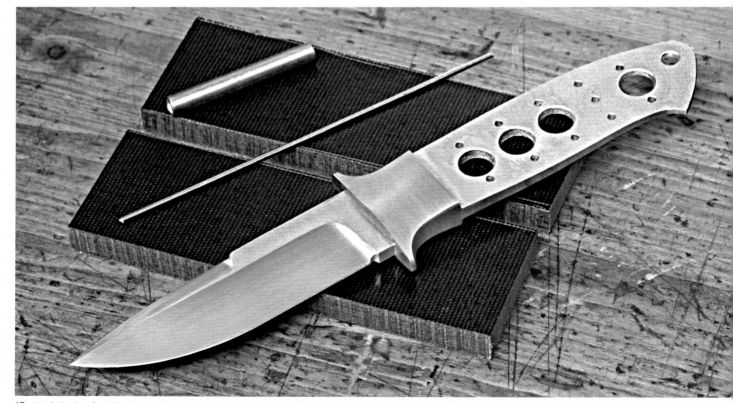

17 Now it is time for Michael to make a decision about what material he shall be using for the knife's handle. An unlucky choice will influence the practical value as well as the aesthetic appearance of the knife. For this specific knife the robust canvas-micarta was his choice. The micarta beautifully enhances the technical character of the Chute-Knife. Hi other favorite among the many different materials available is Desert Iron Wood, which perfectly combines beauty with practical aspects.

18 The material of choice for the handle was maroon linen micarta. The outline of the handle is being transferred onto the material with a steel needle. It is then cut out 1 mm outside the marked line with a band-saw.

19 Drilling the rivet holes and belt's eye is done after the handle parts are glued together.

20 Before final gluing of the handle slabs, the components have to be degreased. During the bonding process, the handle is heated inside an oven to ensure best cohesiveness of the Epoxy glue.

21 After the adhesive has cured, the handle is shaped with a file. To obtain accurate symmetry, gridlines are drawn by pencil on the handle.

22 As soon as the handle reaches its final shape, it is carefully polished with wet abrasive paper of 400 to 2000 grit. The final polish is completed with a leathery cloth and diamond paste.

23 The logo is applied after the knife is completely finished and the cutting edge has been sharpened. It is being electro-chemically etched into the blade to a depth of 1/10 mm, with the aid of perforated foil.

24 Work is done! A final scrutiny and the Chute-Knife is shortly off to to be received by its new and happy owner. "The crafting of Integral-Knives has become my passion. Every single knife I manufacture presents a new challenge. My hand and my instinct both guide and inspire me to the shape forming of my knives. The similarity of my knives to work-pieces of other makers is not due to crude copying, but rather to sharing of a sense for the optimal ergonomic design".

Steve R. Johnson
"David's Fighter", 2004

Born in 1948, in Utah, USA, Steve had the opportunity to hunt, fish, ride horses, camp, play ball, and work on his father's farm for most of his years as a youth. He was fortunate to have Gil Hibben as his Boy Scout Explorer Advisor, and when Gil gave each scout the opportunity to make a knife in his shop, Steve jumped at the chance. Knifemaking has remained a constant in Steve's life, and he enjoys the people and places associated with knifemaking and the personal challenge of making each knife. He presently serves on the Knifemakers' Guild Board of Directors as Secretary/Treasurer and enjoys his association with the Board and the many members of the Guild and the knifemaking community, worldwide. He still sees it as a privilege to work in the custom knife business and is very thankful for the experiences he has had, which have resulted from 40 years in the knifemaking field.

202 E. 200 N. (P. O. Box 5)
Manti, UT 84642, USA
Phone/Fax: (435) 835-7941
email: srj@manti.com
Site: http://www.srjknives.com

"David's Fighter", 2004 This fighter has a 5.5" (140 mm), BG-42 clipped blade and T-416 stainless steel bolsters, handle screws and pins and premium Mother-of-Pearl handles. Overall length 10 3/8" (263 mm).

1 Materials used to make the knife. The red fibrous material is water resistant and its exposed edge polishes up nicely on the finished knife.

4 The outline for the new knife is scribed on a suitable bar of BG-42 steel.

8 Grinding the blade's bottom bevel is done on an 8" (20 mm) wheel, prior to heat treating.

12 Using a "Pin Press", the 3/32" diameter stainless pins that pass through the tang are pressed into the bolsters for an invisible fit. If all goes well!

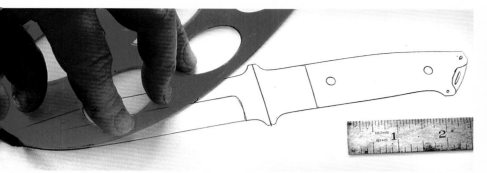

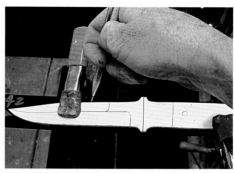

2 After planning the design for this new knife, based on Steve's Classic Fighter design, it is accurately drawn out. For strength and a pleasing appearance, the top grind is terminated forward of the bottom grind by about 5/8" (16 mm).

3 When the design is complete, the pattern is cut out and then glued onto stiff cardboard, plastic or even steel, for transferring its outline to the knife steel.

4 After transferring (or scribing) the pattern onto the bar of steel, the knife is sawn out on a slow-speed band-saw.

6 A line for the center line is scribed on both sides of the blade using a steel scale and a carbide scribe.

7 The guideline for the knife's edge is scribed along the edge of the ground-to-shape knife blank. using a tool designed to place the finished edge exactly in the center of the blade.

8 During the grinding operation, the blade is cooled when necessary in a nearby water container before continuing with the top grind of the rough grinding stage, on a 3" (76 mm) wheel.

10 For the top bevel, a 3" (76 mm) wheel was used. Steve holds the knife's handle with his bare hand but uses a glove to hold the blade end, where the heat is generated.

11 The "thong slot" at the rear of the handle is first drilled out with a 1/6" drill laid out in a line, Then the remaining steel is ground out and shaped with a carbide burr mounted in a very high-speed air grinder.

13 The knife, with polished blade and temporarily mounted bolsters, is now almost ready for attaching the rough-shaped Mother-of-Pearl handle pieces.

14 Bolsters rough-shaped, handle slabs in place, ready to be drilled for handle screws (top). Bolsters shaped (below), MOP mounted and profile-shaped, screws in place, holes for pins drilled.

Abraham (Avi) Koraty
"Royal Dagger No. 1", 2005

Avi was born in 1945, in Tel Aviv, Israel. After studying in technical and art schools, he travelled to Holland, to complete five years of studies in fine arts at the Royal Academy in The Hague. In Amsterdam, while visiting the famous "Old Man" store, he discovered the world of custom knives. Back in Israel, Avi got to meet with local knife collectors and with the help of Alex Shamgar, among others, learnt the basics of knifemaking. Mostly self taught, he began by making several knives based on the designs of other well known makers. Now Avi designs his own knives, daggers being his favorite subject.

"I create fully handmade knives from 01 and D2 steels using the stock removal process, using files. For handle material I am rather traditional, using tropical wood, various organic materials and in some cases micarta. I strive to make knives that are well designed reflecting their purpose, yet remain graceful and, I hope, noble in their presence...".

26 Melchet Street,
Tel Aviv 65234, Israel
Phone: (+972) 3-5607535

1 Avi's work is completely handmade. His knives are created using the stock removal method. The majority of his hand tools are files, some of which are seen in this broad view of his working space.

3 For safety reasons, Avi begins his filing on the handle section, and only later moves on to the blade, with the knife held firmly in a vice.

"Royal Dagger No. 1", 2005 An 01 steel dagger, created by stock removal and hardened to 58 Rc. Ebony, ivory, brass and Sterling silver were used for the handle. The four dots in the brass crown-bolster are pins made of Sterling silver tubes with 9k gold threads. Overall length 9" (228 mm), blade length 5" (127 mm).

6 Drilling is done with the only electric power tool Avi uses. Here, drilling the holes for the bolster and handle, but also to reduce weight while retaining the optimal balance needed for the knife.

8 The knife is about ready for assembly, yet, last inspection and measurements have to be taken to ensure that everything has been done as planned, carefully checking every fit and finish detail.

2 Avi first glues the accurate drawing of the dagger onto the 01 steel stock. Then, using a hacksaw, he removes all unwanted material getting close to the knife's outline. Now the knife is ready to be shaped by hand, using files.

4 During the first stages, rough and medium-cut files are used (flat, round and half-round files) working slowly and carefully up to the exact contour of the knife.

5 When beginning to shape the surface of the blade it is securely clamped by the handle with pieces of protective leather. Beginning with medium and fine-cut files, the process ends with 400 grit abrasive paper. Special attention is given to the most difficult part, namely, the arcs and center line, taking utmost care in handling these challenges.

7 The process of hand polishing the blade begins after it gets back from heat treating (to 58 Rc). This starts off with 400-600 grit paper, 400-600 grit stones, Micro Mesh MX 90 metal-finishing kit and finally, diamond paste.

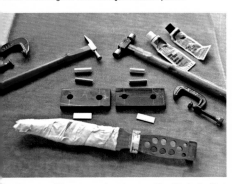

8 The assembly process has begun. The blade is first wrapped for protection while carefully installing all the parts, gluing with epoxy where needed and clamping tight.

10 A broader view of the cross polishing process of the blade, both with abrasive paper and stones. The work is constantly inspected throughout the whole process for all aspects of surface quality. After cross polishing the blade, the final stage is done with diamond paste, achieving an almost mirror-like surface finish.

Mardi Meshejian
"Titanium Damascus San-Mai, #13", 2005

Born in 1970 in Manhattan, NY, Mardi grew up in Queens, NY, and East Northport, Long Island where he still resides. Mardi worked as a jeweler before making the switch to knife making in 1995, when he decided to pursue his life long interest in knives. He started his career after attending several classes at the ABS school in Arkansas. Mardi's knives are sculptural with a focus on color and contrast. He shows his appreciation of the beautiful, impractical and the absurd while retaining function. "When people see my work I want them to stop and think. I want to challenge their preconceived notions about what a knife is and what it can be". After developing titanium Damascus he expanded the process to include steel so it could be used as a functional blade material.

33 Elm drive
East Northport NY 11731, USA
Phone: (631) 757-4541
email: toothandnail13@yahoo.com

1 To make the titanium Damascus, Mardi starts with a stack of alternating titanium alloys, CP3 and 6AL4V, (4"x1" each) enclosed in a steel box, fabricated from a 1" square tube with capped ends.

3 The billet has to be heated rapidly to temperatures in excess of 2300° F while adding the argon. It is then forge-welded and drawn out in a 50 ton hydraulic press.

6 To remove the billet, both ends of the box are cut off with a chop saw. Grinding the edge of the box reveals the titanium billet within, which is then removed by prying it off with a chisel.

10 The pommel is polished.

"Titanium Damascus San-Mai, #13", 2005 The blade is a forty layer titanium Damascus, combining two alloys, 6AL4V and CP3 with a 1084 steel center core. The fittings are copper and superconductor and the handle is mammoth ivory. Overall length 9" (228 mm).

2 A hole is drilled in one end and the box is welded closed. A steel tube is welder around the hole acting as a handle and also enabling the argon gas to enter the billet during heating process.

4 After being removed from the box, the resulting layered titanium billet is ground and cut lengthwise with a band saw. The two titanium bars are re-stacked in a new box with a piece of 1084 steel sandwiched between them.

5 The new billet is heated rapidly to temperatures in excess of 2300° F while adding the argon. It is then forged down using flat dies and the 50 ton hydraulic press. Once the billet is made, the heating and forging processes take less than one hour.

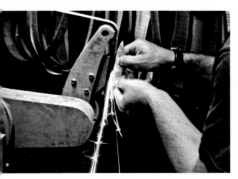

7 Rough grinding the billet to layout the blade design then profile grinding it to shape with a course ceramic belt at a slow speed on a variable speed grinder. The bevels are ground into the blade to a 220 grit finish.

8 A piece of copper is cut to the proper size for the guard and the slot for the tang is milled out in a small Taig mill, fitted with a file.

9 For the pommel, Mardi cuts a slice of a superconductor (niobium in a copper matrix) with a chop saw and then sands its surfaces. A threaded fitting is attached to the pommel disk with screws threaded into blind holes.

11 the copper guard and pommel are heat colored to a light orange color with an oxygen propane torch and then quenched in cold water.

12 The mammoth ivory handle receives its finishing touches. Scratches are removed from the carving using a dowel wrapped with sandpaper in the rotary tool. The ivory is polished with an unstitched buffing wheel.

13 The exposed steel of the blade is masked with nail polish. The titanium is then anodized using a brush and distilled water, with a teaspoon of sulphuric acid as an electrolyte, connected to a DC current.

Tracy Mickley
"The Twins", 2005

Born in 1957 in Fargo, North Dakota, he now calls southern Minnesota home. Tracy came to knife making in 1999. He started cautiously with an inexpensive knife grinder after reading a magazine article on how to make your own knife. After making his first knife, he was hooked and created a 5 year plan to accumulate the tools and skills he needed to make a high quality knife. His first 100 knives were never sold. They were thrown away, destroyed in testing, given away or raffled off for charity. *"Knife making is so diverse that it would be impossible to master every aspect and that is what makes it challenging and interesting. When you master one skill, there is another one that wants your attention".* The majority of his work has

been in stainless fixed blades. As a part time maker with plans to go full time eventually, his day job supports his evening and weekend knife making. He has yet to attend a knife show and depends entirely on the internet site to show and sell his knives. *"I have found that one of the best parts of knife making are the people that are involved with it".*

42112 Kerns Drive
North Mankato, MN 56003, USA
Phone: (507) 947-3760
email: tracy@mickleyknives.com
Site: www.mickleyknives.com

"The Twins", 2005 Hand ground from CPM 154CM steel, a powder technology steel developed specifically for the premium end of the cutlery industry. One handle is Black Line Spalted Maple burl with black accent liner. The other handle is Redwood Burl with rust colored accent liner. Dovetailed 416 bolsters. Overall lengths 9 1/2" (241 mm).

1 Every knife starts as a concept drawing and is then transferred to a metal pattern before it is finally transferred to the raw steel. Here, the pattern is cut out on the metal band saw.

3 The blade edges are dyed with layout fluid and then two lines are scribed on the edge of the blade as a guide for grinding a clean, straight cutting edge.

6 While grinding, the grind line height is constantly measured on both sides of the blade to ensure they are exactly even along its the entire length.

8 The knives have both been trial assembled and inspected to ensure a flawless fit and finish. They are glued, clamped and set to cure over night in a warm food dehydrator that has been modified to hold knives and sheaths.

2 When working on a specific project or design, at least two knives are made at the same time in case one doesn't turn out quite right. Here, both blanks profiled to the final outline compared to the paper pattern.

4 One blade has been beveled to 45 degrees for the initial grind. The other blade shows the double scribed line along the cutting edge.

5 Knife steel in Tracy's shop is purchased in 4"x36" sheets. Here he is cutting out the two blanks on the metal band saw.

7 One bolster has been cleaned up with the shaping and polishing started. The small wheels shown above the knives are used for grinding the finger relief section in the bolsters.

9 Both knives are completed but not sharpened, making the sheath construction safer. The sheaths are custom fit to each knife. The hand stitches are recessed and spaced evenly with the two hand tools shown.

10 These patterns hanging on the wall of the shop have accumulated over the last seven years. The Twins were created by using the handle of one pattern and the blade of another pattern. For this project both knives were finished to completion.

Alain Miville-Deschênes
"The Minotaurs", 2005

Alain was born in 1972, in the small village of Bonaventure, in the province of Québec, Canada. As a young boy he began to collect knives, and to use them during various outdoor activities, while camping and hunting. His knifemaking began late in 1999 when he searched for an artistic form of manual work as a change from his virtual job as a computer artist and teacher.

He set up a small shop in his house and self-taught himself into knifemaking by trial and error with the help of books, magazines, and the Internet. Alain likes to learn and experiment with new things, enjoying knifemaking while exploring various related techniques such as design, metal working, soldering, sculpture, jewelry, leather work and more. Alain makes knives of many styles, hunting knives, tactical knives, neck knives, art knives and folders. He prefers to use natural materials like wood-burl, antler and ivory, but also likes synthetic materials such as G-10 or micarta.

1952, Charles-A. Parent
Québec, QC, Canada G2B4B2
Phone: (418) 845-0950
email: amd@miville-deschenes.com
Site: http://www.amd.miville-deschenes.com

"The Minotaurs", 2005 A pair of knives with ATS-34 blades. One with a 416 stainless guard and spacer, fossil mammoth ivory spacer and a black buffalo horn handle. The other with a bronze guard and spacer, a black buffalo horn spacer and a moose antler-tip handle. Overall lengths 10 1/2" (267 mm) and 10 3/4" (273 mm).

1 The materials used to make this pair of knives. Moose antler tip and buffalo horn tip for the handle, fossilized mammoth ivory and buffalo horn for spacers, 416 stainless steel and bronze for the guard.

3 The two blades are rough cut out from the ATS-34 stainless steel bar, using a vertical/horizontal metal band saw.

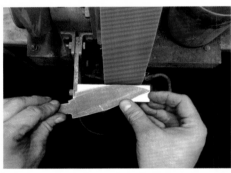

6 The 2"x72" variable speed belt grinder is used to grind the blade and tang contours and bring them flush with the scribed line.

8 The blade shoulder is filed square using a home made filing jig and flat files. A round file is used to put a small radius in the corner to avoid stress in the steel during the heat treating process.

2 The designs for the knife were drawn by hand and then finalized on the computer. The completed drawing is printed out and traced with a scribe onto the ATS-34 bar.

4 The blade is cut close to the previously scribed line. Sometimes, a pushing-block is used to avoid getting one's fingers too close to the saw's blade.

5 A 1"x42" home made variable speed belt grinder is used to grind the small radius on the blade. Various sizes of small contact wheels can be installed on this grinder. A coarse grit belt is used to begin the grinding and then progressively finer belts are used to reach a smooth finish.

7 The contour of the blade is brought to its final shape. The blade is also surface ground on the flat platen of the grinder to remove any scales and pits from the surface of the steel.

9 The grind line is drawn on each side of the blade with a pencil. A home made jig with carbide tips is used to mark two fine parallel lines on the side of the blade. This is the guideline for grinding the blade bevel.

10 The holes for the pins are drilled in the tang before the heat treating process. For hidden tangs, like in these two knives, only one hole is necessary for the pins. On full tang knives many holes are drilled on the tang to distribute the weight correctly and to give more grip for the glue. Each hole is counter-bored to minimize the stress in the steel during the heat treating process.

11 The blade is ground on the variable speed 2"x72" belt grinder with a 10" contact wheel. The guide lines on the blade and scribed lines on its side are used to control the removal of the same amount of steel from each side.

12 Grinding the blade bevel begins with a 60 grit belt and goes on with progressively finer belts. The flat parts of the blade are also sanded to a smooth "scratchless" finish.

14 The spine is buffed to a mirror finish and the flats are hand rubbed to their final satin finish. A home-made knifemaking vise is used to hold the blade during this process.

13 The ATS-34 blade is heat treated by a specializing firm to obtain a high quality result (vacuum heat treated with cryo). When the blade returns, it receives the final hand-rubbed finish with fine grits of sanding paper.

15 The guard is rough cut and polished. The tang is measured and its dimensions are drawn on the guard. Many smalls holes are drilled and then connected to make the slot rectangular, using dental burs on a Foredom flex shaft.

16 Cleaning and squaring of the rectangular slot is done with a small file in a filing jig. Many tests and adjustments are needed to obtain a good and tight fit.

17 "I make many utility knives, intending them to be used. I work a lot on the ergonomic and practical aspects but do not forget the aesthetics and the visual aspects as well. I draw and redraw all my models many times by hand and then on the computer until I obtain a result that pleases me and my customer. A hand made sheath (exotic leather or kydex) is also part of the final product and requires a lot of work and attention too. I work in a little shop and like to use simples tools and many self made hand tools. I also like to build my own knifemaking machinery. The belt grinder, drill press, metal band saw, Foredom flex shaft and caliper are the tools I use most".

19 The raw materials are cut to make the buffalo horn spacer and a mammoth ivory spacer. Spacers are sanded flat and parallel (checked with a caliper). Vulcanized paper spacers are also prepared.

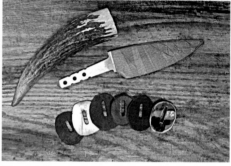

20 A hole for the tang is drilled in the vulcanized paper, buffalo horn and mammoth ivory spacers. The guard and spacers are assembled without glue to check the fit.

18 The flat ends of the buffalo horn and the moose antler are sanded flat (to a 90° angle) on the belt grinder. This end on the buffalo horn and the antler tip is later modified into an oval shape to fit with the guard. A low speed horizontal disc sander, visible in the picture behind Alain, is used to flatten many types of materials such as spacers.

21 The blade and guard are cleaned and prepared for soldering. The blade is plunged into water during the soldering to prevent any ruining of the heat treatment. A jig holds the parts together during the soldering process.

22 Low temperature silver solder is used to solder the blade and the guard together. A small brass chisel is used to remove and clean the solder. A Foredom flex shaft with a small cratex wheel is used for the polishing.

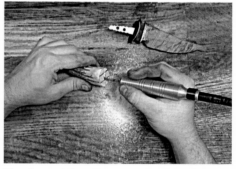

23 Holes are drilled in the handle for the tang and interconnected using the Foredom flex shaft with a carbide rasp. All parts are assembled without glue to check their fit, and the hole for the pin is drilled into the handle.

24 Before applying the glue, all the handle parts are cleaned and roughened with coarse sandpaper. Two-part epoxy is mixed and the knife is assembled with glue.

25 Everything is held together in a clamp during curing. The overflowed glue on the blade and guard is cleaned with acetone before curing.

26 Final shaping of the handles and guards on the belt grinder begins after the glue has cured. Finishing off is done by hand sanding with fine sand paper and finally buffing to a nice polish.

Antonio Montejano Nieto
"Abellán", 2005

Antonio was born in the cutlery city of Albacete, Spain in 1961. He began to etch and engrave at the age of 21, under the tutelage of his Master Engraver father. The honorific title of Master Artisan (Engraver/Cutler) was bestowed upon him in the year 2000. The acid etchings and engravings that he does, utilize traditional artisan techniques inherited from the last century. He has also developed and improved new techniques on his own over a period of several years, expanding his knowledge considerably.

He has participated in cutlery competitions in Spain, and has been awarded numerous prizes. Of these awarded works, five pieces are on display as the property of the Museum of Cutlery of Albacete.

His knives are inspired by classic styles such as Renaissance, Gothic and Art Nouveau, and employ the techniques of the goldsmith. He has a small collection of very special pieces made over a period of several years.

San Cristobal, 19 - 2° B
02003 Albacete, Spain
Phone: (+34) 967-504351
email: monti502@ono.com

"Abellán", 2005 This knife was created in the Art Nouveau style, with Renaissance influences. It is made of Sandwich 12C27 steel and a handle of ivory and nickel-silver with Red Coral inlays. The handle is handmade and hand finished, with the carving polished to a high luster. The blade is acid-etched with traditional methods of the last century, making this a fine collector's piece. Overall length 10" (254 mm).

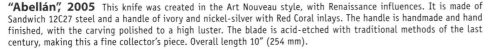

1 Elephant ivory for the handle slabs; German nickel-silver for the handle with Red Coral for the inlays; copper and 12C27 steel for the blade.

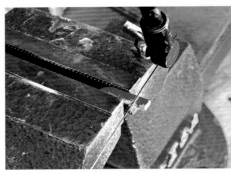

5 Trimming pieces of Red Coral with a very fine jeweler' saw blade, in preparation for inlay in the spine.

9 After polishing with fine sandpaper, and buffing with cotton cloth, the spine is complete.

13 The handle pieces are pinned together with dri bits.

Trimming and filing the nickel-silver that will form the [sp]ine of the handle.

3 Using various files to shape the edge surface all around the handle.

4 Filing of the back spine completed, and a cutout is created to accept the tang of the blade.

[T]He spine is completed with inlays of coral, carefully [c]ut and filed to size.

7 Nickel-silver side plates are clamped to the spine to frame the coral inlays. Plates are 1.5 mm in thickness.

8 Drilling and tapping the plates and spine to accept 3 mm fasteners.

[10] Sawing of the ivory to obtain two pieces for the [sc]ales.

11 Cutting the ivory scales with a jeweler's saw after drawing the scale profile.

12 The scales and the spine with all holes drilled for later assembly.

[1]4 The handle pieces are clamped while pinned together [w]ith drill bits to keep them properly positioned during [su]bsequent work.

15 The holes are being tapped for 3 mm threaded rod which will be used to hold the pieces together.

16 Using a milling machine to make two grooves in each handle scale to accept nickel-silver inlay pieces. This allows for a perfect fit.

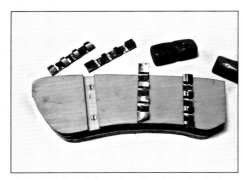

17 Test fitting of the nickel-silver inlays in the ivory indicates success.

18 Cutting Red Coral pieces to be inlaid in the nickel-silver pieces.

19 The coral is epoxied into the already close-fittin mortises.

20 A perfect fit is achieved.

21 Rough shaping of the whole handle assembly with a file.

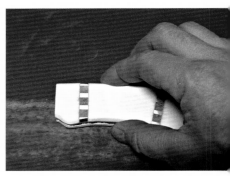

22 After the filing, a very fine finish is achieved on th ivory by sanding from 300 to 2000 grit.

23 Handle with an excellent surface finish is polished to a high luster. After laying out a design, ivory carving begins using a Dremel tool and gravers, as need dictates.

24 Using a magnifying visor helps to assure a quality carving as seen here while working with the Dremel tool.

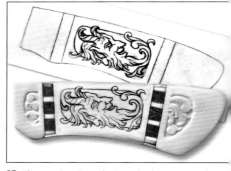

25 After carving the ends, Antonio chose a gargoyle mas and drew it out on paper with a pencil. He then copie the design directly onto the ivory, allowing him to begi to carve it out.

26 The handle assembly clamped in a vise for carving. While carving, the drawing gets smeared, so the silhouette is carved first. The handle is seen here in an advanced stage of the carving.

27 One side is now finished.

28 The highly polished detail of the mask carving is no evident.

29 A different theme is drawn on the other side of the handle.

30 Finished and polished carving of the second side.

31 Laying out the design for the guard.

32 Filing the guard to shape.

33 Drilling out the hole in the guard to accommodate the tang of the knife blade.

34 Embellishing the edges of the guard with filework.

35 After grinding the blade by hand on a belt grinder, fine sanding is required (beyond 1000 grit). The blade will then be polished with a cotton cloth and polishing paste.

36 Fileworking the spine of the blade is done after heat treating, so a diamond file is used.

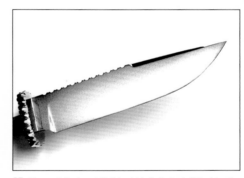

37 The polished and finished blade is test-fitted to the guard.

38 The initial drawing of the design is transfered in ink onto the steel.

39 After etching, the background now removed to a lower level to emphasize the embellishment.

40 The knife is completed after shading is added by engraving the high relief etching on the polished blade using diamond burs.

Dusty Moulton
"Sliver", 2004

Dusty Moulton was born in 1951, in the Eastern Oregon town of Lakeview, a small lumber and ranching community. He grew up hunting, fishing, riding motorcycles and horses and working on ranches. Dusty's knife career began in 1991, being totally self-taught in his knife making and engraving. He has evolved over the years to create knife and engraving designs that are unique. *"I currently build and engrave up to 60 knives and sheaths a year on a full-time basis. I could possibly make more but then the quality would go down. I am always evolving and learning. I have plans laid out for the future that include learning to do some sculpturing of*

handle materials for a more artistic look, and to add a quality tactical lineup to my offerings which is a departure from my usual repertoire."
As of 2004 Dusty has won 26 knife-show awards. He currently attends only 3 to 4 knife shows per year.

*135 Hillview Lane
Loudon, TN 37774, USA
Phone:(865) 408-9779
email: dusty@moultonknives.com
Site: http://www.moultonknives.com*

1 The basic components used for building a double bolstered fighter called the Sliver.

5 After cleaning and flattening the steel using a 12 then a 320 grit on the platen with a hand held magnet, th guidelines for grinding are marked along the sides.

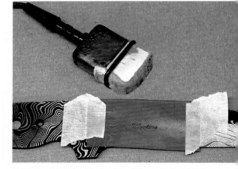

9 Dusty signs the blade after it is etched. With Damascu steel the process is different than with plain steel. H electroetchs it as usual but then the process varie a bit.

13 The bolsters are ground flat on a 1 1/2" thick piece c surface ground steel with a sheet of sand paper glued t it, making sure they end up completely flat.

"Sliver", 2004 The handle material is Paua shell and the Damascus is 1095 & nickel by Jim Ferguson. Overall length 10 3/4" (273 mm).

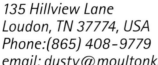

The knife-profile pattern has been traced out on the [b]ar of Damascus steel and is now ready to be cut out with [a] bandsaw.

3 After roughing out on the bandsaw, it is off to the profiling grinder, which is set-up to run at a high speed to hog off material for the final profile of the knife.

4 When profiling is finished, holes are drilled using a drill press. The holes are then chamfered before heat treating to help avoid stresses that could cause cracking.

The grind for the top false edge is done first, as it is a [s]maller and more precise grind; Dusty likes to get it right [fi]rst and only then proceed to the main blade grind.

7 The main blade grind is taken down to 320 grit and then hand rubbed to 400 grit until all traces of grind lines are removed, before proceeding to heat treatment.

8 The top tang is marked with the appropriate spacing so it can be file-worked before heat-treating. Dusty uses only two files, a small triangular file and a round chain saw file.

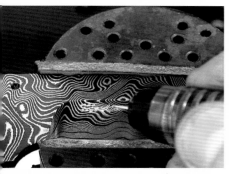

[1]0 Using a microscope and a high-speed rotary tool, [h]e delicately goes over the acid etch with the carbide burr [to] highlight the logo on the dark Damascus.

11 Next are the bolsters. Double-sided tape is used to hold them to the knife for drilling the pin holes.

12 There are front and rear bolsters on the Sliver. After they are profiled and drilled, the bolsters are taken to the disk grinder to grind the dovetail angles.

[1]4 Fitting the handle material (in this case some beautiful [p]aua shell) comes after the bolsters have been pinned to [th]e knife.

15 A large scale drawing of the engraving patterns are drawn out first before they are reduced down to fit the bolster.

16 The engraving design is cut out, and the backgrounds relieved and flattened. Next come the final shading cuts to give detail and depth. Inking darkens everything up.

Hidetoshi Nakayama
"Kawazu" (Frog), 2005

Hidetoshi Nakayama was born in 1971, in Kawagoe City, Japan. He began making traditional style knives in 1990, at the age of 19, under the guidance of a one of the top knife makers in Japan, Nobuyuki Uekama. Three years later, at the age of 22, he started studying netsuke carving, under the netsuke artist, Yasufusa Saito. In 2000, he began taking his carving skills to his knife making, creating his own style by merging his knives and his netsuke art. Hidetoshi felt that the art knife had the same basic feel about it as the netsuke. Both being objects one can enjoy

holding in ones hand while appreciating their beauty. In 2001, he sold his first knife at the Blade Show West held in Los Angeles. He usually participates in 4-5 shows each year and has won several awards both in Japan and overseas. Hidetoshi also displays his netsuke at exhibitions every year.

1131-27 Fujima, Kawagoe, Saitama
350-1142 JAPAN
Phone: 090-2400-5264
email: chima_chima365@infoseek.to

1 The material Hidetoshi chose to use for the knife handle and sheath is Boxwood, a hard and fine texture wood. Here it is being cut to size with a hand saw.

"Kawazu" (Frog), 2005 Carved and dyed Boxwood handle and sheath. Buffalo horn bolster and carbon steel blade. Overall length 7 7/8" (200 mm).

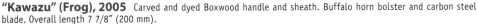

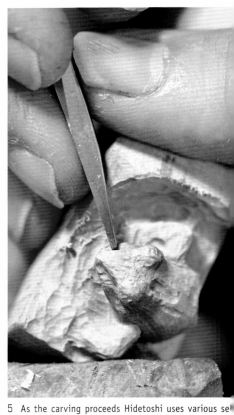

5 As the carving proceeds Hidetoshi uses various self made tools for each stage. Carving the frog and the bark of old pine tree on the handle took 30 hours t complete.

Hidetoshi uses more than 50 kinds of carving tools, all made by himself. There is no comparison between these handmade tools and mass-produced tools.

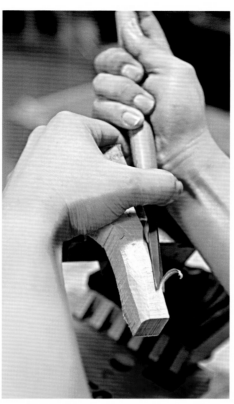

3 One of the first stages after cutting the rough shape of the handle and the sheath with a hand saw is to chisel out their general shape using paring gouges and the flat chisels.

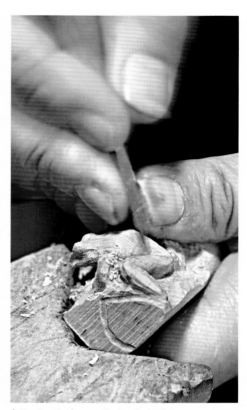

4 Carving the frog on the handle begins.

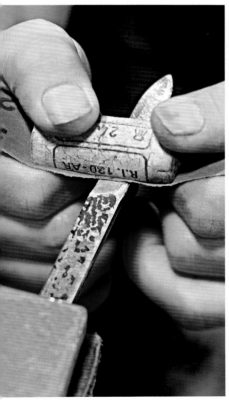

The blade is ground freestyle on the belt grinder and nd shaped with bastard files. It is brought to a luster sing progressively finer sand paper attached to a piece f cork.

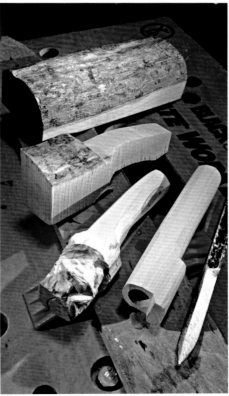

7 The handle, the sheath and the blade are roughed out, before beginning the long and detailed final carving.

8 The finished knife after all carving and dyeing has been completed. The dyes are a mixture of chemical and vegetable dyes. The frog's eyes are sheep horn inlays.

Francesco Pachì
"Skinner Hunter", 2005

Francesco Pachì was born in 1961, in Genoa, Italy. Today he lives in Sassello, Italy, in a house surrounded by woods and meadows, with his wife, Mirella, and daughter Gaia. After finishing his scientific studies, in 1983, he started a publicity photography company that within a few years became one of the most successful in the city of Genoa. Francesco loves nature and outdoor activity and is an expert archer and hunter. In 1991 he became deeply interested in steels and the components used in creating them. Completely self-taught, his first experiments with grinding, led him, in 1994, to his first exhibition. In 1995, after a trip to the United States and a few days spent in the studio of the great American master Steve Johnson, he decided to devote himself full-time to knifemaking. The special characteristic of his blades is

the chipped appearance of the flat of the blade, creating a pleasant contrast to its perfectly polished, mirror-like finish. Many of his creations are finished using fossil ivory for the handles, both mammoth and walrus, on which his wife, Mirella, a well known scrimshaw artist, creates true masterpieces.

Via Pometta, 1
17046 SASSELLO (SV), Italy
Phone/Fax: (+39) 01 9720086
email: info@pachi-knives.com
Site: www.pachi-knives.com/homeita.htm

"Skinner Hunter", 2005 RWL-34 stainless steel blade, 416 stainless steel bolsters, Mosaic pins, mammoth ivory slabs, scrimshaw by Mirella Pachì. Overall length 9 7/16" (240 mm).

1 Using a model made of paper, the knife pattern is scribed on a bar of RWL-34 stainless steel.

5 Drilling the holes in the steel.

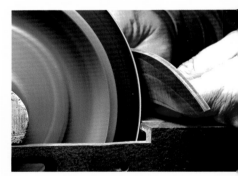

9 Grinding is done on a 8" contact wheel, starting with a 50 grit belt and going up to 220 grit.

13 A premium piece of fossil mammoth ivory is chosen for the handle slabs.

2 With the belt grinder the excess steel is removed.

3 The steel is now flattened out with the surface grinder.

4 The blade is marked for drilling the holes to connect the handle slabs and the bolsters.

6 Center lines are traced along the edge as guiding marks for grinding the blade.

7 Center lines are traced to mark the tapered tang.

8 After marking the center lines along the edge, Francesco begins to grind the blade.

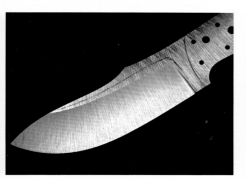

10 The grinding is complete

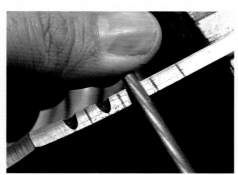

11 File-working the spine.

12 Before the heat treating process, the blade is wrapped in stainless steel foil with a piece of paper inside to burn all the oxygen.

14 After the heat treatment, Francesco starts to grind the tang.

15 This grinding is done to reduce the steel in the tang and help out when moving on to the plate of the belt grinder.

16 Shaping the tapered tang is finish on the plate of the belt grinder.

17 The logo is etched onto the blade.

18 The chipping that is a characteristic of all of Pachi's knives is created on a small contact wheel.

19 The 416 stainless steel pins and steel for the bolsters.

20 The bolsters are ground to create perfect alignment.

21 With a tapered end-mill francesco works on the guard holes.

22 All the components are ready to be assembled.

23 Peenning the bolster's pins.

24 The slabs of mammoth ivory and a thin foil of black fiber are prepared to finish the handle.

25 The front part of the handle slabs that will come in contact with the bolsters is ground flat.

26 The slabs are glued in the correct position.

27 After the glue is dry, holes for the pins can be made.

28 The hole for the tube is drilled at rear end of the handle.

29 Mosaic pins are chosen for their visual beauty.

30 The mosaic pins are glued in position with super-glue.

31 When the super-glue is dry, the handle is finished on the grinder.

32 One wall of Francesco Pachi's shop is covered with the many templates of knives he has made over the years.

33 Finishing the handle by hand continues, using finer and finer abrasives.

34 Much attention and care is used when finishing the sides of the handle, where steel and mammoth are are exposed side by side.

35 The final polish.

Rik Palm
"Crane", 2005

Born in 1959, Rik grew up in small rural Maine City. He loved playing outdoors with his dad and brother, hunting, fishing and kayaking. His interest in knifemaking started when he was in high school. It wasn't until the year 2000 when Rik had the pleasure of meeting Rob Simonich who encourage him to give knifemaking a try. He was immediately hooked. With the intrigue of unexplored design freedom, craftsmanship, sculpture and new experiences, he signed up with the American Bladesmiths Society and has not looked back ever since. Rik received his Jouneyman Smith rating in June 2004. He enjoys making fixed-blades but is interested in making folding knives too, everything from simple utility workers to art knives. Rik is currently exploring many different directions in knife design and construction. He prefers to use natural materials like bone and ivory on his knives. In the future he plans on learning to cast and engrave giving himself more options while planning and building his knives.

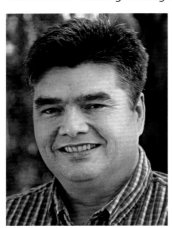

10901 Scripps Ranch Blvd.
San Diego, California 92131, USA
Phone: (858) 530-0407
email: rikpalm@knifesmith.com
Site: www.knifesmith.com

"Crane", A Nature Series Knife, 2005 A carved 152 layer 15n20/1084 pattern welded full tang knife. The blade is 5" long with a full distal taper. The handle has wave file work around its edge and carved elephant ivory scales with a 22k gold eye pin on top of a textured nickel silver pinned background. Overall length 9 3/4" (248 mm).

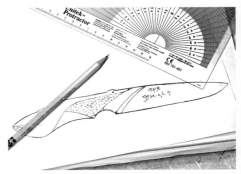

1 Rik refined his original sketched drawing of the Crane knife to be a nice size, and easy to carry hiking knife. He will clay harden and balance it at the finger choi with a tapered tang.

3 After grinding out the blade's profile, he flattens it before cleaning up the bevels. Once the blade is square and cleaned up, he does a quick etch to check the welds and the pattern in the steel.

6 Rik engraves the ricasso lines deeply on both sides of the blade before he uses carbide ball burrs for shaping the scallop indentions between the lines, making sure they flow over from one side to the other.

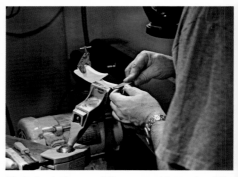

10 A jeweler's saw and files are used to rough out the elephant ivory scales to match the blade's profile after heat treatment. The scales will have hidden pins to secure them to the tang.

2 He welds a 19 layer stack and folds it 8 times resulting in a 152 layer billet. He then forges the knife's profile as close to shape as possible. Using his sketch pattern, he traces it onto the pre-form.

4 Using his sketch again, Rik makes a template out of an index card to help him mark and match both sides of the blade's carved pattern. Each curve is a little different so he makes 4 templates.

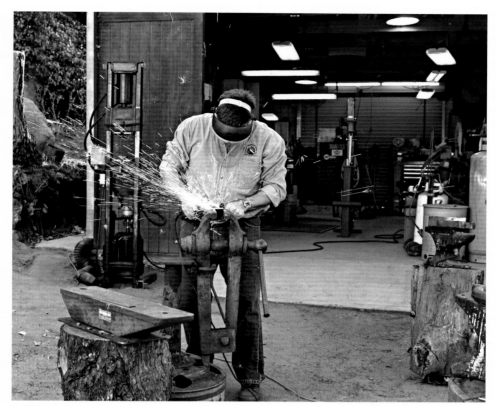

5 Rik is cutting the pattern into the billet with a small angle grinder after the last weld and before he forges the knife. *"I have a small shop with a hydraulic press for welding billets, a 100 lb. Little Giant power hammer, Foredom, Hardcore variable speed grinder, a variable speed small wheel grinder, variable speed disc grinder, 3 anvils, three old 2, 3 and 4 pound sawyer hammers, an engraver and ball vise, a gas torch, a mig welder, a post vise and welding and forging forges".*

7 He uses needle files to refine the general shape of the carved ricasso in the finger choil and on the blade's back. Different grits of sand paper with specially shaped sanding rods are used to finish it all to a 600 grit.

8 Rik thermocycles the blade to sphereodize and normalize it before re-finishing it to 220 grit.

9 Satinite is used for differentially hardening the blade during heat treating. Using it allows Rik to target exactly where he wants the blade to be hard and where the steel can remain softer.

11 While carving the crane's shape, Rik uses needle files that he modified. To hold the pieces together he uses a drill bit inserted through the eye and twist clamps to keep the ivory scales registered.

12 After Using Windex to neutralize the effect of the etchant, Rik carefully knocks off the oxides with 2500 wet/dry sand paper to reveal the pattern in the steel.

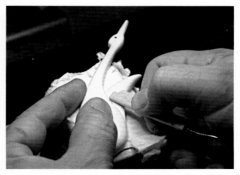

13 Before final assembly, the crane shape is cleaned with sanding sticks progressing to finer and finer grits. A small 2" floppy buffing wheel is used to bring the ivory to a bright polished finish.

Bertie Rietveld
"Ballerina", 2005

Born in 1962, in Johannesburg, South Africa, Bertie Rietveld lives on a farm and creates his knives in his well equipped workshop. For 26 years now this craftsman has chosen the medium of fine knives to express his artistic talents. The many facets of this pursuit stretch to stonework for handles, gold inlay work and beautiful Damascus that he forges himself. He is very passionate about sole authorship, including the Stanhope lenses which house his logo, if peeped through. Machines are another one of his passions, and his workshop is filled with all sorts of quality machines, each having its specified task. He believes that the Damascus steel used in a knife must compliment the overall design and spends hours designing and then choosing the appropriate materials that will enhance the final result, in both form

and color. The design of "The Ballerina" dagger has an Art Deco flavour, depicting a ballerina wearing a plumed headpiece and dancing with her toes pointed and her skirt flying up around her waist. The curves of the design represent the waist, hips and the elegant slenderness of the dancer.

P.O. Box 53 Magaliesburg
1791 South Africa
Phone: (+27) 14-577-1294
email: rietveld@netdial.co.za
Site: www.batavia.co.za

"Ballerina" Dagger, 2005 The blade is a 3-bar composite Damascus billet, with a tapering nickel lined center, flanked by Dragonskin damascus on either side. The S-guard is nickel Damascus that flares from the middle outward. The ferrule above the guard is anodised titanium, and the handle is exhibition grade Barberton Verdite. Overall length 16 1/3" (415 mm).

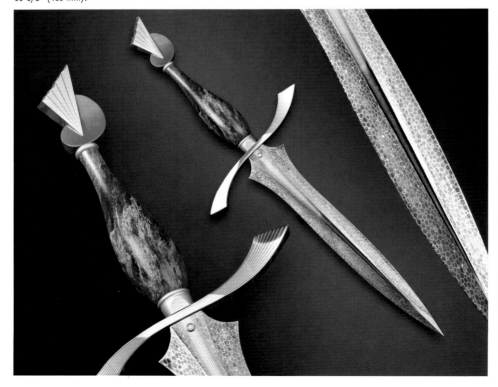

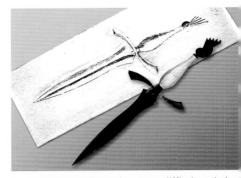

1 Designing the dagger is a most difficult and time consuming task. Sketches are made and altered till the final drawing is completed. A wooden model of the knife is then made from hardwood.

4 The dies used to bend and compress the Damascus for the guard have to be lined up correctly to produce the correct shape. These dies will never be used again, as the daggers are one-of-a-kind.

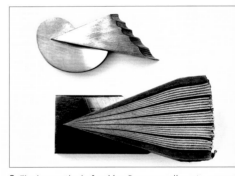

8 The box method of making Damascus allows to arrange the shim in any given pattern, as seen here in 2 stages of the pommel flare. It is silver-soldered to a scroll cut from Dragonskin Damascus.

12 The rough blade billet is cleaned on a Brown & Sharpe hydraulic surface grinder with a grinding belt conversion. The blade is ground taper towards the tip.

2 Shims of carbon-steel and nickel are forge-welded to make the Damascus billets. Dragonskin Damascus used in the blade, is forged from thousands of steel balls.

3 Dies are made specifically to forge the flare on the pommel. The middle layers of the Damascus billet will compress to nothing as the die squeezes it under the hammer to produce two flares.

5 The blade is a three-bar composite, with tapering nickel lines in the centre piece, flanked by Dragonskin Damascus all fitted together precisely to avoid distortion when forged together.

6 The forged guard and blade and parts that make up the pommel are the the Damascus building blocks for the dagger. Now the fitting, grinding and finishing can commence.

7 Bertie is seen forging the flare of the pommel on his 500 pound Massey powerhammer that was built in England in 1944 and then restored (a 6 year process) to its former glory.

8 A diamond core-drill is used to cut the Verdite stone cores for the handle. As it was difficult to predict what the stone looks like on the inside, it took twelve cores to find an acceptable piece.

10 The stone core is placed in the lathe, a hole drilled through the centre using a smaller diamond core-drill and a titanium sleeve glued in place. Now the grinding of the profile can commence.

11 A specially built belt grinder, using diamond belts, is bolted to the lathe and used to grind the stone to its required profile. It is then carefully hand-sanded until fully polished.

13 The tapered blade is profiled, a centre line scribed on the edge. The main bevels are ground on a belt grinder. At first just a rough grind, then heat treated, then a perfectly symmetrical final grind.

14 When grinding the blade it looks like any other steel with no visible pattern. Etching in ferric chloride brings out the Damascus pattern. It is dipped in the solution and then rinsed off.

15 The real thrill comes when all completed parts are laid out to resemble the finished knife. For the first time one can get a good idea of what the finished knife will look like.

Ariel Salaverria
"No-Hammer-Marks Cable Damascus Fighter", 2005

Ariel Elias Salaverria was born in 1965 in Buenos Aires, Argentina. He made his first knife when he was only 12 years old. Growing up, he worked as a diesel locomotive mechanic, in electric facilities and in artistic bladesmithing shops among other places, gaining experience for his knife making path. After several years of part time knife making, he decides, in 2002, to become a full time knifemaker and has been doing it ever since. Ariel's knives are individually crafted and completely hand made in his small shop. Most of the knives he makes are forged from his Damascus. Ariel has shown that his innovative mind knows no

boundaries when combining the various metal elements he uses for his blades. He is constantly pushing the envelope, trying new ways and techniques for creating Damascus as well as home made micarta, every one of his knives is unique and mesmerizing.

Leon Gallo 4006, San Justo
B1754DNZ, Buenos Aires, Argentina
Phone: (+54) 011-4691-2145
email: ariel@aescustomknives.com.ar
Site: http://www.aescustomknives.com.ar

"No-Hammer-Marks Cable Damascus Fighter", 2005 A 10" (254 mm) blade, including bolsters, in Cable Damascus (1085) with a 7 1/2" (190 mm) cutting edge. Handle made of deer stag with a 1" (25.4 mm) handmade ornamental inlay. Leather and bronze spacers. Hand stitched and worked leather sheath. Overall length 15" (381 mm).

1 The cable section and a 1030 steel rod are the materials that will be used to forge the blade. The rod will be inserted into the cable, to replace the inner strand. One end, left protruding, will provide a secure tang for the handle.

3 After heating the cable to get rid of the oil substances found between the strands and to make it more ductile, it is placed in a vise, where it is twisted tight. The wire ties prevent the cable from coming apart.

6 Hammering the hot pipe after it has been taken out of the fire. Encapsulating the cable inside the pipe prevents it from coming in direct contact with the flames, keeping it from decarburizing.

10 During the grinding process Ariel makes sure the edge is properly welded and only then begins to grind the bevels of the already shaped blade. Ariel uses masking tape to mark the blade on both sides for an even grind.

To replace the inner strand, the cable needs to be secured a vise. Ariel proceeds to center the rod on the cable d starts to hammer it in, pushing the inner strand out om the other side.

Cable already inserted into a stainless steel pipe that ll protect it from the hammer marks. Both ends of the pe are welded closed. Now the canister is ready to be aced on the forge.

After several heating and hammering sessions, the ade is flattened out. The bolster area is intentionally ft untouched so that the original shape and patterns of e cable will be displayed in the finished knife.

1 The ground and polished (not etched) blade, along ith the stag and decorated pin for the handle, and pieces f bronze and leather that will later become the spacers tween the cable and the stag.

5 Ariel built his workshop by closing and roofing a patio in his house. Measuring 10 feet square (3x3m), it is relatively small, but keeps all the tools and equipment in one place. Using a disk-grinder Ariel is cutting a piece of cable in the process of making the Cable Damascus fighter. Specializing in Damascus steels, Ariel likes to make San Mai blades that provide an excellent cutting edge.

8 Removing the cable blade from of the pipe. First, Ariel grinds the flattened pipe along its edge and opens it up. Then he uses a chisel to separate and remove the blade.

9 After removing the blade (they don't weld together because the pipe is made of stainless steel) it is evident that the pipe that held it in place during the entire process, protected it successfully from hammer marks.

12 Detail of the now finished knife, showing the bolster with the exact same shape and pattern as the original cable, as well as the blade with no hammer marks and the already etched bevels.

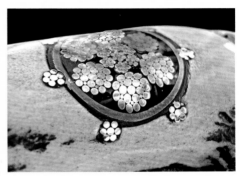

13 Close-up of the handmade "decorated pin" located on the handle. It was created from a piece of cable inserted into a copper pipe filled with with clear epoxy resin. A view of the individual strands emerges after polishing.

Joe Szilaski
"Presentation Pipe Tomahawk", 2005

Joe was born in 1949, in Hungary. His training in metal work began in 1963 at a trade school in Hungary, as a blacksmith's apprentice. Part of his training was to make knives and cleavers for local butchers. Since that time he has worked in various metal-working trades, as an ornamental ironworker and a senior detailer in an art foundry specializing in bronze, silver and steel sculptures. He has earned the rank of Master Smith with the American Bladesmith Society, is a voting member of the Knife Makers Guild and is currently a field editor for BLADE Magazine, who publish his bimonthly column "Joe Szilaski's Q and A". Most of his pieces are one-

of-a-kind designs, specializing in carved ivory, pearl and Damascus. All of his knives and hawks are fully hardened, functional pieces, not wall-hangers, done by himself, from the forge to the final embellishments.

Custom Knives & Tomahawks
29 Carroll Drive
Wappingers Falls, NY 12590, USA
Phone: (845) 297-5397
email: Joe@Szilaski.com
Site: http://www.Szilaski.com

Presentation Pipe Tomahawk, 2005 The owner wished to have a bladed hawk made to match and complete his set. These hawks are fashioned in a style typical of hawks made in the 1800's, though spike-pipe tomahawks were rare and few original specimens have been found. This hawk has an 8" (203 mm) head with 3 1/2" (89 mm) wide cutting edge. Overall length 20 1/2" (520 mm).

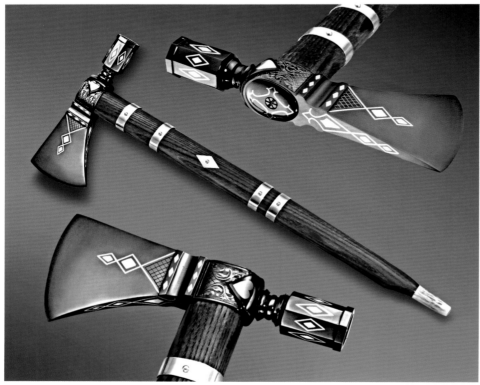

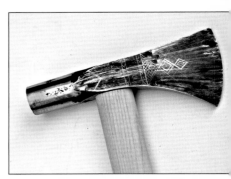

1 After the hawk head is forged it is allowed to slowly co in a hot box for 24 hours. Joe will then rough grind it remove any scales formed during the forging process.

3 The eye of the head is filed smooth and the haft tightly fitted. The head is covered with layout ink and t design is laid out.

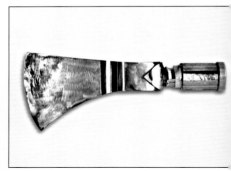

6 This hawk will have an octagon shaped bowl. After t neck of the bowl is filed down, Joe uses masking tape mark out the sides of the bowl.

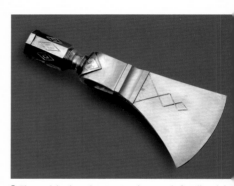

8 The cavities have been cut and are ready for silver inla Joe cuts the cavities deep to ensure the silver stays secu when the hawk is used to chop or throw.

A piece of hickory wood is cut to size and a smoke hole is carefully drilled, before it is fit to the head. A hand-forged spade bit measuring 22 1/2" (570 mm) is used.

Joe begins to shape out the chevron (top photo) and then undertakes the fuller section between the eye and the blade (bottom). Most of this work is done with files.

To make the job easier, the head is placed in an engravers block. As one can see, there are few surfaces that will not receive some inlay work.

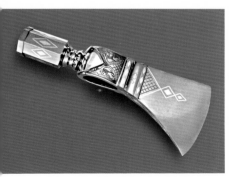

The silver work is now complete and has been sanded smooth. Joe engraves a period design over the eye and blade. The piece is now ready for heat-treating, polishing, and gun-blueing.

5 To forge these presentation pipe tomahawks, Joe starts out with 2 inch round W2 tool steel, which is an excellent all around steel. With correct forging temperature and heat treatment it will make a tough and reliable tool. Joe also uses S5 and S7 for his throwing tomahawks because of the shock resistant properties of these steels.

10 The six pound hammer Joe is using will move some steel. He also has a 50 pound Little Giant power hammer as his helper. In this photo, you can see the hawk head starting to take on its shape. The hawk head will be put through several thermal-cycles before it takes its final shape.

Michael A. Tyre
"Damascus Southwestern Bowie", 2005

Michael Tyre was born in 1950, in Logansport, Indiana. In 1968 he Joined US army and proudly served two tours in 101st Airborne Division in Vietnam, returning home a disabled veteran. He then attended university and majored in arts. Visiting a knife show he was hooked for life. Later he was introduced to knifemaking by D'Alton Holder. *"I have gained so much from every knife maker I met. They all share their knowledge and friendship which I shall always treasure. My goals are to make the highest quality knives, using the finest materials available, to increase my knowledge of metallurgy and to have a lot of fun while doing this".*

Mike specializes in folders, hunters and survival knives, using natural materials for his handles.

1219 Easy Street
Wickenburg, AZ 85390, USA
Phone: (928) 684-9601
email: azbiker88@hotmail.com

1 This is the fun part, when beginning the process of creating something from one's thoughts. Mike draws out the design on paper then on the blank piece steel, this time choosing Jim Ferguson's Damascus for the blade.

3 Flat grinding the blade on a hardcore grinder with flat platen and a work rest. This stage of the knifemaking process usually takes about 15 minutes.

6 The blade is now ready for the heat treatment. The oil for quenching the blade is being warmed to about 125° F.

"Damascus Southwestern Bowie", 2005 Cowboy style knife made of Jim Ferguson Damascus, fileworked all along the top of the blade. Hidden tang juniper burl handle with a "salt and pepper" agate, four stainless steel spacers and four black and white spacers. 420 steel guard and butt plate engraved by Barry Lee Hands. Overall length 12 3/4" (324 mm).

8 A close view of the finished knife. The Damascus blade has been etched and marked with the maker's mark using a chemical etching process. Now it can be sent for engraving.

The design is cut out on the bandsaw following the drawn outlines very closely. This blade will be 8" (203 mm) long. It will be a Southwestern style Bowie, or cowboy knife.

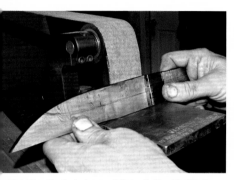

Finishing the last stages of flat grinding the blade.

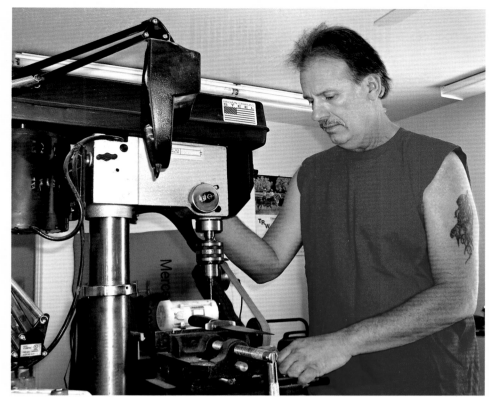

5 "My second day in the new shop. The equipment I use: Hardcore belt grinder with attachments, 9" disc sander to keep things flat, metal cutting bandsaw, drill press, milling machine, oven kiln for heat treating and tempering, anodizer for titanium parts, chemical etching machine for marking my name. My focus is shifting to high performance folding knives, but I shall continue making hunting knives, Bowies and kitchen cutlery".

The blade is heated up to 1250° F, to a non magnetic state, and is dipped point first in the oil quench. Then it is tempered twice at 400° F for one hour, to produce the correct blade hardness.

A close view of the finished knife after returning from the engraver, Barry Lee Hands.

10 Quality check of the finished knife. Checking the knife for uniform blade thickness, fit and finish of the various components as well as the acid etching of the Damascus. If everything is satisfactory, it is time to send it off to its new owner.

Michael Vagnino
"California Bowie", 2005

Michael was born in Kansas City, Missouri, in 1948. Introduced to knife making through a forging class in 1995 with Karl Shroen in California, Michael continued to hone his forging and knife making skills receiving his Mastersmith rating in 2003 from the American Bladesmith Society. He is best known for his folders, but also enjoys making fixed blades, his favorite styled after a George C. Shreeve bowie from the mid 1800's. He chose this style of knife for its simplicity. *"It's harder to make a simple knife well. There are only a few lines and details for the eye to see, so if anything is out of place, it will stick out like a sore thumb".* Michael also enjoys sharing his knife making expertise with others. He teaches in his shop and at the Sierra Fire and Forge School of Fire Arts

in Exeter, California. His degree is in Art Education, and though his past career opportunities took him on other paths, he is happy that knifemaking has brought him back to his passion to create and teach. *"Knife making has been a perfect blend of expressing my artistic side and the ability to share with others what I have learned over the years".*

P.O. Box 67
Visalia, CA 93279, USA
Phone: (559) 528-2800
email: mvknives@lightspeed.net
Site: www.mvknives.com

"California Bowie", 2005 A California Bowie, styled after a knife made by George C. Shreeve of San Francisco in the mid to late 1800's, along with a tip-and-throat sheath. Overall length 12" (305 mm).

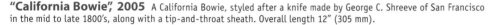

1 The Mosaic Radial pattern Damascus chosen for the blade of this knife is made by Michael. It starts out by drawing the initial billet into a square bar using a press.

3 The bar on the right shows the initial stage of shaping the triangle; the bar on the left has been worked further.

6 Truing the bar up on the anvil, eliminating any kink or bends. Michael then cuts and welds four equal lengths of the triangular bar together and draws it out to a 1" square bar.

The square bar is then pressed into a triangular shape.

Michael pays close attention while sizing the bar so that it will be uniform, making it easier to fit together for the next stage.

5 The final pass on the press.

Here one can see four equal pieces of the 1" square bar welded into the final billet.

8 Once the final billet is welded and drawn out to size, Michael cuts an accordion shape into it with a band saw. This brings the end grain of the pattern to the surface.

9 Ready to flatten the accordion and draw it out to length, bringing out the end grain of the pattern to the surface.

11 The finished billet is now ready to be forged into a blade.

12 Michael starts making the blade by forging in the tip. The hammer he uses is a Bill Fiorini Japanese style hammer. He really likes the way it feels and works.

10 As the billet is drawn out, it is continuously checked for being true and straight.

13 Getting the tip to the exact shape as planned. Once the tip is forged, the edge is drawn down, then the shoulders, dealing with the tang only after the rest of the blade has shaped out satisfactorily.

14 The completed forged blade along with the aluminum template below it that was used as a guide. Michael uses template when forging new blade shapes or shapes he ha not forged in a long time.

15 Once the blade is forged, it is normalized several times making sure the blade is straight and flat. He then surface grinds the ricasso and approximately 1/2" of the front of the tang.

16 After surfacing the flats, Michael does the initial grind prior to heat treatment. When the heat treatment is complete, he finishes the grind.

17 The guard material is fit on the blade, then the width shoulders and top and bottom center lines are marked. The aluminum guides used for this step are milled to various depths to accommodate different thickness of blades.

18 Marking the guard face. Michael uses a soft tip marke on an inked surface to avoid scratching the guard, making the final clean-up easier.

19 Once the center lines are marked on the guard, it is removed from the blade and a template is used to draw the final shape of the guard.

20 Shown is the guard sequence, from marking the width and center lines, marking the guard shape and the cut out guard.

21 Filing a decorative groove in the guard using a chain saw file.

22 After the interior of the scales (handle material) are surfaced flat, the tang of the knife is traced on them making sure it is centered on both pieces.

23 Here one sees the jig Michael made to use in his mill. He glues the scale to the jig, clamps it in a mill vise, then uses an end mill cutter to remove the material from the scale, leaving a void for the tang fits into.

24 Another jig, made to hold the .030 nickel silver spacer to be file worked. The spacer fits between the scales.

25 A dry fit of the guard and handle, prior to etching the blade. Once the blade is etched and marked, the guard is refitted, the handle is peened together and the edges are rounded and smoothed.

26 Close up of the file worked spacer on the finished knife.

27 File working the spacer. This Bowie one of Michael's favorite knives, styled after a George C. Shreeve Bowie from the mid 1800's. He chose this style of knife for its simplicity. *"It's harder to make a simple knife well. There are only a few lines and details for the eye to see, so if anything is out of place, it will stick out like a sore thumb"*

Stephen Vanderkolff
"Dark Star" Dagger, 2005

Born in 1959, Steve currently resides in the small town of Mildmay, Ontario. He began making knives in 1998 but had carried a passion for them all his life. What started as an attempt to save money on a set of throwing knives quickly became a hobby, and then an obsession. The purchase of the KMG grinder in 2003 was a turning point; it allowed him to start creating some of the knives that had danced in his head for years. In 2005 he won Best of Show Art Knife at the Wolverine Annual Spring show. He continues to specialize in fixed blade knives ranging in size from the five-inch Gent's Pocket Knives to full sized Bowies and Art knives. Dark Star, the knife pictured here, was one of those knives that he had thought

about for a long time but was reluctant to attempt. The opportunity to be part of this book was the impetus that he needed. He knew he would need some very high contrast Damascus and therefore turned to Matt Walker to create the Ladder pattern Damascus. Matt's steel worked perfectly and is truly an integral part of this project.

5 Jonathan Crescent
Mildmay, Ontario, Canada N0G 2J0
Phone: (519) 367-3401
email: Steve@vanderkolffknives.com
Site: Vanderkolffknives.com

"Dark Star" Dagger, 2005 A double edged dagger with a Matt Walker Ladder pattern Damascus blade and bolsters and Mother-of-Pearl inlays. Overall length 14 1/2" (368 mm).

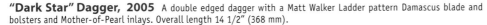
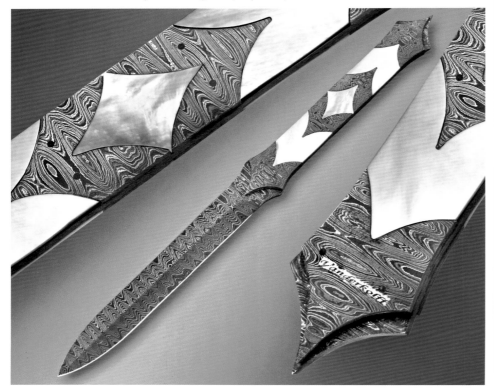

1 "Dark Star" was a knife that Steve had been designing for many years without actually drawing it out on paper. Once it was drawn out, he knew that high contrast Damascus with Mother-of-Pearl inlays were required.

3 To ensure the inlays would be permanently attached to the knife, holes are drilled in the tang to create epoxy pins. The holes are also used to remove the inlays throughout construction.

6 Installing the bolsters so that they are lined up in all dimensions was a very time consuming and frustrating process. Before this step was completed Steve had to regrind three of the bolsters.

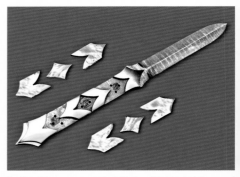

8 The inlays were sanded flush with the bolsters and polished then removed so the finished knife could be etched. Each inlay and corresponding place on the knife was marked using kydex.

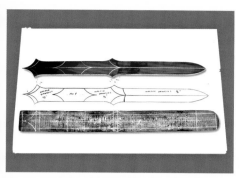

2 First step after drawings for Steve is always the aluminum blank. This lets him get a rough feel of the blade, check dimensions and see if the design translates into reality.

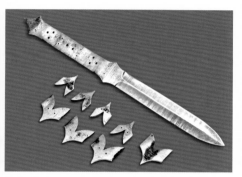

4 The blade was ground to 400 grit on the KMG and then hand sanded to 1200 before heat treatment. This process helps to bring out the Damascus pattern. Grinding and sanding the eight bolsters took about twenty hours.

7 The bolsters were attached with 1/16" 01 pins so that they would not be visible in the Damascus once they were etched. All the bolsters were now hand sanded to 1200 grit.

9 Final assembly required epoxy to hold the inlays, vaseline to ensure the epoxy did not stick to the surface Damascus and plenty of anxious moments.

5 As the project began to develop and Steve started the actual construction, he decided to change the design of the inlays. He hoped that four additional bolsters and more intricate inlay work would elevate this knife to a different level. The thirty one-step plan just became a forty seven-step plan.

10 Each Mother-of-Pearl inlay was a two to three hour project. Luckily Steve had ordered 4 extra pieces of Mother-of-Pearl, and needed them all. Each inlay piece was first traced out using stencil paper, then rough ground on the horizontal grinder, then painstakingly hand filed using needle files. It was a case of three or four strokes with the file, check the fit, repeat, repeat and repeat.

Gustavo C. Vilar
"Carcará Feather", 2005

Gustavo Colodetti Vilar was born in 1978, in Vitoria, the capital city of the beautiful state of Espírito Santo. Neighboring the famous Rio de Janeiro state, Espírito Santo has beautiful beaches and Gustavo grew up to become a professional triathlon athlete. At the age of 18, he started to practice bladesmithing as his father too was a blacksmith artist for many years. His great interest in knives began as a childhood fascination that grew into a deep passion as he grew older. Gustavo took classes, studied from books, consulted every bit of information on the internet and did his own research. He became a full time knife maker in 1999 and from that time on has been collecting titles and prizes in the local São Paulo Knife Show and the Brasilia Custom knife Hall. In 2002 he became a member of the Brazilian Knife Makers Society and joined the American Bladesmiths Society, intending to submit for his Journeyman test.

Rua 25, número 34 – Vila Nova
Vila Velha / ES
Cep. 29105-160 Brazil
Phone: (+55) 27 3349 7079
email: gustavofacas@hotmail.com
Site: www.brazilianbladesmiths.com.br/
gustavo.htm

"Carcará Feather", 2005 Named after a large Brazilian hawk, the blade and bolster of this knife are VCO and 5160 Damascus. Handle is Canafistula burl (Cassia fistula). Overall length 13" (330 mm).

1 First, the Damascus billet is forged and drawn to the proper length and pre-planned number of layers, using a power hammer.

3 One of the twisted bars is left with an extra length that will become the tang. The two are forge welded to form a simple Turkish Damascus pattern.

6 After the blade has been ground, the filework on the bolster begins. Gostavo carefully uses a hacksaw to mark the design, and then a round file to cut the deep groove all around the bolster.

10 The blade is cleaned of oxides and polished to a satin finish, removing minor imperfections and power grinding marks prior to revealing the Damascus pattern. This starts with 200 grit sandpaper and goes up to 800 grit.

2 The bar is cut in two and each section is then twisted in opposite directions.

4 Now the knife is forged and ground to shape, using a special 1" diameter roller on the belt grinder. This creates a perfect flowing transition from the blade to the bolster.

5 Gustavo keeps his workshop clean and organized. This enables him to function with a clear mind and makes the long hours he spends in there much more productive.

7 Heat treatment is done using a special digital oven. It includes full annealing, hardening and very little tempering at this stage. Just enough to keep the blade from cracking.

8 The blade is now selectively tempered with a small torch. This must be done very carefully and without haste. When the back of the blade starts to turn blue with oxides it is ready.

9 Knife and handle are ready for assembling and finishing.

11 The pattern is now revealed and the blade wrapped in tape for protection. The handle can be glued with epoxy and set aside to dry.

12 The handle is very carefully ground to shape, checking constantly for proper grip, visual harmony and overall looks. The flowing transition between grip and bolster is one of Gustavo's trademarks.

13 Finally the handle is buffed with a special wood polishing compound to bring out a beautiful shining finish.

Ricardo Vilar
"Paulista Utility", 2005

Ricardo Vilar was born in 1972, in the city of São Paulo, the biggest metropolis in Brazil. Ricardo began making knives as a hobby in 1988, while running the family marble business. In 1993, he started "PERCOR Cutlery", the name inspired by "The Great Art", a novel written by Ruben Fonseca. Ricardo made knives by the stock removal method until 2001, when he hosted the workshop taught by Jerry Fisk, a major event in Brazilian knife making history. From that point on, influenced by Jerry's teachings, Ricardo abandoned stock removal and began forging all his blades. In 2003, Ricardo was elected as president of the Brazilian Knife Makers Society, the SBC, founded by knifemakers from all over the country who attended Jerry's workshop. Ricardo was also the first South American to receive the Journeyman Smith rating from the American Bladesmith Society. He is one of the foremost Brazilian knifemakers in the international scenario and attends at least two international shows every year.

Alameda dos Jasmins, 243-Parque Petrópolis
Mairiporã / SP
Cep. 07600-000 Brazil
Phone: (+55) 54 3281 4512
email: vilarknives@terra.com.br
Site: www.rvilarknives.com.br

"Paulista Utility", 2005 Blade, bolster and butt cap are made of 15N20/1095 Damascus. The handle is stag antler. Overall length 11 1/2" (292 mm).

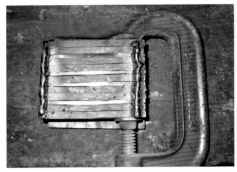

1 The initial billet is created from 01 tool steel and 2767 steel, rich in nickel, from Thyssen Krupp. Ricardo starts out with 9 layers and will end up with 258 layers.

5 The blade is forged to its approximate size using the power hammer. It is important to leave enough material on the blade to cut the Wolf Tooth pattern properly. The corner of the die is used to pull the edge back.

9 Using a belt grinder the blade begins to take shape. Proper edge geometry will be created along with the gentle curves of the knife's silhouette. A lathe is also used to round out the bolster and fit it to the handle.

13 A stag handle is then fitted on the knife and the butt-cap screwed on. All adjustments to be made are carefully marked.

2 Forge welding begins and the billet is drawn and folded until is reaches the number of layers required.

3 Using a blacksmith's simple spring fuller, Ricardo marks the beginning of the blade and is very careful that the fuller is symmetrically positioned when it strikes.

4 The power hammer is used to draw the steel into what will later become the blade.

6 The stock is separated from the handle and the pattern cut with an angular grinder using a thin disk. The grooves are not deep, going one third of the edge's thickness into the blade. The beginning of the tang is also marked.

7 The tang is now forged from the remaining stock on the bottom end of the bolster. The grooves that were cut into the steel are also forged into place to set the layers and expose their different patterns.

8 The final shape is forged, leaving a good amount of material for corrections, if needed, at a later stage.

10 To set a smooth transaction from the blade to the bolster, a special 1" diameter roller-belt grinder is used. This grinder also perfects the faces of the knife creating a full flat from spine to cutting edge.

11 The bolster is now hand filed to create the characteristic spherical detail of a gaucho-style knife. The knife is then heat treated with proper annealing, selectively hardened and tempered and a 400 grit hand finish is applied.

12 A screw nut is made on the lathe and securely silver-welded to a Damascus plate forged from the same billet as the blade.

14 The butt-cap and the fit of the handle to the bolster are ground to shape and the stag handle is polished and prepared for final assembly.

15 The knife is taken apart and the patterns on the blade and butt-cap are revealed by etching with ferric chloride acid. Depending on the solution's concentration, this process can last for an hour or so.

16 The parts are ready to be assembled and glued together, using high quality epoxy resin.

Rudi Zirlin
"Everlasting Ribbon", 2005

Rudi was born in 1964, in Chelibynsk, a city in the Ural mountains in central Russia. He graduated as an engineer/metallurgist from the Polytechnic university and after graduation, he spent some time directing a team of locksmiths at a local foundry. Being deeply interested in making edged weapons, he became an apprentice to a trained blacksmith in Zlatoust (the most famous arms and armor making center in Russia). In 1993 he immigrated to Israel and worked as a blacksmith ever since, making edged weapons exclusively. In 2002, Rudi made a presentation at a seminar of Japanese influenced artists at the Tikotin Museum of Japanese Art. He also made several replicas for the Israeli National Maritime

Museum. Rudi makes knives, swords, axes and other edged weapons of any style, using almost any available correct steel, including his own pattern-welded Damascus. His working methods are traditional and he hand forges (no power hammer!), files, engraves, does inlays, polishing, casting of precious metals and scrimshaw. He also does his own heat treatment.

email: rudi2@013.net
Site: www.rudiknives.com
Israel

"Everlasting Ribbon", 2005 Dagger with a 1095 + nickel Damascus blade. The stylized cross-guard (designed after the guard on the Katzbalger sword) and the pommel are made of 1040 + nickel Damascus. Ebony handle with silver and bronze fittings. Overall length 13 1/2" (343 mm).

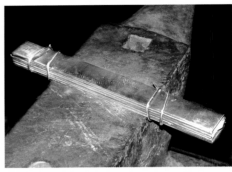

1 Preparing the raw materials for the primary billet. Nine layers of 1090 steel and eight layers of nickel.

3 The billet, after forge-welding, is being cut with a hot chisel.

6 The soon to be pommel.

10 The finished Damascus pattern after the acid etching, a symmetrical alternating "Butterfly" pattern along the spine. Rudi's personal mark is deeply hot-struck.

Heating in the forge while all the metal segments are
bund together with iron wire prior to forge-welding.

First fold before the welding.

5 Heating an additional bar stock, to create the cross guard. Rudi's working methods are traditional and he hand forges (no power hammer!), files, engraves, does inlays, polishing, casting of precious metals and scrimshaw. He also does his own heat treatment.

Re-heating the pommel.

8 Forging the pommel to shape.

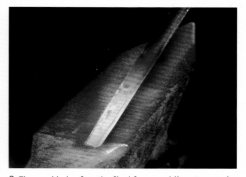

9 The raw blade after the final forge-welding stage, prior to shape forging.

1 The finished dagger prior to final assembly, stripped to its parts after heat-treating and all the fit and finishing ages. All the steel parts, the blade, the cross-guard and the pommel, are made of 272 layer Damascus.

12 A view of the stylized cross-guard, designed after the guard on the Katzbalger sword.

Making Folding Knives

Opposite:

Dr. Fred Carter, USA
"Hand Made Prototypes", 1996-1999
Recognized world wide for his exquisite custom art knives, Dr. Carter is equally known for designing high-quality production knives. The seven handmade prototypes shown here are only a small part of approximately 40 designs he created between 1996-2000. The third knife (from the top) is considered one of the most copied knives ever, having been counterfeited by many factories. Since 1999, Dr. Carter has been designing his knives using various CAD (Computer Aided Design) programs and only occasionally has a handmade prototype been needed to be made. Today his designs can go directly from vector files to CNC produced prototypes and then on to possible production.

Ron Appleton
Phil Booth
Jim (Coop) Cooper
Ron Duncan
Antonio Fogarizzu
Chuck Gedraitis
Jeff Hall
Koji Hara
Jeff Harkins
Howard Hitchmough
Des Horn
Dave Kelly
Jeremy Krammes
Don Morrow
Stephen Olszewski
Francesco Pachi
Nico Pelzer
Andy Shinosky
Mike Skellern
Josh Smith
Stefan Steigerwald
Johnny Stout
Bill Vining
Stan Wilson
Owen Wood
Richard S. Wright

Ron Appleton
"Arwen", 2004

Born in 1954, in Colorado, Ron grew up in his dad's machine shop. He predominantly runs the shop since moving to Texas in 2004 as his father, Ray, is all but retired. Ron was introduced into the Art Knife Invitational after his designs at three AKI shows displayed strengths in design differing dramatically from Rays while still integrating unique and innovative mechanisms. Ron's designs incorporate flowing curves and sweeping concave arcs. His current projects include automatic mechanisms, engravings and collaborations with Scott Pilkington, Master engraver and new locking/opening works of different kinds. He uses titanium and many other rare metals as well as wood, bone, horn, stone and shells. Preferred blade

steels include ATS-34, CPM-3V, O1, D2, S7 and A2. Fitting and overcoming future engineering problems is a constant process during the creating of a new knife. His knives are each built from the ground up thus presenting a whole new set of problems with every new knife. Producing one knife can take 400-700 hours of hard labor. Ron and the love of his life Angela spend a lot of time together working in the shop.

315 Glenn Street
Bluff Dale, TX 76433, USA
Phone: (254) 728-3039
email: ron@helovesher.com

"Arwen", 2004 A three-position push-dagger. Overall length 8 5/8" (220 mm)

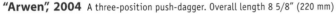

1 Raw cutout pieces, titanium handle halves, 416 SS buttons, ATS-34 Blade, Beryllium-copper round stock for the button cages. The cage and buttons are the heart of the multalock mechanism.

5 Our Agietron Electrical Discharge Machine (EDM). It holds tolerances to within a few ten millionths of an inch and was built in the mid-60s. It precisely removes sections of any metal using spark erosion.

9 Here are essentially all of the internal and external parts for the mechanism. There is still a huge amount of work to do. At this point the knife is 15% completed.

13 With almost all of the machine work done, hand work becomes predominant. Hundreds of hours of hand fitting forming, finishing and polishing are still ahead.

2 Machining the pivot diameter in the blade. This step sets the dimension of the ball lock detents.

3 Drilling indexed ball detents with progressive drills. The number and pattern of the holes define the number and location of blade stops.

4 Great care is involved in machining beryllium due to its toxicity. This is one of two buttom cages, which rotate with the buttons in the handle.

6 This setup in the big Charmilles EDM, forms the interlocking lugs which fit into the blade. It allows the buttons to turn the blade open and closed.

7 Cutting off the residual button length. This button was used as an EDM electrode tool which cut out the button design in the button cages. The shortened buttons will be stoned and polished to size.

8 This is what the texture of an EDM surface resembles. The electrode has been retracted for inspection. There were a minimum of one thousand separate machine operations involved in making this knife.

10 After the blade pivot-well has been machined from the titanium handle halves, the blade will have its final configuration ground using a surface grinder and some very unique techniques.

11 This is the first time the pieces all start fitting together. Visualizing a knife at this point is becoming less of just a concept.

12 With the mechanism operational, shaping the handle begins. Machining titanium requires constant attention. Sharp tools and cutting aggressively help keep the material from work-hardening.

14 The finished product. Anodizing the handle will reveal any flaws. I usually finish anodize the handle six or seven times before satisfied with fit and finish, color and tone.

15 Finish-lapping of the sides. I finish all anodized surfaces of titanium to 1200 grit. Using a machinists surface plate I can get an optically flat surface.

16 The handles have been anodized for the last time, finished to many exacting specifications. Careful assembly is all that separates these handle halves from being a finished knife.

Philip Booth
"Double Blade Auto Bartender Knife", 2005

Born in 1951, in Hillsdale, Michigan, Philip comes to knife making via the fine arts. He is a lifelong award-winning artist working in the mediums of painting, printmaking and knifemaking. Taking the time to paint small watercolors from life is one of his great pleasures; however, knifemaking takes up most of his creative hours. A Knifemakers Guild member, Philip lives with his wife Cheri, in a very small town in central Michigan, surrounded by fertile farm land, lakes and woods. His days are divided between working at the town's hardware store and making art. Choosing to work in the store a few days a week rather than spend all his time in his basement

shop has been a real bonus. "It is just better for my creativity, to be able to step back and think about what is being worked on". Philip makes many styles of knives all of his own design and has over a dozen different automatic mechanisms to choose from in his repertoire.

301 S. Jeffrey Ave.
Ithaca, MI 48847, USA
Phone: (989) 875-2844
email: pbooth@chartermi.net
Site: http://www.philipbooth.com

"Double Blade Auto Bartender Knife", 2005 A two blade automatic, push-button lock bartender knife, with a gun blue finish. A hand filed, fully useable corkscrew which works as a slip joint, completes this unique folding knife. Damascus by Delbert Ealy (3 different patterns). The knife employs a fully file worked single spacer bar which is the stop for both blades and the spring for the cork screw. Overall length 6" (152 mm), closed 3 1/2" (89 mm).

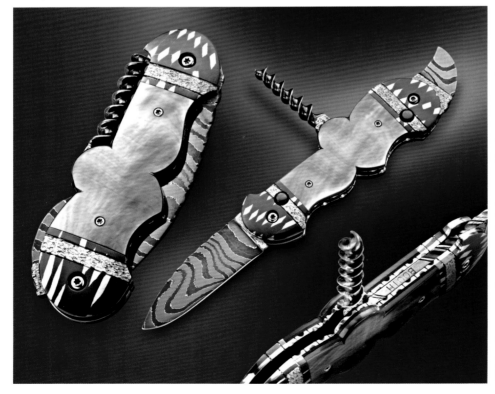

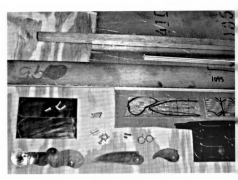

1 The initial layout of all the materials contained in the knife. This serves the same strategy used by painters as they lay out the colors of the pallet to be used. Now, pattern, texture and finish are decided upon.

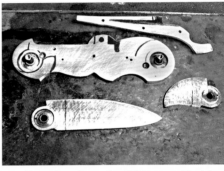

3 No high tech equipment here! Philip uses a blue ink pen to draw onto the spacer/spring and liners. These are guide lines for the next stage of cutting and grinding. Each piece of the knife will then be individually fit and finished.

6 The corkscrew starts out as a 1/2" bar of Damasteel. Philip first grinds it square and fits it to the knife and spring. After meticulous measuring and marking, the flutes are hand-cut with a jeweler's saw.

8 Philip does his own heat treating, heating the Damasteel to 1500° F before quenching in warm oil. This knife requires two different tempers: the blades for hardness and the corkscrew and spacer for flexibility.

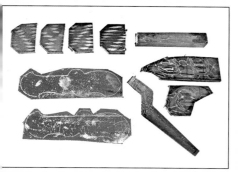

2 Outlines of the parts are scribed on the steel and then rough cut. The actual cut is outside the lines. This provides some flexibility in changing lines or curves and not remaining "locked" onto a specific shape concept.

4 These are the scales in an early and somewhat rough stage. The beauty of the final knife is still well hidden under what will take many hours of hand rubbing to get rid of all grind marks.

7 Time now for the final fitting, before the decorative filework is completed on the blade and spring. All the parts are then hand rubbed to a 400 grit finish before they move on to heat treating for hardening.

8 A very careful oxidation process achieved these dramatic carnival colors. The two automatic spring powered blades coupled with a wine bottle opener, make this such a fun package, the colors just add to the aura of celebration.

5 This wide shot shows one room in Philip's shop, located in the basement of his home. The floors are painted a bright yellow which contrasts with the screws and small parts that constantly drop while working on his knives, making them easy to spot. The added primary colors of the shop provide a fun, playground feeling, which comes through in much of his work.

10 "The actual making of a corkscrew from rough Damascus to the finishing polish takes me an entire day of hand labor. I use a new chainsaw file for each corkscrew produced. The process requires constant turning of the Damascus bar during the filing process to keep each flute even and correctly spaced. File marks are then removed with rope and polishing compounds. Each of my handmade bartender knives is tested by pulling a cork and sharing the wine".

Jim (Coop) Cooper
"Darrel Ralph-designed 'GX6' folding dagger"
by KnifeKits.com, 2005

Born in 1953, Jim has lived in Connecticut all his life. He is lovingly married to his wife Susan, and his only son Trevor was born in 2003. 'Coop', as he is known in the knife community, is also a prolific collector of custom knives. Coop was a longtime racer and technician in motorcycles, and his fabrication and working skills lent themselves nicely to the newly-available KnifeKits.com folders. *"I found that understanding the mechanisms and going through the finishing processes helped me appreciate even more what a true custom maker achieves"*. Coop has handfinished over thirty kits, and has done versions with full filework and damascus hardware. His interest in displaying them led to learning photography on the Knife Network

Forums and beyond. Now, 'SharpByCoop' has become a formidable knife photographer, with his client's work shown in publications in the US and abroad. He is a consistent presence on many internet knife forums and he has created tutorials for both kits and photography.

9 Mathew Court
Norwalk, CT 06851, USA
Phone: 203-838-8939 home/studio
email: jcooper@sharpbycoop.com
Site: www.SharpByCoop.com

"Darrel Ralph-designed 'GX6' folding dagger" by KnifeKits.com, 2005 AUS-8 blade, SS hardened liners, Spalted maple scales and backspacer. Spalted maple scales and backspacer. Overall length 6 5/16" (160 mm). Knife concept, finishing and final montage image, all executed by Jim Cooper.

KnifeKits.com GX6 Folding Dagger by Jim Cooper   Image~ SharpByCoop.com

1 After cutting both scales and a section for the backspacer from a block, Coop is measuring and trimming the backspine scale to the exact thickness needed (blade width plus 2 washers). The dimension is critical for fit.

3 After attaching party-plate plastic liners with glue, the pilot holes are now drilled from the outside with a special step drill. The depth is critical to get enough threads to catch while not protruding.

6 Removing the bolsters, the scales can be sanded in steps for a final profile. This is slow and careful work, looking from directly above. This one was made intentionally rounded.

8 Final finish on all the edge profiles and the blade comes with working on the buffer. Grey to start, and white rouge for finish. The outside of the bolsters are hand-sanded, buffed, and sanded again for the final 400 grit finish.

2 The scales have been flattened and the bolster edge squared true. The scales are attached to the liners with double-sided tape. Now he drills pilot holes through the existing tapped holes in the liners with an undersize drill.

4 After screwing all the rough components together, the horizontal grinder shapes the profile right up to the liner, from rough to finish grits. Safety equipment: goggles, mask and a dust collecting vacuum hose.

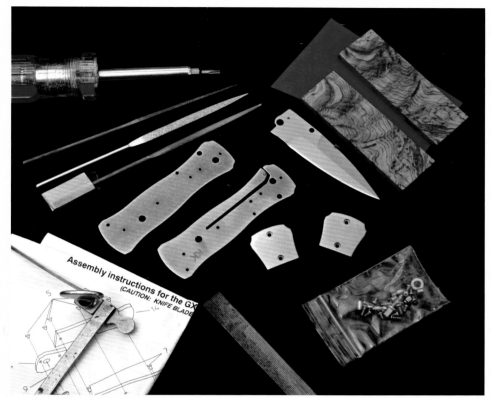

5 The raw components before work begins. "80% of the hardest and smartest work on these knives is purchased from the outset. The geometry, engineering, and hardware are already sorted out, and I get to enjoy the finishing aspect with confidence". KnifeKits.com supplies many different scales although these were cut from a larger block. The red liners are from a party plate! You can finish these just as nicely with hand tools, saws and files.

7 Using the horizontal grinder again, the final bevels are applied in finishing steps. This is the most delicate work since the materials cut so easily. A steady and consistent hand is needed.

9 Good workmanship starts with organization and being crafty. Many of the tools necessary for the project are here. Coop uses TV dinner trays to organize all the components for cleaning and final assembly.

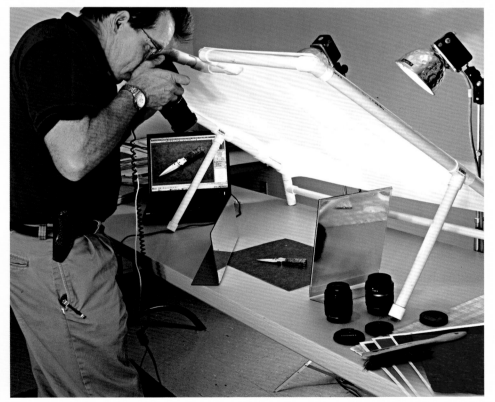

10 Coop has photographed many knives for Dr. Darom, and he is working on his own. His setup is as shown: Canon SLR Digital Camera and lenses linked to a laptop computer, the PVC Frame and diffuser is backlit by 2-3 powerful strobes, while the light is reflected back in with mirrors. Because he has plentiful light, he can shoot at a higher shutter speed and not have to use a tripod. He uses an assortment of backgrounds to compliment the individual knife.

Ron Duncan
"Stacked-Handle Hunter", 2005

1 Ron, working in his shop, holding a stack of steel made of alternating layers of 1080 high carbon and 15N20 medium carbon/high nickel steel, soon to become the Damascus billet from which this knife will be forged.

Ron was born in 1955, in Missouri, where he grew up and developed his life long love for hunting, fishing and the great outdoors. Ron's knife making career began while he was attending a shop class in high school in 1970 where he made his first knife. In the mid 80's he was fortunate enough to meet Corbin Newcomb, a long time knifemaker and voting member of the Knife Makers Guild who has been a friend and teacher, inspiring Ron to always make the best knife he can, one that is functional, attractive and a tool anyone can depend on to operate as expected when called upon. Ron has strived to create a style that is recognized as being his own. His varied and beautiful stacked handles, made of different materials, and the gentle curves throughout his knives, attest to that quit well. Lacey, Ron's daughter, born in 1985, is one of Ron's

four daughters but the only one to follow her dad's love for making beautiful things out of leather and steel. Lacey joined the Ron's business and makes all of the heavy leather sheaths for his knives as well as for anyone else in need of a good functional and attractive leather sheath.

4 The blade is now forged, ground to the desired shape, heat treated and ready to have the tang threaded so that the pommel nut can be later screwed onto it.

"Duncan Made Knives"
3938 County Road 1440
Cairo, MO 65239, USA
Phone: (660) 263-8949
email: duncanknives@mcmsys.com
Site: www.duncanmadeknives.com

"Stacked-Handle Hunter", 2005 Stacked handle made of 32 individual pieces of material and a nickel-silver guard and pommel. Damascus by the maker and sheath made by his daughter, Lacey Duncan. Overall length 9 1/2" (241 mm).

7 Ron stacks one piece of material at at a time onto the tang of the knife to make sure everything fits and is in line.

10 The blade is etched to bring out the pattern and texture of the Damascus. During this process, the guard is covered with figer nail polish to avoid contact with the etching acids.

2 Creating the blade. Ron is seen working on the Damascus billet that will later be used in making several blades for his knives.

3 The 34 individual pieces of material that will make up the guard, stacked handle and pommel, are laid out in their "stacking" order. These consist of copper, brass, nickel-silver, aluminum, black micarta spacers, white and black vulcanized spacer material along with two pieces of stag all of which will go into making the handle for this knife. The guard and pommel are nickel-silver.

5 The rough nickel-silver guard is silver soldered on the blade and the solder joint has been cleaned up. The round pommel nut is also soldered into the counter sunk rough pommel that will eventually keep everything secure and held together.

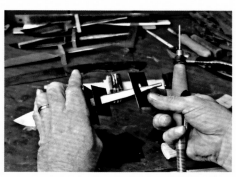

6 Ron is making the slots in the materials to be "stacked" on the tang, pre-fitting all the different pieces that will be used in the construction of the handle.

8 This is the knife after all the pieces are all drilled, fitted and in their final resting place on the tang. Now the whole construction will be taken apart, epoxy will be applied to each individual piece and everything will be reassembled for the last time.

9 Ron tapes sections of the knife that should not be exposed to epoxy while the handle parts are being reassembled and glued together. When dry, the handle is sculptured on the grinder and then finished off.

11 Lacey, at her table, carefully hammering a basket weaving tool (punch) on a piece of heavy leather, creating the all-over pattern that will cover the sheath.

12 Lacey uses the drill press as leverage to force the needle and waxed thread through the heavy 13 ounce leather as she stitches the sheath them one stitch at a time.

13 After making sure that the knife fits properly in the sheath, Lacey will give it the finishing contouring and dying.

Antonio Fogarizzu
"Tursiops", 2005

Born in 1971, a native of Pattada, Sardinia, Italy, Antonio Fogarizzu found himself following in his father's footsteps, and when he began making knives they were traditional Sardinian fixed blades and folders. Having plans to enter the 21st century in style, he began devoting his time to making custom knives. A member of the Italian Knifemakers Guild, Antonio not only makes fine custom knives, but he is very involved with Damascus patterns, forging his own steels. He initially worked at duplicating existing patterns until he arrived at the point where he believed he knew the basics. Antonio was the first Italian maker to forge his own Mosaic Damascus and use it in many of his knives. He also makes stock removal blades from ATS-34 stainless stock, and uses 416 stainless steel for bolsters and handles, the latter ideal for engraving embellishments.

Via E. Fermi 5
07016 Pattada (SS), Italy
Phone/Fax: (+39) 079 755003
email: a.fogarizzu@tiscali.it
Site: www.fogarizzuknives.com

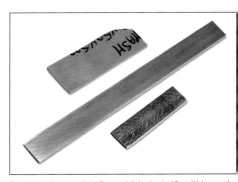

1 The basic materials from which the knife will be made. A bar of Double Twist Mosaic Damascus made by Antonio, 416 stainless steel for the handle and MA5M steel for the spring.

3 Using a pre-made template on the pantograph, Antonio has cut out the two pockets for inlays in the handle. Two holes were drilled into each piece to secure them on the pantograph while cutting the pocket.

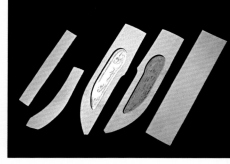

6 All of the knife parts, the handle, spring and blade, are ground to exact shape before begining the drilling process.

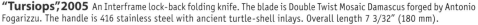

"Tursiops", 2005 An Interframe lock-back folding knife. The blade is Double Twist Mosaic Damascus forged by Antonio Fogarizzu. The handle is 416 stainless steel with ancient turtle-shell inlays. Overall length 7 3/32" (180 mm).

10 Using the pantograph again, Antonio cuts out the turtle-shell inserts for the handle.

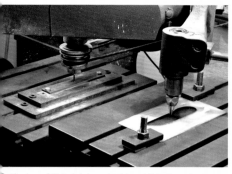

2 The bar of 416 stainless steel is cut into two pieces, one for each side of the handle. Each piece is attached to the pantograph and pockets for the inlays are cut into them.

4 After shaping the handle slabs, they are ground completely flat on the surface grinder.

5 Antonio is using the pantograph to accurately cut the frames. He is carefully guiding the way into the 416 stainless steel by following a pre-made template.

7 After drilling the pivot hole in the blade, Antonio begins grinding the lock on the belt grinder. He will finish it by hand to the needed exact fit, using small files.

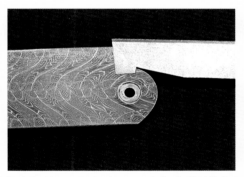

8 The locking mechanism is now ready for the final fitting and finishing which is done by hand.

9 Knife mechanism is assembled and tested before going on to the hardening process.

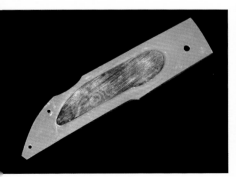

11 The handle, immediately after a turtle-shell insert is glued into its pocket. Excess glue exits from the spring hole on the inside of the frame. When the fit is perfect, no glue will squeeze out on the outside.

12 Using the pantograph once more, Antonio cuts the inside of the handles to accommodate the Teflon bushings.

13 Using abrasive materials from 200 grit to 3,000 grit, Antonio removes all marks of the grinding process before buffing the handle with paste to create the mirror finish typical of his knives.

Chuck Gedraitis
"Balisong #11", 2005

Born in Worcester, Massachusetts, in 1976, Chuck Gedraitis had a fascination for knives since a very early age. His grandfather gave him his first pocketknife when he was 5, and it was that moment that set his future for him, starting to make knives by taking apart his mother's kitchen knives. "My parents thought that there was something "wrong" with me because I had a fascination with sharp objects. That all changed when I took them to a local knife show and showed them a whole room of people interested in knives". Chuck began making knives seriously when he was 16 and has never stopped since. Since 1999 he has concentrated on making one-of-a kind folding knives and automatics of his own design. He is now making knives full time.

444 Shrewsbury Street
Holden, MA 01520, USA
Phone: (508) 963-1861
email:cgknives@blademakers.com
Site: http://cgknives.blademakers.com

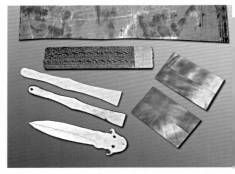

1 Hand drawn blade and handle patterns, titanium fo liners, Eggerling Mosaic Damascus for the blade, Al May Damascus for bolsters, and Gold-lip Mother-of-Pearl fo the scales.

3 The pockets have been filed to the planned depth. Note the drilled pivot holes and screw holes for the bolsters and scales.

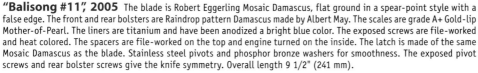

"Balisong #11", 2005 The blade is Robert Eggerling Mosaic Damascus, flat ground in a spear-point style with a false edge. The front and rear bolsters are Raindrop pattern Damascus made by Albert May. The scales are grade A+ Gold-lip Mother-of-Pearl. The liners are titanium and have been anodized a bright blue color. The exposed screws are file-worked and heat colored. The spacers are file-worked on the top and engine turned on the inside. The latch is made of the same Mosaic Damascus as the blade. Stainless steel pivots and phosphor bronze washers for smoothness. The exposed pivot screws and rear bolster screws give the knife symmetry. Overall length 9 1/2" (241 mm).

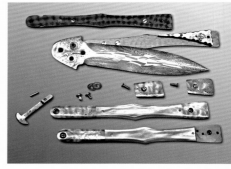

6 The front bolsters and scales are attached to each line first. Spacers and dowel pins are installed next. The pivot for one side of the knife is installed into the liner, a bronze washer added and the pivot is inserted into its hole.

8 The rear bolsters are attached and the latch and its pivot pin are installed.

2 The rough ground liners have a pocket filed into each side. This is where the tang pins in the blade sit when the knife is in the open and closed positions. They are filed only into the liners giving the knife elegance.

4 Final pre-assembly inspection of the knife. The blade has been ground, heat treated and etched. The spacers have been file-worked and tang pins inserted in the blade. This is when the final open and closed positions are set.

5 Grinding on a 2x72" Bader BII belt grinder. Adequate lighting is very important when grinding blades. Chuck does all his profiling and rough grinding on this machine. When working he always wears an apron, safety glasses, a respirator and hearing protection. *"My shop is very simple with a couple of drill presses, 2 grinders, a buffer and a bandsaw. I do most of the work the old fashioned way by hand".*

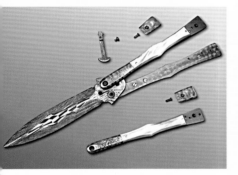

7 One handle is complete except for the rear bolsters which go on last. The second handle is assembled in the same order as the first.

8 The knife is finished and seen here in a semi-closed position. The pivot screws and the rear bolster screws have been left exposed to give symmetry to the handles, they have also been file-worked and heat colored.

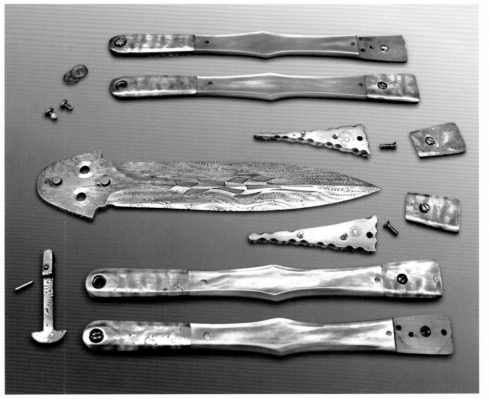

10 A view of all 24 finished parts of the knife before begining the final assembly. All the embellishment has been done, the spacers and screws are file-worked. The titanium liners anodized, the Damascus bolsters, blade and latch etched and the pearl polished. In the final assembly of the knife, there are many parts that have to be assembled in a specific order.

Jeff Hall
"Maverick", 2005

Born in Chicago, IL in 1963, Jeff Hall began making knives in his mid-30's. Despite suggestions from others, he started with folders and sold his first in 1998. The Maverick tactical folder shown here is typical of 85% of his knives. While Hall still builds elegant gentleman's folders that feature natural materials like pearl and ivory, the rugged, over-built folder is what he's become known for. Thick titanium liners, durable handle materials, and unusual grinds are common on his

tactical knives. Open to just about any fun and challenging project, Hall often exchanges ideas and collaborates on unique tactical items with his friend Joel Pirela. Whether working by himself, or with someone else, Hall continues to develop interesting designs, learn machining techniques, and search for new materials.

P.O. Box 435
Los Alamitos, CA 90720, USA
Phone: (562) 594-4740
email: jhall10176@aol.com

"Maverick", 2005 Tactical folder with a 3 5/8" (92 mm) S30V stainless blade, bright green canvas micarta handle and 0.105" thick titanium liners. Titanium pocket clip and ambidextrous thumb studs. Overall length 8 1/2" (216 mm).

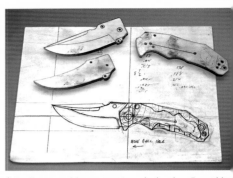

1 It all starts with an accurate scale drawing. Everything is thought-out and located on paper before templates are made in metal or plastic.

3 Pilot holes are drilled in the titanium liners with cobalt drills and cutting fluid. Each hole will be drilled to final size and finished later.

6 Using an imported 2 HP milling machine and 3" abrasive disk, the lengthwise cut for the lock is made at about 1,500 RPM.

10 A few minutes of hand sanding with 120 and 320 grit sandpaper makes uniform, rounded frame edges that feel nice in one's hand.

2 Red Dykem machinist lay-out fluid is sprayed onto titanium and steel sheets. Parts are scribed, transfer punched, and then cut using a two-speed Wilton metal cutting band-saw.

4 Titanium produces a lot of sparks! Here, the band-sawed parts are profile ground on a variable speed Bader B3 grinder using 50 grit ceramic belts.

5 A well-lit workbench provides plenty of space for planning and assembly, and ready access to hand tools.

7 More layout fluid. This time it is used to locate the short cut in the liner that will be band-sawed to finish the lock.

8 After initial assembly, the parts begin to look like a folder frame. A horizontal sander with an 80 grit ceramic belt squares the entire frame.

9 Removing the work-rest and changing the belt on the same machine allows for quick chamfering of the frame's edges.

11 With the frame completed, it's time to finish the blade. Here, it's hand-held against a 100 grit belt and 5" contact wheel with a homemade push stick.

12 A Hardcore grinder and 220 grit belt grinds the edge, but buffing of the wire edge and testing is necessary before the knife is shipped.

13 Just before clean-up and final assembly, the maker's name is electrically etched onto the blade through a stencil.

Koji Hara
"Fairlady X", 2005

A native of Japan, Koji Hara was born in 1949, in Imari City, Japan. Koji is a premier knifemaker carrying on the tradition of superb Japanese blademaking. Koji's knives are unique, innovative and well designed pieces. By combining the esthetics of Japanese form and function with modern techniques and materials, Koji creates a knife of distinction. His blades are made of a proprietary Japanese steel known as Cowry-Y, holding an excellent edge, and polishing to an extremely high

mirror-finish. Although one of the drawbacks of powdered steel is its weakness towards lateral impact, this can be corrected through proper heat-treating. Koji is a Knife Maker's Guild member and very active on the international Knife Show circuit. His knives have attained worldwide recognition and awards.

292-2 Osugi Seki-city
Gifu-pref. 501-3922 JAPAN
Phone: (+81) 575-24-7569
email: info@knifehousehara.com
Site: http://www.knifehousehara.com

1 First the design is scribed onto a sheet of steel. The each part is roughly cut out with a band saw.

5 Milling out the three sided pockets for the Black-li pearl inlays on both sides of the handle.

"Fairlady X", 2005 A liner lock folding knife with a mirror polished Cowry-Y steel blade and a 316 stainless steel handle inlaid with Black-lip pearl. Overall length 7 11/16" (195 mm).

9 Both sides of the finished handle with the clamshel pattern bolsters and the Black-lip pearl inlays, before th final polishing stages.

11 Hand polishing the blade is done in five stages Sanding with 320 grit, progressing through 600 grit 1000 grit, 2000 grit and finally creating a mirror polis using diamond paste.

2 The roughly cut pieces that will eventually become a beautiful liner lock folding knife.

3 Working on the handle with a fraiser milling bit.

4 Milling the slots on the back-bar to accommodate the Black-lip pearl inlays.

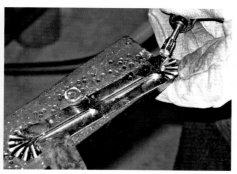

6 Carving the front and rear bolsters in a clamshell pattern. Koji wears thick leather gloves to protect his fingers from the high speed cutting tool.

7 Carefully grinding the Black-lip pearl inlays to perfectly fit each of the four pockets milled into the handle.

8 Fitting the inlays of Black-lip pearl into the handle.

10 Jeweling work is done on the liner, eliminating the visible scratches and creating a beautiful looking finish.

12 All the parts laid out before final assembly.

13 Final assembly of the folding knife. Peening all pins very carefully with a hammer.

Jeff A. Harkins
"KRACKED ALPHA" Single-Action Automatic, 2005

Born in San Bernardino, California in 1964 and raised in Montana, Jeff joined the army after leaving high school. In 1988 his father showed him the possibilities surrounding a custom knife by sending him a production knife that he had inlayed with some precious stone, along with a copy of the "blade" magazine. *"I wore out the pages of that magazine, as I had finally found a venue to exercise my desire to metal sculpture utilizing a tool for my art"*. In 1989, after spending 9 years as an army machinist, Jeff began making swords and fighting knives fulltime. Around 1990 Jeff began making folders and a year later delved into the world of automatic knives. *"I enjoy auto's because of the mechanisms and the interrelated workings that*

each part has on the next, its like building a little machine". Jeff belongs to the U.S. Knifemakers guild and the Montana Knifemakers association. He attends 2 or 3 shows per year and has numerous "Automatic" designs licensed to different knife companies.

P.O. Box 218 Conner, MT 59827, USA
Phone: (406) 821-1060
email: kutter@customknives.net
Site: www.customknives.net
www.blackholeforge.com
www.switchblades.info

"Kracked Alpha", Single-Action Automatic, 2005 A folding fighter with a flush button (trap door) automatic mechanism. The blade is ATS-34 and the frames are heat-treated 416 stainless steel. "This Knife is a very contemporary design in that the lines and flow of the knife are almost futuristic. It is a study in stainless, in angles, flow, and finish". Closed length 5 2/5" (145 mm).

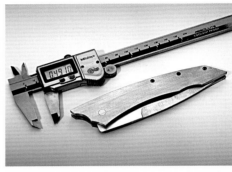

1 The rough profiled parts along with the hardened 416 stainless steel bar stock. The frames are hardened to allow for a brighter finish as well as increasing the corrosion resistance of the steel.

3 After installing the button, the knife is surface ground on both sides to ensure the faceting process has equal amounts of material on either side of the frame.

6 For the purpose of etching away the hardened stainless steel and creating the lines of the Kracks, a stainless steel cutting electrolyte is used at 14 volts DC. The Electrolyte is applied to a pad and the pad is applied to the stencil.

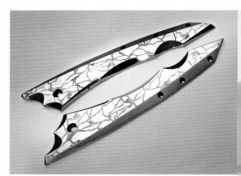

8 The frames after the etching process. The lines were purposely exposed for an extended period to create an aged and eroded look. A resist (nail polish) is applied to each facet to protect the finish during these final stages.

2 The button is hammered in and out of its pocket 30 to 40 times, the bright contact marks are filed and sanded away. Then it is rocked back and forth with lapping compound until it rocks with ease. This process takes 2 days.

4 The facets and concave areas are hand ground, stoned and completely finished in an alternating manner to insure a crisp edge where one facet meets another. The concave areas are hand polished.

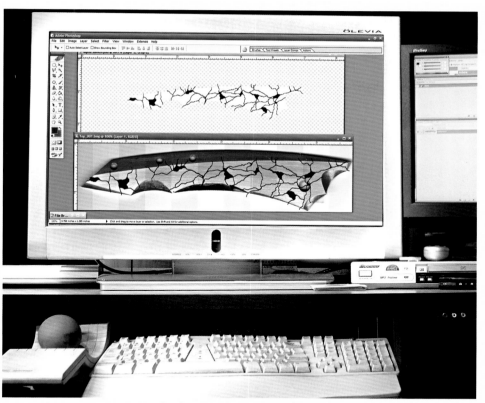

5 After scanning the knife frame into Photoshop, a drawing of the planned design is generated to match the flats of the knife. From this drawing a transparency is produced. From the transparency a stencil is created for the purpose of etching the lines of the Kracks. The stencil is carefully positioned on the desired area and secured to prevent any movement during the etching process.

7 The combination of stainless steel cutting electrolyte and voltage, when applied through the stencil onto the steel part, eat away the metal to create the desired "Kracks" design.

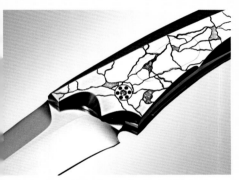

9 A detail of the finished knife showing the "Kracks".

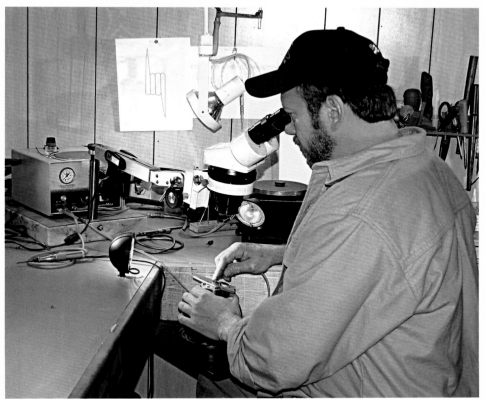

10 After etching, the frames are hand engraved with a graver-max using a stereo scope. The lines are cut at different depths to aid in the visual effect of a dried lake bed. The frame flats are then refinished and the knife is assembled for the last time.

Howard Hitchmough
"Wave Dancer", 2005

Now living in New Hampshire, Howard was born in London, England in 1942, where he spent nearly thirty years making surgical instruments. A full-time maker for the past 20 years, he began creating knives in the 1960's. Making high quality knives requires particular attention to design, the most difficult part of the process. Moving from drawings to aluminum patterns and then to steel templates ensures that everything will work correctly before the actual knifemaking begins. Howard believes it is imperative that a knife look good both open and closed. He gives much thought to selecting suitable materials for the handle, blade etc.

so the resulting knife is visually pleasing. Attention to detail is vital. All his lockback and linerlock folding knives are assembled with screws. These enable adjustments that make a knife work with the smoothness and precision expected of a top quality folder.

5 Old Street Road
Peterborough, NH 03458, USA
Phone: (603) 924-9646
Fax: (603) 924-9595
email: howard@hitchmoughknives.com
Site: http://www.hitchmoughknives.com

"Wave Dancer", 2005 A lockback folder with a 3 1/4" (82 mm) flat ground blade made from "Odin's Eye" pattern Damasteel. The handle frame is machined from 01 tool steel, then carved and textured to resemble tree bark. Hot gun-bluing gives it a rich black oxide finish. The opening lever is made from stainless Damascus and is decorated with rope file-work to match the file-work on top of the blade and spring. Handle inlays are premium quality Mother-of-Pearl. The blade opener is 18k gold and is set with a sapphire. The handle screws are also 18k gold as are the collars around the main pivot screws. Overall length 7 3/4" (197 mm).

1 Original concept drawing showing the knife with various options. To the left is the working pattern cut from cardboard.

5 With the handle side securely clamped to a fixture on the milling machine, the recess for the main screw and its collar is bored out.

8 Fileworking the top of the locking lever prior to heat treating. Now the blade is carefully heat-treated and cryogenically quenched in liquid nitrogen to ensure the correct balance between hardness and toughness.

12 The assembled knife. Various screwdrivers are used to tighten the stainless steel screws that hold the knife together. The handle is now ready for shaping and texturing.

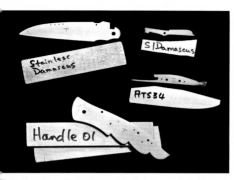

2 Hardened steel templates with all the screw holes in their correct positions are made following the cardboard pattern. Howard believes in make accurate templates to ensure that everything will work correctly.

3 The lock notch being machined into the tang of the blade using a 1/8" end mill in a Bridgeport milling machine.

4 Relieving the area around the main screw on the inside of the handle is done on a rotary table of the "Bridgeport" using an end mill. This prevents the blade from scraping when the knife is opened and closed.

6 After being roughly flat ground, the blade is finished to size by careful hand filing. This is followed by hand polishing using progressively finer grades of abrasive paper until all scratch marks are removed.

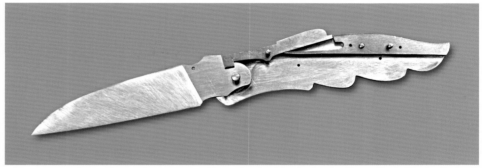

7 Knife assembled showing the locking lever accurately filed to fit into the lock notch in the blade. The spring is held in place with studs. The holes for screws that will hold the handle frame together can be seen. Next step is to decorate the top of the lever and spring with filework. All the pieces are then properly heat-treated.

9 Turning the main pivot screws in the lathe. At this stage, great care is taken to make the screws as accurate as possible. This ensures minimum "play" in the finished knife.

10 The main pivot screws before being parted from the rods. Also shown are the 18k gold collars that will surround these screws.

11 Carefully hand shaping the white pearl to fit the steel handle frame.

13 Securely fixed to a block of wood, the steel handle is shaped and textured using a carbide burr in a rotary handpiece.

14 Hot gunbluing the handle frame. Although this is a nasty procedure requiring the use of hot and hazardous chemicals, the finish obtained is far superior to other bluing processes.

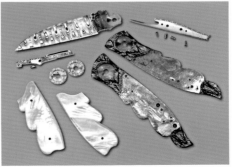

15 Finally the various pieces are finished and ready for assembly.

Des Horn
"Elements of Sharp Art", 2005

Des was born in 1947, in Johannesburg, South Africa. This is where he went to school and then on to Wits University and it is where he spent many years in the dental practice, before finally moving to Cape Town. He started knifemaking as a schoolboy after receiving advice from the legendary Bo Randall on how to make a good knife and what steels to use. He feels that his first true quality knife was made in 1970, using O1 steel heat treated to 59 Rc. Since then many things have changed but few more dramatically than the quality standard of steel available for making the ultimate cutting tool, as well as high-tech materials such as titanium and silicon nitride ceramics. In 1990, Des started going to international knife shows and has, on many occasions, won awards for his designs and for the quality of his work in South Africa and internationally. In 2004 he decided to stop dentistry and follow his passion, becoming a full time custom knifemaker.

P.O. Box 322
Onrusrivier, 7201
Cape Town, South Africa
Phone: (+27) 2831 61795
Fax: (+27) 2831 61795
email: deshorn@usa.net

"Two Folding Knives", 2005 From the left: **"Ball Release Liner Lock"** This folding knife has a stain resisting Damasteel blade and grade five titanium liners. The indent and release balls are silicon nitride and the handles are Gold-lip pearl with titanium bolsters inlaid with 24k gold and engraved by Armin Winkler. Overall length 6 11/16" (170 mm). **"HBP-2"** model, with Gibeon Meteorite handles estimated to be 4.6 billion years old. A concealed hinge pin is internally threaded into blind holes tapped into the handles. Gold pins are 24k. The blade is double tempered and sub zero quenched stain resisting Damasteel. Overall length 6 1/2" (165 mm).

1 Pattern modification at the forge to suit the particular blade profile for the planned folding knife.

3 Diamond lapping of the pivot hole achieves perfect roundness and the best finish for a smooth and long lasting action. The three-sided lap removes any possible ovality and polishes the pivot hole square to the pivot pin.

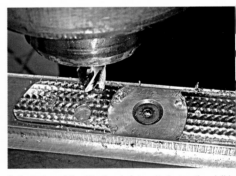

6 Texturing of the titanium bolster eliminates the visible scratches. Done in the dividing head of the Bridgeport milling machine, using a modified carbide end mill at high feed and slow speed, it creates a beautiful looking finish.

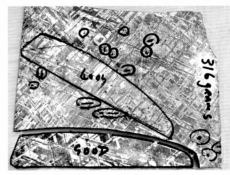

8 Getting flawless inclusion and crack-free Gibeon Meteorite for the concealed pivot pin model HBP-2 folding knife. The circled areas are inclusions to be avoided. There is a large wastage factor in order to get flawless material.

2 Partial grinding of the blade before heat-treatment allows for minimal grinding after the hardening process, but leaves a full-thickness point for stability at a later stage, on the magnetic vice.

4 Slitting of the liner for the ball release knife in the Bridgeport milling machine after all other machining is completed.

5 Sub-zero liquid Nitrogen quench is essential to get the best out of high-tech modern steels. The down draught of cold air is clearly visible.

7 Rockwell hardness testing of all blades. *"A knife is first and foremost a working tool regardless of how fancy it is finished and therefore correct heat treating is essential"*.

9 The partially assembled HBP-2 showing the components as well as an enlargement of the pivot pin (in the lower right corner), used for fitting into the internally threaded blind holes in the handle slabs.

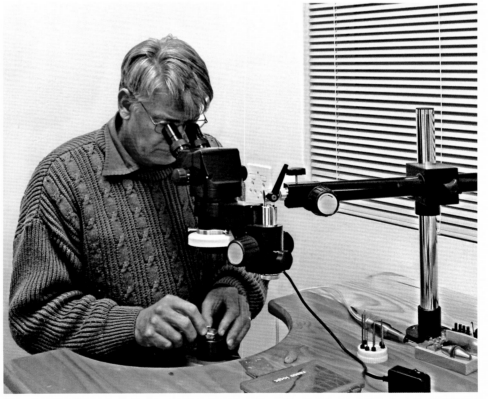

10 Des uses the the stereoscopic microscope for engraving and very often in order to minutely check the final fit and finish of all the knives he makes.

Dave Kelly
"Woolly Grouse" 2005

Dave Kelly was born in 1952 and spent over 20 years as a general building contractor with an interest in building custom cabinetry and furniture. He had his last major back surgery in 2002 and being unable to continue woodworking, he discovered hand made knives. While recovering, he purchased books and videos as well as materials and tools, and began studying and designing folders. Dave finished his first knife in April of 2003. He continues to make folders and recently made his first fixed blade. Dave's knives have been inspected and approved by four voting members of The Knifemakers Guild. He hopes to fulfill his ambition of

showing his knives at a guild show and becoming a member. The support and information shared by the community of knifemakers has made being part of it a great experience.

865 S. Shenandoah St.
Los Angeles, CA 90035, USA
Phone: (310) 657-7104
email: dakcon@comcast.net

1 All the components of the knife are drilled, rough profiled, and ready for assembly. Also shown are the pivot, bronze bushing and washers, stop pin, frame screws, and bolster spacer dowels.

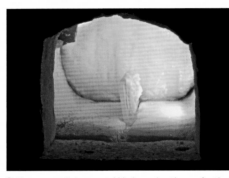

3 The oven and clay coated blade are heating up for the 3 normalizing cycles. The blade is rotated during this process to get it evenly heated. After the third cycle it is ready for the final heat treatment and quench.

6 Profiling the liners on a variable speed edge-sander. Dave loves this machine and uses small wheels for the radius profiles and the platen for straight edges. He usually cuts the 2" belts lengthwise in half so they last much longer.

8 After bringing the bolsters to a near mirror finish, a blackening agent is dabbed on using a cotton tip applicator, washed and rubbed with fibril wool. This is done several times and finished with baked-on oil and a wax buff.

"Woolly Grouse" 2005 After approving the design, collector Michael Gettier helped choose the materials to be used on this knife. Blade is 3 5/8" (92 mm) clay treated 1084 steel. Bolsters are blackened 1084 and the spacers titanium and 1084. Mammoth ivory scales, rope file worked and blackened 1084 back spacer. Overall length 8 1/8" (206 mm).

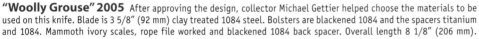

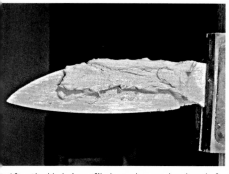

After the blade is profiled, rough ground and ready for heat treatment, the clay is applied to the spine. The area beneath the clay cools slowly in the quench and will be softer than the rest of the blade.

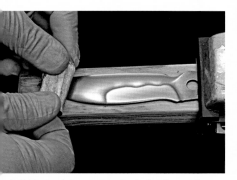

Polishing to bring out the hardening line, or hamon. Dave repeatedly dips the blade in a diluted ferric chloride solution for about 30 seconds each time, rubbing with fine fibril wool in between and finishing off to 8,000 grit.

Stippling the pivot pin with a variable speed rotary tool and a 1/8" round carbide burr. Using a foot pedal to adjust the speed frees the hands. Most of the texturing on bolsters, liners, and pins is performed with this setup.

Polishing the blackened file-worked spine with polishing cloth wrapped around a wooden dowel. When polishing, Dave uses different sanding sticks and pads made of rubber, leather, wood, plastic, and steel.

5 Dave is using a variable speed horizontal disk to flatten the bolsters and scales. He doesn't have a surface grinder, so he uses this machine quite often for hogging off and flattening material. Finishing is done using an abrasive sheet on a surface plate.

10 "This is my small workshop, not seen in the picture are 2' (60 cm) to the left, where my 2"x72" belt grinder, belt rack, buffing cabinet, storage cabinet, and surface plate reside. I am standing at the end of my workbench, 3' (90 cm) away at the other end, rests my main drill press with various small parts and an assortment of hand tools".

Jeremy Krammes
"Peregrine", 2005

Born in 1977, Jeremy Krammes grew up outside of a small rural town in eastern Pennsylvania. Spending most of his time in the outdoors, hunting and hiking, he was always interested in knives. After an injury at work, and while looking around for something to do with his spare time, Jeremy met knifemaker and engraver Ron Nott. Ron got him started on the basics of grinding steel and folding knife mechanisms. He completed his first folder in March 2004, and sold his first knife later that year. Some of Jeremy's future plans include engraving and forging his own Damascus.

138 West Penn Street
Schuylkill Haven, PA 17972, USA
Phone: (570) 385-2462
email: blade@jkknives.com
Site: www.jkknives.com

1 The materials for this project were .080" 6AL4V titanium for the liners, S-30-V steel (.125" thick) for the blade, G-1(steel for the spine and .125" carbon fiber for the scales.

5 Profiling and rough grinding.

"Peregrine", 2005 This folder is named "Peregrine" after the falcon. The blade is 3 3/4" (95 mm) of S-30-V, heat treated by Paul Bos. It is a liner lock with carbon fiber scales. The liners are 6AL4V titanium. Overall length 8 5/8" (219 mm).

10 Drilling .125" holes in the back of the liners.

Profiling the liners to shape after cutting them out on e band saw.

3 Jeremy "match drills" the pivot and stop pin holes with the liners super glued together.

4 Fitting the blade to the stop pin.

Drilling the holes for the spine, and carbon fiber ales.

7 Hollow grinding the blade on a 10" wheel. After the grinding, the blade is off to Paul Bos for heat treatment.

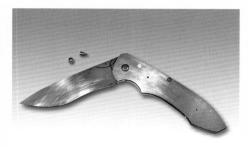

8 Liners and blade together, and getting ready to install the dual titanium thumb studs.

9 Contouring the scales with the Dremel tool, to make them more ergonomic.

Bead blasting the liners with medium glass beads.

12 Filing grooves in the lock bar for a comfortable grip.

13 Finally, the finished knife with the pocket clip installed.

Don Morrow
"Double Blade Trapper", 2005

Born in 1941, in San Diego, Don is a relativly "newcomer" to knifemaking. He made his first knife in October, 2000, and sold his first knife in December of the same year. The opportunity to learn how to make "slip joint" pocket knives was irresistible. Slip joints continue to be his main interest and are primarily what he makes. Since that time, Don has retired from his career as a school administrator and become a full-time knifemaker living and working in Texas. Don is committed to quality and takes whatever time necessary to finish a knife to his exacting standards, whether building a single, double, or three blade knife. Along with Bill

Ruple, he co-hosts a knife forum on knifeforums.com called "Custom slip joint talk with Bill and Don". Don is a member of The Texas Knifemakers and Collectors Association (TKCA), and enjoys getting to know people in the knife-making world, many of whom have become good friends.

P.O. Box 79
Helotes, Texas 78023, USA
Phone: (210) 695-2770
email: don@morrowknives.com
Site: www.morrowknives.com

"Double Blade Trapper", 2005 A pocket size, double blade trapper with ATS-34 stainless steel blades and backsprings, 416 stainless steel bolsters, 410 stainless steel liners and abalone pearl scales. It is fileworked on the blades, backsprings and liners and also has jeweling on the liners. It has a clip blade and a wharncliffe blade and measures 3 3/8" (86 mm) closed and 6" (152 mm) open. The knife was designed for a particular client.

1 Raw materials consisting of abalone pearl scales and ATS-34 stainless steel blanks for blades and backsprings. The steel blanks are scribed with the patterns for the blades and backsprings.

5 The two blades after being hollow-ground using a 6 grit abrasive belt.

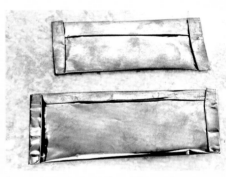

8 After cutting the nail nicks and stamping his name, Don wrappes the blades and backsprings in heat treating fo and places them in the heat treating oven. Don does h own heat treating.

11 The bolsters, made from 416 stainless bar stoc are welded to the liners using a spot welder. After th procedure the bolsters and liners will appear to be on piece.

2 Don Morrow wearing protective equipment while working on the belt grinder, grinding the blades and backsprings.

3 Blades and backsprings are beginning to take shape after being profiled on the grinder. The blades are now ready to be hollow ground.

4 Here, one of the two blades is being hollow-ground on a grinder using a 10 inch wheel.

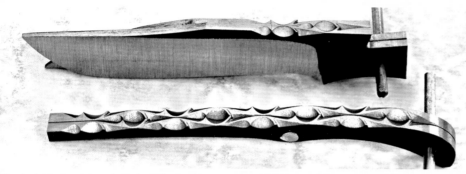

For the beginning cuts on the blade and backspring Don uses a 1/4" round file. The next step is to make the same cuts on the other blade and backspring so that all of the filework matches. The finished filework on the blades and backsprings seen here is done using only three files. An 1/8" round file, 1/4" round file, and an extra slim triangle file. The trick is to make sure everything is in alignment when finished.

7 After completing the filework, the next step is to cut the nail nicks in the blades. This is done on the milling machine using a fly cutter and bit as shown here.

Blades and backsprings after heat treating. The next step is the final grinding and polishing of the blades and preparing the backsprings for layout.

10 Layout is done on blades and backsprings using stainless steel liner material and holes are drilled in the liners on the milling machine. Next the bolsters are made from 416 stainless bar stock and their dovetails are ground on the disk sander. The bolsters and liners appear to be one piece on the finished knife, but they are made of two separate pieces.

2 Grinding the knife to its rough shape on the belt grinder.

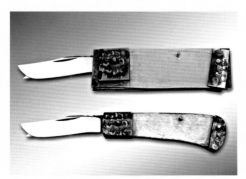

13 Knife assembled after the welding, profiled into a rough shape so reliefs can be milled on the blade end of the knife (top). It is then ground to a rough shape using a 40 grit abrasive belt (bottom).

14 Knife parts ready for assembly. They appear quite different from the raw materials. On this type of knife, the parts are actually hammered together using a 4 ounce ball peen hammer and 416 stainless steel rods or pins.

Stephen Olszewski
"Art Deco Folder", 2005

Born in North Kingstown, Rhode Island, in 1953, Stephen always had a love for the outdoors and nature. As Stephen got older, he developed a love for all the shooting sports along with hunting. This inevitably involved the use of knives. He would throw knives and play different games with them as well as use them to carve and whittle. One day Stephen was out deer hunting with a friend when his friend showed him a hand made knife that a blacksmith had made for him. That was it. He wanted to make his own knife to use in his sporting adventures. This led to the making of drop point fixed-bladed hunting knives. He soon got bored with this style of knife and began making lockbacks. Stephen's background in art and

his career of over 30 years in sculpting, led him to develop his own style of highly ornamented and fully carved one of a kind art knives. He likes to use precious metals as well as Damascus steels, fossil ivories, and pearl. Stephen builds lockbacks, liner locks and automatics.

1820 Harkney Hill road
Coventry, RI 02816, USA
Phone: (401) 397-4774
email: blade5377@yahoo.com
Site: www.olszewskiknives.com

"Art Deco Folder", 2005 A liner lock with titanium liners, a 440C steel blade and Sterling silver scales. The main figure is 18k yellow gold, the sash is 14k rose gold, all other gold is 14k yellow. Overall length 7 1/2" (190 mm). From the collection of Don Guild, Hawaii.

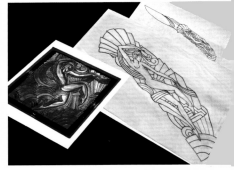

1 The original photo of a Follies Bergere plaque that wa the inspiration for this folder project. Next to it are th enlarged sketch of the front of knife with details of th figure along with a smaller view showing the blade.

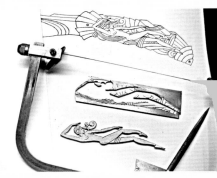

3 The figure of the dancer glued onto metal and pierce out with a jeweler's saw.

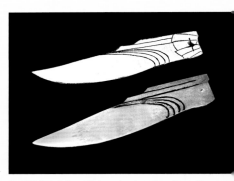

6 440 C stainless blade cut out and profiled. The roug lines are then drawn on the blade blade with a magic marke to show where sculpting will be done.

10 The rough parts are now put together to check ho everything looks.

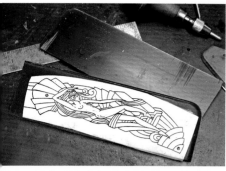

A copy of the original sketch glued onto special carving wax.

A view of some hand tools used along with the sculpted figure and the carved wax for casting the scales.

5 All of the parts for this knife were hand sculpted out of carving wax and pure tin stock. These prototypes were then taken to a company that does "investment casting" and. The cast rough parts were then cleaned up and put together to build the knife. Here, in a general view of the workshop, Stephen is seen tapping parts on the drill press using a Tapmatic.

View of the Sterling silver scale and the 18k gold figure ready for cleaning up and soldering together. These parts were cast using the "lost wax" process. This is the same process used by manufacturers of fine jewelry.

8 The dancer is being soldered onto the Sterling silver scale.

9 View of all the major rough parts including the carved blade, titanium liners, backbar and the front and back scales of the knife.

1 Front and rear completed scales are being "antiqued" so as to take on the look of an authentic metal sculpture of the 1920's.

12 Fully carved and heat treated blade being hand finished. Note that there is no thumb stud or nail nick on blade. Ribs along its spine are raised above the rest of blade for ease of opening and for maximum aesthetic appeal.

13 The finished knife showing the spine and the raised carvings. 14k rose gold and 14k yellow gold are used for the inlays along the spine, maintaining the Art Deco look.

Francesco Pachì
"Folding Skinner", 2005

Francesco Pachì was born in 1961, in Genoa, Italy. Today he lives in Sassello, Italy, in inland Liguria, in a house surrounded by woods and meadows, with his wife Mirella and his daughter Gaia. After finishing his science studies in 1983, he started a professional photography firm that became one of the most successful in the city of Genoa. Forever a nature and outdoor-activity lover as well as an expert archer and hunter, he also became interested in the world of custom knives. In 1991, completely self-taught, he began his first experiments with grinding, which led him, in 1994, to his first knife exhibition. In 1995, after a trip to the United

States and a few days spent in the studio of the great American master Steve Johnson, he decided to devote himself full-time to knifemaking, thus it became his primary occupation. He is now president of the Corporazione italiana Coltellinai and voting member of the American Knifemakers Guild and of the Deutsche Messermacher Gilde.

Via Pometta 1
17046 Sassello (SV), ITALY
Phone/fax: (39) 19 720086
email: info@pachi-knives.com
Site: www.pachi-knives.com

"Folding Skinner", 2005 Blade and bolsters are "Butterfly" Mosaic Damascus made by Aldo Conto (Italy). Locking button with a citrine stone and the screws are solid gold. Fossil mammoth ivory handle slabs with scrimshaw by Mirella Pachì. Overall length 7 3/8" (187 mm).

1 Using a bandsaw, Francesco cuts the bolsters fro the bar of "Butterfly" Mosaic Damascus forged by Ald Conto (Italy).

3 Francesco briefly treats the blade and bolsters in a acid bath to check the pattern in the Damascus and see he is positioning the pieces correctly.

6 Francesco drills the blade and then reams the hole f the pivot pin.

8 Drilling the hole for the pins that open the blade.

Blade and bolsters are brought to the correct size on the surface grinder.

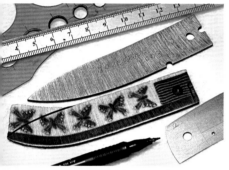

The final design of the blade is traced on the Damascus and the pivot point is marked.

5 The various items used to make the knife. Mosaic Damascus for the blade and bolsters, titanium for the liners, mammoth ivory for the handle slabs, screws and washers.

Using the belt grinder to contour the blade.

All the file work is done before the heat treating process.

10 The shop is always a mixture of many tools and various projects.

11 Francesco has a workshop full of quality equipment which is necessary for the precise work of making his high-end custom fixed-blades and folding knives. Here he is seen next to the pantograph.

12 The heat treatment is done and the blade was brought to a temperature of 830°C before cooling in oil.

13 The handle pattern template is traced onto the liners.

14 The contact point between the liner and blade flattened out carefully.

15 The liners are contoured.

16 The back spacer and the two liners are drilled while held together in place.

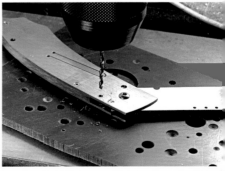

17 After the knife is assembled, Francesco drills the two liners for the the stop pin.

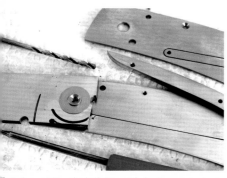

18 Before drilling the ball détente hole, Francesco checks it is positioned correctly with regards to the blade.

19 checking the milling process for the correct depth.

20 Milling the back side of the bolsters to accept the hidden screws.

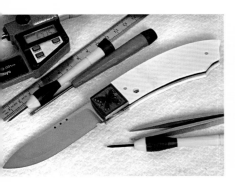

21 The knife is assembled before beginning to work on the handle.

22 Francesco begins to shape the handle on the belt grinder.

23 Continuing by hand, Francesco uses finer and finer grits of abrasive paper to reach a perfect finish.

24 The ball détente is inserted in position into its hole.

25 With a hard steel punch Francesco marks the exact point where the ball will be captured by the blade and then creates a small hole in that spot with a carbide point.

26 After revealing the beauty of the Mosaic Damascus in acid, Francesco peens three gold pins in the blade to assist in its opening.

Nico Pelzer
"Backlock with Damascus Interframe", 2005

Nico, born in Pretoria, South Africa, in 1970, made his first knife as a school project at the age of 14. These humble beginnings were the start of a lifelong passion for knives, pocket knives and art. He started creating knives as a hobby in 1998, whilst he was a poultry farmer in Northern Kwa Zulu Natal, an area steeped in history, and started making knives fulltime in 2004. Nico's love for the art of knife making has resulted in him progressing from just making fixed blade knives to making folders and to making his own Damascus steel. Nico makes knives of his own design, but will also manufacture knives according to customer's specifications. Nico takes enormous pride in the making of each knife, and will not allow any knife to leave his workshop if he is not 100% satisfied with it. Currently Nico makes mostly folders using exotic materials, but also enjoys making daggers and fixed-blade knives.

P.O. Box 414, Vryheid
3100 South Africa
Phone: (+27) 34 980 7388
Mobile: (+27) 82 323 5992
email: nico@nicoknives.com
Site: www.nicoknives.com

1 Each knife project begins with detailed drawings and th final placement of all pins and moving parts is finalize at this stage.

3 All of the various parts for the knife are surface groun before any profiling or drilling is done on them.

"Backlock with Damascus Interframe", 2005 A backlock folder with Damascus interframe and Damascus blade. blade carved to match both the radius of the ricasso and the bolsters. All pins are 16k gold with a hidden lock-bar pivot pin and blade stop pin and a titanium spring. Length closed 3 11/16" (94 mm), overall length 6 9/16" (164 mm).

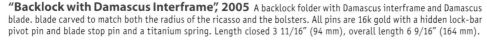

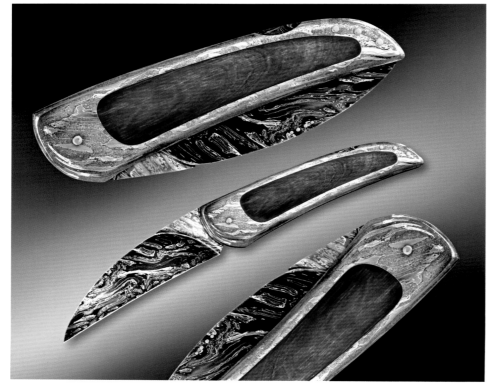

6 The blade gets carved to match the radius of the grin and the radius of the front end of the bolster, making us of riffler files before doing the final finish wit sandpaper.

8 The templates used to create the inlays and the cutout for the inlays, as well as the files used to do the carving work on the knife.

2 All the jigs and templates for drilling and assembly, as well as the templates for creating the inlays on the pantograph are completed before starting any work on a knife.

4 The surface ground parts are profiled as close as possible to the final profile.

5 To ensure accuracy, precision vice and clamps are used to hold the verious parts when drilling the holes. This is a critical stage that is carefully executed in order to ensure the smooth action of all moving parts after the final assembly.

7 The frame, with inlays already cut, is shaped as close as possible to its final shape before the inlays are fitted.

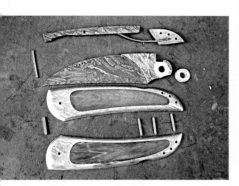

9 All parts ready for final assembly, including 16k gold pins and the anodized titanium spring.

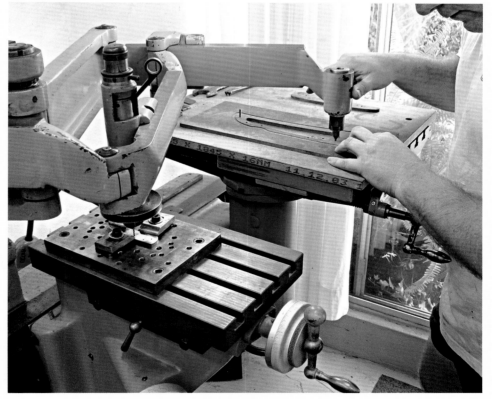

10 The Deckel GK 21 pantograph used to create the inlays. Note the universal machining plate with multiple taped holes allowing the work piece to be clamped down in almost any position.

Andy Shinosky
"Single-Action Automatic Dagger", 2005

Born in Warren, Ohio in 1959, Andy attributes his earliest attraction to knives to a day when, as a small child, a neighbor showed him a small pearl handled folder he kept in his pocket. Andy says he was mesmerized by that knife and never forgot that moment. Today if you should ask him what attracts him to knives he would tell you of his great love for tools in general, and for Andy there is no more personal tool than that of a folding knife. He feels that because of this personal nature that is attributed to knives, he choses to embellish and adorn them, making them even more unique and one of a kind. To his surprise he was met with much early success earning the Best New Maker Award at the annual Blade Show. Currently Andy enjoys making interframe and integral frame-locking folders as well as traditional locking liner

folders. His favorite handle materials are various Mother-of-Pearls due to their inherent stability and natural beauty. Because Andy loves all aspects of the knifemaking craft he has taken time away to learn the art of engraving so that he can further embellish his knives.

3117 Meanderwood Dr.
Canfield, Ohio 44406, USA
Phone: (330) 702-0299
email: andy@shinosky.com
Website: www.shinosky.com

"Single-Action Automatic Dagger", 2005 A folding dagger with a button-activated single-action automatic mechanism. The blade and lockbar are ATS-34. Handles are 416 Stainless. Inlays are Black-Lip Pearl. Closed length 4 3/8" (111 mm).

1 Computer drawings along with the hardened an tempered blade, lockbar and spring. Shown are som fixtures and inlay templates and the rough handle slabs

3 Rough sawing of the 416 Stainless Steel handle slab using a push block to guard against injury.

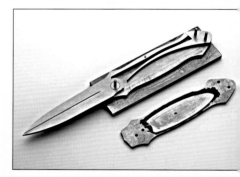

6 An early test fit of the knife components while utilizing a fixture to protect the holes from elongation due to the incomplete assembly of the knife.

10 Pearl inlays are attached to the inlay templates using lapidary dop wax and then routed to final shape using special diamond burrs. This is done wet to avoid heat and loading of the tool.

2 Using an expandable barrel lap to create a polished and true pivot hole helps to ensure a clean smooth action between the blade and bushing.

4 The handle slabs are glued to a fixture using Black Max adhesive and then rough milled for the inlay pockets and the rough profile.

5 Contouring of the side case using progressively finer belts: The inside of the knife is packed with tissue. Then the entire perimeter of the knife is masked off to prevent any grit from entering into the mechanism of the knife. The handle sides receive their final belt finish prior to engraving. The end finish will be attained during the engraving process as there is additional sanding done at that time. The inlay will be polished after the engraving is done.

7 By using a slow speed shop built sanding disc Andy can bring the flats of the blade to a near polish prior to the grinding of the main blade bevels.

8 Grinding the blade bevels after heat treatment ensures the stock removal will not happen too quickly and more control is afforded to achieve a symmetrical grind.

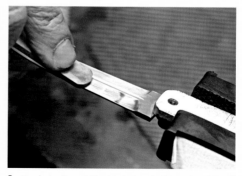

9 Hand stoning of the blade bevels to work out small imperfections and prepare the blade for it's final finish.

11 Using a milling machine with a shop built fixture to create relief areas on the inside of the handle slabs.

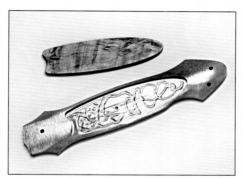

12 Handle inlays prepped and ready to be seated in the pre-glued handle pockets.

13 All knife components ready for final assembly. All internal parts have been sanded to their final finish and are cleaned and demagnetized.

Mike Skellern
Two "Mastiff" folders with Warthog Tusk Handles, 2005

Born in 1939, in Rugby, England, Mike emigrated with his parents to South Africa in 1947. Always being involved with outdoor pursuits, he currently lives on a banana farm in Natal province. He qualified as a medical practitioner in Pretoria, in 1965, and later became involved with Banana plantations and with Game farming. His interest in knife making began in 1986 influenced by his good friend Owen Wood. Sheath knives soon gave way to the challenge of folding knives, being intrigued by both modern and old pocket knives. Other than occasional embellishment by

scrimshander wife, Toi, his knives are completed in house, though Damascus steels are acquired from others. Mike is an active hunter and most tusks or horns used for his knives are procured personally. Bone and wood handle materials are similarly selected via his various farming ventures. He is an active member of the Southern African and the Italian Knifemakers Guilds.

Skema Farm, P. O. Box 323
Munster 4278, South Africa
Phone and fax: (+27) 39 31 92 53
email: skellern@venturenet.co.za

1 Warthog tusks. Only the upper-jaw tusk of the male (in the middle) can be used for making a knife handle (should be 10" or longer). Both lower-jaw tusk of the male (top) and the female tusk (bottom) are not suitable.

3 Tusk portion ground flat to the required depth so as to show the shape and color required for the knife in progress Knife handle traced onto blank with pencil to visualize final appearance.

Two "Mastiff" folders with Warthog Tusk Handles, 2005 Mike names his knife models after dog breeds. Titanium frames/bolsters and blades of Damasteel hardened to 59 Rc. Overall lengths 7 5/16"(185 mm).

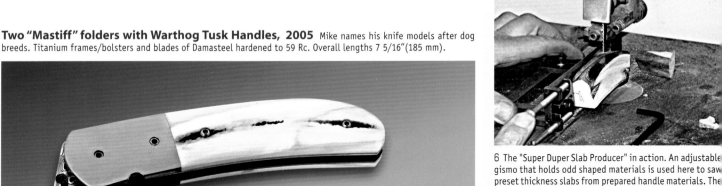

6 The "Super Duper Slab Producer" in action. An adjustable gismo that holds odd shaped materials is used here to saw preset thickness slabs from prepared handle materials. The slab is indexed on the side held against the appliance.

8 Knife parts ready for assembly. Handle slabs start off 2 mm thicker than the bolsters. They are then clamped to the frame and drilled for the screws. Once the entire "sandwich" is assembled, they are ground down to size.

2 This shows flat grinding of the tusk portion chosen for the handle slabs, grinding down till the desired texture and appearance are reached. This process is applied to each of the two natural 'flats' of the tusk.

4 Sawing the prepared tusk to the overall length of intended handles.

5 Mike uses a tapping accessory with a safety clutch to cut threads into titanium knife frame for micro screws. G-e-n-t-l-y does it, or the tap will fracture! Mike has gradually brought into his workshop all the equipment he needs, including a recently acquired Deckel pantograph, allowing him to have his knives completed in-house.

7 The rough-cut handle slabs have been sawn from the tusk 'cylinder' then go off to the surface grinder for precise smoothing and shaping to the correct thickness.

9 Several slabs under selection for fitting to the knife. The center slab is from the tusk core and has more subtle colors and texture making it suitable for scrimshaw or carving.

10 Hand filing the flat slabs to suit the knife contours. Sanding with decreasing size grits, down to 1500, comes only after after completing the file work. The knife is gripped between padded jaws onto an old file that itself is fastened to the vice.

Josh Smith
"Abalone Auto", 2005

Born in 1981, Josh began making knives under the direction of Rick Dunkerley at the age of 11. His parents bought him one of Rick's Damascus hunting knives for Christmas and shortly after that Josh was invited to his shop to make a knife. Over the next few years Josh began to buy knife making equipment with money he saved from his lawn-mowing business. At the age of 15 he passed his Journeyman Smith and in 2000, at the age of 19, he became the youngest person to ever attain the Master Smith rating in the American Bladesmith Society. Fortunate to have supportive parents, Josh was able to advance his knife making skills quickly. In 2002 he became a full time knifemaker and has been enjoying it ever since. *"I specialize in Mosaic Damascus, liner lock folders, automatics, bowies, and fighters. In 2002 I married my wife Jodi and in 2004 we were blessed with our first child, a girl we named Demi Jayne. We are expecting our second child in 2006. Raised in Montana I enjoy hunting, fishing, and golf".*

P.O. Box 753, Frenchtown,
MT 59834, USA
Phone: (406) 626-5775
email: josh@joshsmithknives.com
Site: www.joshsmithknives.com

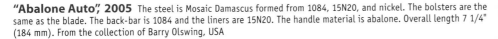

"Abalone Auto", 2005 The steel is Mosaic Damascus formed from 1084, 15N20, and nickel. The bolsters are the same as the blade. The back-bar is 1084 and the liners are 15N20. The handle material is abalone. Overall length 7 1/4" (184 mm). From the collection of Barry Olswing, USA

1 Once he has forged the Damascus and decided on a knife design, Josh uses this abrasive 3B surface grinder to flatten the steel for the knife. This knife will be an automatic so it is crucial for the parts to be flat and true.

5 Josh hand taps all of the holes to the correct screw size.

9 After heat treating the knife, the handle and liners are sanded to a finish. Then Josh grinds and finishes the blade. Everything is buffed and ready for etching and blueing.

2 The 8x24" magnet on the surface grinder holds the blade stock down as it is ground to the correct thickness. Josh also surface grinds the back-bar, spring material, and bolsters at this time.

3 Pre-drilling all the holes in the knife with a 1/16" bit. Later Josh returns to drill and ream all the holes to the correct size in preparation for tapping and fitting.

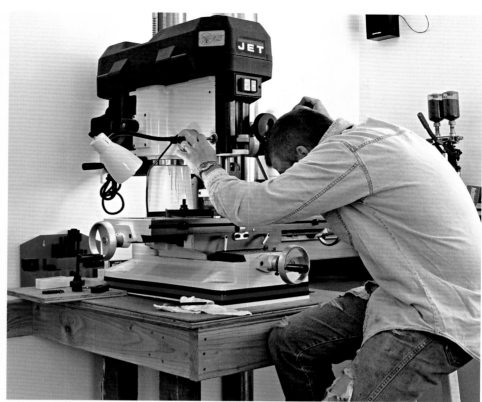

4 "I use my JET milling machine to drill accurate pivot holes in the blade and liners. It is very important to have good pivot holes. It is not a necessity to have a mill or a surface grinder but it does make some of the jobs much easier. I feel it was good to make knives without this equipment at the beginning. It makes one understand and appreciate the machine when you do eventually get one".

6 On his disc grinder, Josh flattens the abalone to the correct thickness. "The disc grinder is the most important piece of equipment I have".

7 Here all the pieces of the knife are laid out and ready for the lock to be cut and the button hole to be milled. Then Josh makes the spring and rocker. Once the auto mechanism is working properly, he grinds the handle to shape.

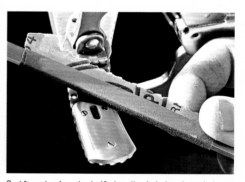

8 After shaping the knife handle, it is hand sanded to a medium finish. Then Josh file-works the back bar and liners and later heat treats the knife.

10 Using a pin vise Josh file-works all of the screws, then sands and buffs them. File-work on a knife really dresses it up and everyone loves it.

11 Here Josh is heat coloring the screws with a small torch. He likes to think about the overall look of the knife, visualizing ahead how the final colors will compliment each other.

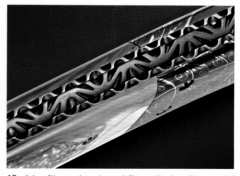

12 Crisp file-work and good fit on the handle material really catch a collector's eye.

Stefan Steigerwald
"Relict", 2005

Stefan Steigerwald was born in 1968, in Nuremberg, Germany. He likes outdoor sports and always needed a reliable knife with him. Commercial knives didn't satisfy him, neither in shape nor in function, he therefore decided to make his own. Working as a pattern-maker and a precision mechanic, helped him to realize this and he has been making knives since 1990. Most of Stefan's custom knives are design oriented. In 1999 he joined the German Knifemakers Guild and in 2001 he became a full-time knifemaker and material reseller. His first book about knife materials and knifemaking tricks was printed in 2005. His extraordinary style is obvious. Serrations and optical elements from nature turn his knives into biomechanoides and true collector objects. He usually incorporates elements of ancient materials in his knives making them one-of-a-kind and giving them a special aura. Stefan sees the joy of working with these unique materials as an attempt to let time run a bit slower.

Schwander Str. 12a
90 530 We, Germany
Phone: (+49) 9129 402151
email: info@steigerwald-messer.de
Site: http://www.steigerwald-messer.de

"Relict", 2005 Handle made of Sikhote Alin Meteorite from Russia. Liners are D-2 steel and the blade is Wilbert Torsion Damascus steel. Overall length 7 3/16" (182 mm).

1 Choosing a nice looking combination of "raw" materials so that the steel and Meteorite colors will go well together in the finished knife.

3 The cut piece of Meteorite is fixed to the drill plate while drilling the holes for the pivot.

6 The counterpart of the Meteorite handle is made of D2 steel. Here it is being drilled for the pivot and for its cover.

10 The cover is being fitted onto the liner.

2 Stefan first makes samples of every new knife out of cardboard. He makes these simple working models in order to check compatibility between the design, its dimensions and the functioning of the mechanism.

4 The pivot, made of Damasteel, is being cut to shape and size on the lathe.

5 *"This is the workplace, where I spend most of my time. Everything is arranged for me to do an efficient job comfortably. Most of my machines are overworked and then painted unique green (The color of hope, ha, ha...) Deckel, Weiler, Thiel and Kugelmüller. All of them quality brands, doing a good job for many years".*

7 A round piece of Damasteel is turned on the lathe for inserting into in the liner and covering the pivot.

8 Now the handle is decorated/carved using the milling machine and a radius milling cutter.

9 To assure a smooth performance of the opening and closing of the blade, an extra bearing, made of bronze, is turned out on the lathe.

1 The liner is being skeletonized, first by drilling, then with a jeweler's saw and finally with files.

12 Both the Meteorite and the liner are being drilled together for the connecting pins. Plastic fillers hold the meteorite in a position so that the holes are truly parallel.

13 In his workshop, Stefan has one room for the "clean" machines and his knife finishing and assembling workspace and another where he works with his grinders and compressor. An additional room is the storeroom.

14 After drilling and reaming the pivot hole in the blade, the outline of the blade can be worked on, using a milling cutter to machine the rounded section.

15 The "locking pocket" gets the right geometry by cutting it out accurately. The bronze bearing is set in place for the first test assembly of the folding knife.

16 The Damasteel blade is ground out on the belt grinder.

17 The surface of the blade is finished by hand using progressively finer grits of sand paper.

18 The locking lever, produced from the same Damasteel as the blade, is worked into shape on the milling machine to create a perfect fit with the blade.

19 All the parts receive the finishing touches by filework and buffing.

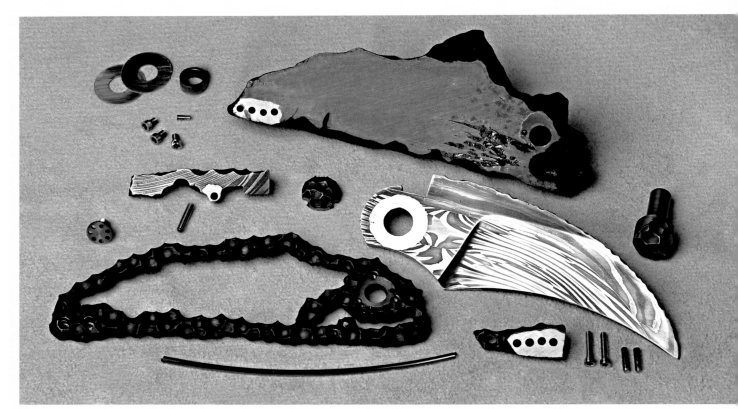

20 All the various parts that go into the making of this one-of-a-kind folding knife before going for heat treatment.

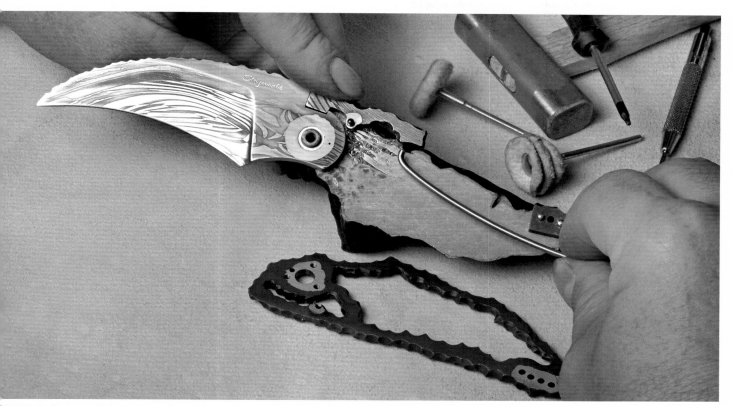

1 With the final assembly in progress, only the spring is left to be dealt with before the final fitting.

2 Assembly has been completed and fit, finish and the smoothness of the opening mechanism have been carefully checked. Now Stefan can find a moment to admire this little piece f art in which he used modern technology to combine modern materials with an element from outer space.

Johnny Stout
"Double-Action Automatic Folder", 2005

Born in Alpine, Texas, in 1943, Johnny's earliest memories of pocket knives are from an early age of five when he regularly went on the trap-line with his grandfather who handed down his old knives to Johnny to carry proudly as though they were new. In 1983 Johnny was first exposed to handmade knives while visiting the shop of Jim Moore in Texas, where he made his first knife, the High Country Classic Hunter, which he still offers today as one of his standard models. He soon purchased his first few pieces of shop equipment and set up his own shop in a small storage building, in his back yard. Later, as he was exposed to more of a national audience, his work was in demand for more elaborate knives, mostly folders. Today he offers a variety of

folders, with various locking devices, as well as slip joint models. A favorite is his "Zodiac" Double Action Auto. He loves to blend ancient materials such as mammoth ivory and Damascus with the more high tech metals like titanium.

1205 Forest Trail
New Braunfels, Texas 78132, USA
Phone: (830) 606-4067
email: johnny@stoutknives.com
Site: www.stoutknives.com

"Double-Action Automatic Folder", 2005 A folder with a button-activated double-action automatic mechanism. The button locks the leaf spring, allowing the blade to function both in manual and auto mode. The blade and bolsters are "Paisley Pattern" Damascus steel, the back spacer bar is A2 tool steel. Handles are stabilized mammoth ivory, bolsters are engraved by Joe Mason. Closed length is 4 7/8" (11 cm).

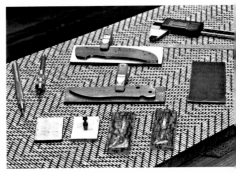

1 Materials used to build the double action auto. Blade and handle patterns clamped to the Damascus billet, and the titanium liner materials, rough cut mammoth ivory scales, the push button and steel for the lock bar and spring.

3 The blade is cut out of the Damascus billet using an 18 tooth-per-inch bi-metal bandsaw blade. After the blade is profiled to the scribed line it will be ready for initial shaping.

6 After the heat treatment of the blade, it receives a final pass on the surface grinder using a Ruby Wheel, bringing it to its final thickness.

10 The blade is being ground on a Bader B3, 2"x72" belt grinder using a 10" (254 mm) wheel.

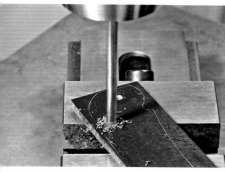

The Damascus billet is surface ground, the blade pattern
scribed on the billet, then the pivot and thumb stud holes
re drilled undersize. The pivot hole will be enlarged later
s further assembly and heat treating are done.

The blade is shown during the final profile step on the
lat platen of the John LeBlanc 2" x 72" belt grinder, using
220 grit 3M ceramic sanding belt.

5 The pivot hole is now reamed to .001" under size with a carbide reamer. The hole will be enlarged to final dimensions
after heat treating, using diamond paste and an expandable barrel lap. This process takes extra time but polishes the
pivot hole so that a good tight fit is accomplished, creating a positive lock-up on the push button both in the open
and closed positions.

The bolsters are rough shaped to a popular "S" pattern,
atched and super glued together, then using a die mill
utter the bolsters are hand held, and the pattern is
fined, on a variable speed drill press.

8 The liners with the oversized bolsters are attached using
the pivot pin and screw, and a 2-56 button head torx screw.
Note the hole in the left bolster for the push button to be
fitted and installed later.

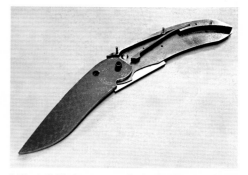

9 The individual components for the double action: blade,
liner with oversized bolster attached, and back spacer with
heat-treated leaf spring installed. Pocket in the right liner
and bolster is for the button and its coil spring.

1 The finished components for the Zodiac ready for final
olish, etching, assembly. Liners with finished bolsters,
ory scales ready for final installation, washers, button,
ack spacer with leaf spring and hollow ground blade.

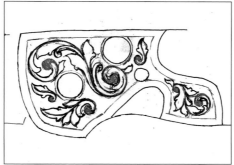

12 Rough layout of the engraving design by Joe Mason.

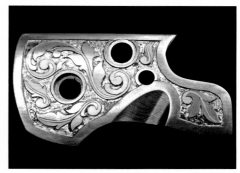

13 One of the stages in the engraving process of the
bolsters. After being rough-engraved and gold inlayed, the
background on this bolster has also been removed.

Bill Vining
"Snake and Dragon", 2005

Bill Vining was born in 1956, a lifetime native of Massachusetts. Knife making has been a part time hobby for Bill since late 2002. He has always had a fascination for knives and actually being able to make one still amazes him. Bill's skills have been acquired through reading books, the Internet, trial and error and some priceless advice from several of the best knife makers in the world. He does not specialize in any particular style, making liner locking folders, lock-backs, slip-joints, boot knives, hunters and the occasional kitchen knife. Although he will take an order for a specific style, Bill likes to make what his creative instincts suggest. He tends to favor making fancy folders with exotic materials such as ivories, pearl, bone and Damascus and he really enjoys the embellishment work.

9 Penny Lane
Methuen, Mass. 01844, USA
Phone: (978) 618-9970
email: billv@medawebs.com
Site: www.medawebs.com/knives

1 Bill uses CAD software to design his knives on the computer as it makes it easier for him to fit pieces together and make changes if needed.

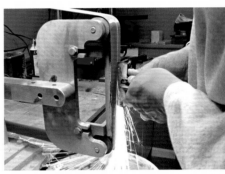

5 The liners have been pinned together for rough shaping on the KMG. Using a 80 grit belt, the sparks are really flying.

"Snake and Dragon", 2005 The knife is named for the two Damascus patterns used, polished and nitre-blued to a subtle bronze color. Bob Eggerling's Snakeskin Damascus bolsters and Delbert Ealy's Dragon Damascus blade and backspine, which is also fully fileworked. The scales are exhibition grade Mother-of-Pearl. The .060" titanium liners have been fully fileworked and anodized blue/purple with gold edges giving a sparkling effect to the knife. The thumbstud is stainless steel inlaid with a 2 mm sapphire in a 14k gold bezel. Overall length 6 1/2" (165 mm).

9 Here is the knife as it begins to take shape. All the pieces have been roughed out and checked for fit.

11 Scales have been mounted and rough shaped.

2 After the patterns are glued to the steel, it is time to start cutting out all the pieces. This is done on the trusty Harbor Freight band saw.

3 Drilling out the pivot. This is done on the blade and liners.

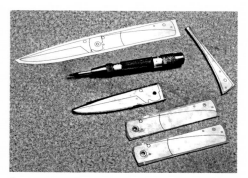

4 Here are all the parts roughed out. The pivot holes have been drilled.

6 Bill needs 3/16" holes in his washers so they fit over the bronze bushings. They come with a .125" hole. He made this little jig out of 01 steel to punch out the inner diameter to the required .1875".

7 Once he drills the stop pin, Bill swings the blade around to drill the stop on the blade. The stop on the blade is then shaped and polished.

8 Beginning to rough fit the backspine. Bill makes his folders using an aluminum plate. This insures correct alignment every time when drilling or fitting.

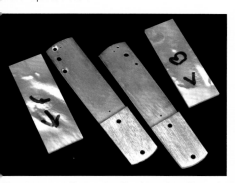

10 Bolsters are all ground to fit. The scales will now be drilled and counter-bored to accept the 0-80 gold plated screws.

14 Anodizing the liners. These liners will have 2 colors. Their basic color will be blue/purple and the outer edges will be gold.

12 Cutting the lock face on the mini mill. This is the part that scares Bill the most. If he makes this too short, it is back to the drawing board.

13 Applying some filework to the back-spacer. The filework on the spine will be continued on to the end of the blade. The liners will be fully fileworked all around as well.

15 A view of all finished parts of the knife before beginning the final assembly. All the embellishment has been done; the spacer and blade have been file-worked. The titanium liners anodized.

Stan Wilson
The "Advisor", 2005

Born in 1958, Stan grew up with knives and remembers the day when carrying a pocket knife to school was part of growing up. Although he had always enjoyed tools and making things, it wasn't until 1999 that he tried his hand at making a knife. It wasn't anything fancy, just a knife. Later that year he found out about an organization called the Knifemakers Guild and he attended the show. *"That show changed my life, I walked around amazed at what I saw, and it inspired and humbled me"*, stated Stan. He decided then and there that if he tried to make each knife

better than the last one, he might become a knifemaker someday. Today Stan Wilson is a full time knifemaker plus a member of the Knifemakers Guild and he still lives by the creed, that he will make each knife better than the one he made before that.

1908 Souvenir Drive
Clearwater, Florida 33755, USA
Phone: (727) 461-1992
email: swilson@stanwilsonknives.com
Site: www. stanwilsonknives.com

The "Advisor", 2005 A liner locking folder. The blade, spine, bolsters and thumbstud are Damascus by Robert Eggerling. Handles are mammoth ivory. The blade is partially file-worked as well as the spine, liners, thumbstud and screws. Closed length 4 9/16" (116 mm).

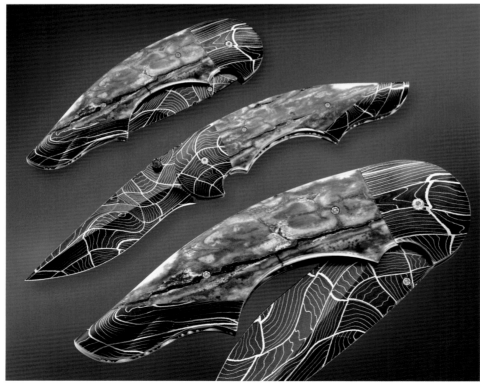

1 It begins with and idea and the raw materials, in th[...] case a bar of Robert Eggerling Damascus, some titaniu[...] sheet and a nice set of mammoth ivory slabs.

3 The bolsters are held in place from the back so n[...] screws will show. They are hand tapped using a modifie[...] tap with a stop.

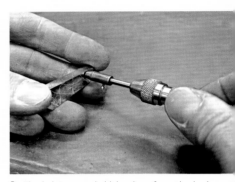

6 The file work is progressing nicely. The blade and spin[...] are attached to one of the liners. This allows a seamles[...] transition of the pattern from the blade into the spine.

8 Getting up-close and personal with the dovetailing o[...] the handles, Stan sands a little and checks the fit. H[...] repeats this till a perfect fit is achieved using a home-buil[...] sander made only for this purpose.

2 The Blade and bolsters are flash etched to bring out the pattern. The blade is then installed into the frame and the bolsters are lined up for maximum pattern match.

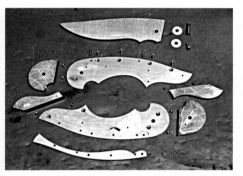

4 All the main parts have been fabricated. After the file-work is completed the blade, spine and bolsters will all be heat treated to insure a consistent etch.

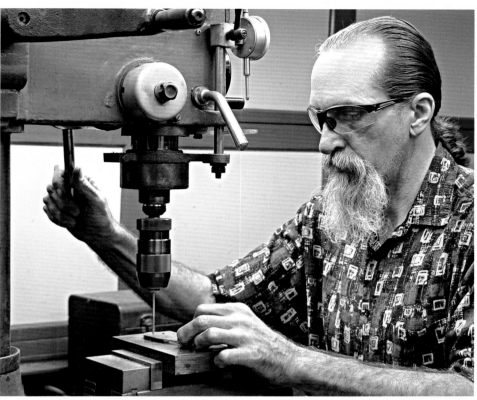

5 Reaming the bolster and liner to size for the pivot pin. For the knife to open smoothly and close centered in the frame all the holes must be drilled and reamed perfectly square to the frame and in perfect alignment. All parts are first surface ground, and the bolster has been screwed to the liner to be drilled and reamed as one unit.

7 The handle slabs have been carefully sanded flat from the back to get them to the required thickness. Next they will be cut oversized the dovetailed to match the bolsters.

9 Turning the thumbstud from the same Damascus used for the blade. The inset for the thumbstud will be turned from the same mammoth used for the handle.

10 *"It's the details that make a difference, or make you cross-eyed. Here I am file working the handle screws. Later, when finished, they will be gold plated"*. The liners will be anodized to a color that fits nicely with the Damascus and the mammoth and then the knife is ready for the final assembly.

Owen Wood
"Art Deco folder", 2005

Owen, born in 1951, grew up in Africa spending much of his time outdoors in the bush. Knives, particularly pocket knives, were items of everyday use and as a child he always had a knife around. During His college years he met Des Horn who helped him make his first knife in 1979. When Damascus steel first appeared in the modern knife, Owen was immediately intrigued by its beauty and its enormous potential in knife making. Sid Birt taught him the basics of forge welding, laminating and patterning in his Indiana forge. Back in Africa Owen started forging steel, and creating striking pattern welded blades still captures his imagination and remains his favorite task. He primarily makes folding knives, but daggers have always fascinated him. Many of his knives are being embellished by other artists, creating

objects of rare beauty. A founder member and Chairman of the Knifemaker's Guild of Southern Africa for many years, Owen started exhibiting at shows in the US and Europe in the early 80's, and has won awards for his work at many of them. In 1999, Owen moved to the United States with his wife and family.

6492 Garrison Street, Arvada
Colorado, CO 80004, USA
Phone: (303) 456-2748
email: wood.owen@gmail.com
Site: owenwoodcustomknives.com

"Art Deco folder", 2005 A Warnecliff liner lock folder. Composite blade using Explosion Damascus and a spine of nickel/1095 layers. Bolsters are 18k gold, fluted along the front radius and engraved in art deco style by Amayak Stepanyan. Scales are Mother-of-Pearl and Black-lip pearl. Spacer is 303 stainless steel decorated in a diamond pattern and blued. Overall length 5 11/16" (145 mm)

1 Materials for a precise composite Damascus blade. Rough bars of Explosion pattern Damascus, ground to perfect rectangular sections and bars of Nickel/1095 laminate, are the raw materials for this Art Deco blade.

3 The forge welding of the blade parts is done in a mild steel box. The Parts of the blade are carefully shaped and fitted, surrounded by fitted mild steel spacers, a sacrificial anvil and side plates.

6 The blade parts in their box, red hot on the anvil. Because the parts are well fitted and the surfaces to be welded have a high finish – a perfect weld is achieved using a relatively light, 1kg hammer.

9 The stop bar in this knife cannot be seen as it runs in a hemispherical slot, machined into the back of the blade. A 2 mm carbide cutter is used for this purpose.

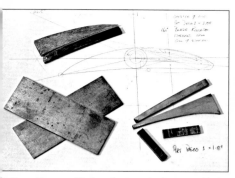

2 The pattern used in Owen's composite Damascus blades is given serious thought. Here the cutting edge consists of a narrow bar of Explosion pattern Damascus welded to a spine of layered Nickel and 1095 set at a dramatic angle.

4 Blade parts, anvil and spacers are laid out on one of the side plates using cyanoacrylate to hold each in place before the seams of the assembly are arc welded, sealing them in a box. Here several boxes are ready for the forge.

5 A large billet of raw material for Explosion Damascus coming out of the forge. All forge welding is done using a flux-less technique. Sometimes this requires that the materials to be included in the billet are sealed in a mild steel box before forging. This protects them from oxidization and produces flawless welds.

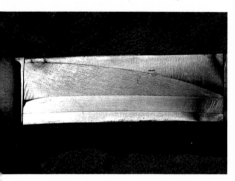

7 After careful forging with a small hammer the box is allowed to cool before stripping the sides to reveal the blade inside.

8 After drilling the pivot hole in the correct place and shaping the profile of the blade, a dividing head is centered under the spindle of Owen's Deckel FP1 milling machine, to machine the stop bar slot.

0 The finished slot in the back of the blade. The two ends of the slot must be precisely positioned allowing the blade to be opened and closed in the correct position.

11 Blades have to be correctly heat treated for good cutting performance. The blade goes through a hardening and tempering cycle and the exact hardness is checked using the Wilson hardness tester.

12 Blades are heat treated in a vertical furnace at 890° C. The blade is protected from the atmosphere by sealing it in a stainless steel envelope. Tempering occurs for 1 hour at 260° C.

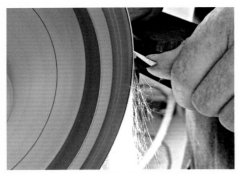

13 The blade is carefully hand ground after first marking out the bevels. Carbon steel Damascus creates a shower of sparks, as it is ground.

14 Rough grinding on a 60 grit belt is complete. Polishing on an A 45 trizact belt is followed by hand rubbing to ensure a good finish. The ball détente hole in the blade is seen at the end of the crescent shaped stop bar slot.

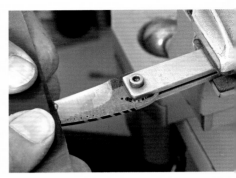

15 Using 600 grit wet and dry paper, the blade is carefully hand polished to ensure that all scratches left by the grinding process are removed.

16 The spine and lower edges of the blade are also brought to a high finish.

17 To achieve a flawless action on a knife with a Damascus blade, the pivot area must not be etched. Here a stop-out is applied to the areas to be protected from the action of the Muriatic acid in which the blade is etched.

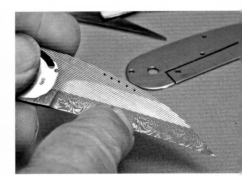

18 After drying at room temperature, the stop out is baked onto the blade at 120º C, before the blade is etched in warm Muriatic acid. In the finished blade the non-etched area can be seen under Owen's thumb.

19 This knife has the added color and value of 18k gold bolsters. Here the flutes in the front edge of the bolster are being milled. This process will be followed by careful polishing of the flutes.

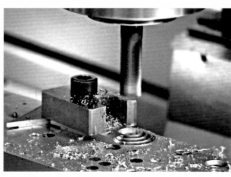

20 The recess in the bolster, made to accommodate the head of the pivot, is being milled. Careful attention is taken to collect all the gold chips produced during this machining process.

21 The Deckel Toolroom milling machine is used for many precision operations in the making of a folding knife. The accurate positioning and machining of the holes in the liners and spacer as well as the tapering of the lock are all accomplished using this machine.

22 Liners and bolsters must fit properly. Here the fit is scrutinized after which the Mother-of-Pearl scales will be fitted and glued into position using modern high strength adhesives.

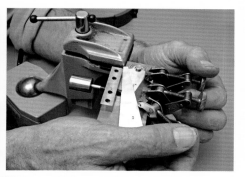

23 A special fixture holds the scales and liners in position, whilst clamps are used only after applying the adhesive.

24 High-speed and super sharp carbide drills are necessary when drilling in pearl. A sensitive down feed is provided by Owen's Hamilton sensitive drill press. The passage of the drill through the pearl can be felt when using such a machine, ensuring a perfect hole with no chipping where the drill breaks through. Here the holes for the gold screws attaching the scales to the liners are being drilled.

25 Titanium liners are profiled using a Deckel GK12 pantograph. By tracing template, this machine ensures that liners and other parts, such as bolsters, are perfectly profiled.

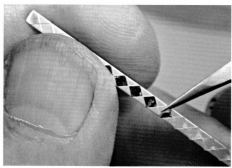

26 High-quality tape is applied to the back spacer before carefully scoring the diamond pattern decoration through the tape. Portions of the tape are picked out before bead blasting and bluing.

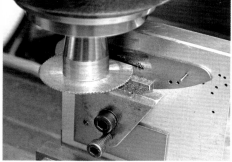

27 In a liner lock, the lock is often a part of the liner. A slitting saw in Owen's milling machine is used to seperate the lock from the liner on two sides. This part of the liner will be tapered to provide clearance for the ball détente.

Richard S. Wright
"Double Bladed Ambidextrous Bolster Release Switchblade", #100, 2005

Born in 1949, Richard lives in a small town in Southern Rhode Island, with his wife and creative consultant of 25 years, and their four Yorkshire Terriers. His background is as a welder, toolmaker and gunsmith. Making knives since he was a boy, Richard became serious about it after he made his first switchblade in 1991. He finds the mechanical intricacies of automatic knives to be what he likes about making this type of knife. He tries not to make two knives alike but

will occasionally make several variations of a particular design. While not making his own Damascus he does forge his blades to shape from other maker's Damascus. Richard strives to make a knife that is both functional and pleasing to the eye, being influenced by the old-world-look of late 1800's Sheffield folding Bowies and other older classic designs.

P. O. Box 201 Carolina,
Rhode Island 02812, USA
Phone: (401) 364-3579
email: rswswitchblades@hotmail.com
Site: www.Richardswright.com

"Double Bladed Auto" #100, 2005 Both blades (5 1/2" and 1 1/4") are made from five bar Rados Turkish Twist Damascus, forged to shape. They open via Wright's "Ambidextrous Bolster Release" mechanism. Either one of the four bolsters can be rotated slightly on the blade pivot axis to release the blade. Bolsters are a composite of Sterling silver and Rados Turkish Twist Damascus, the liners and back bars are titanium, and the scales are abalone. Overall length is 13 3/8" (340 mm)

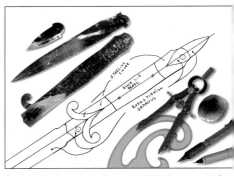

1 Initially, the knife design is established on paper, after which a working sheet-metal model of the knife is made to accurately locate the holes and internal parts of the auto mechanism.

5 The sheet metal template is used to measure how close the final forging is to the desired shape before the forging is complete.

7 The lathe is set up to turn pivot head screws out of titanium round stock. The first stage is cutting the screw diameter.

10 Cutting off the threaded screw blank with the cutoff tool in lathe after threading is completed.

172   RICHARD S. WRIGHT

2 The liners and back bar parts are pre-drilled, roughed out and the Rados Turkish Damascus for the blade is readied for forging to shape.

3 A coal fired forge is made ready for the process of hand forging the blade to shape.

4 The raw Damascus bar is drawn down to a profile as close to the finished blade as the tools and my skill will allow.

6 The templates for both blades show how close the finished forging is to the actual blade shape.

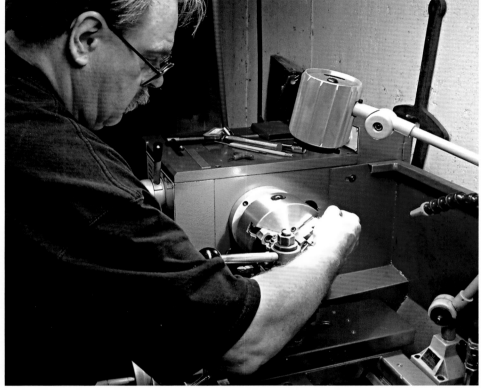

8 Checking the turned diameter of the screw blank with the micrometer before threading is completed.

9 All of the pivots and pivot head screws, and occasionally other screws and knife parts are made one at a time on my engine lathe.

11 The screw blank held in place to machine the screw slot with a saw.

12 The 0.025" screwdriver slot is machined using a jeweler's saw.

13 Finished screw blanks before the final fitting to the knife.

14 A tapping fixture that was made by Richard, insures the threads are cut square to the surface of the back bar.

15 The screw holes are countersunk so that the flat head screws will sit flush with the surface.

16 The Turkish Twist Damascus blade is heat treated, quenched in oil and then stress relieved.

17 The smaller "skull crusher" blade is also heat treated, quenched in oil and stress relieved.

18 Once the Sterling bolsters are cut out and profiled, they are shaped by hand with files and chisels and then hand finished with abrasive paper.

19 The double headed 2""x48"" belt grinder that Richard made for many of his roughing and shaping operations. This belt sander was built when he first started making knives and he has added many attachments to it over the years, making it a very flexible machine.

20 The Damascus inserts in the Sterling silver bolsters are being shaped on the home made 1"x42" horizontal belt grinder.

21 A vast array of files are used in the shaping and finishing of each individual part of the knife before assembly.

22 Once the parts are roughed out, they are then assembled for final fitting, shaping and finishing.

23 One of the two titanium back bars is held in a vise while the vine and rope designs are carved into them.

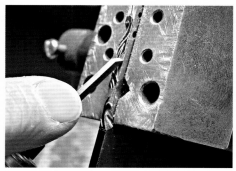

24 Engraving tools as well as files are used to carve the design in the back bars.

25 After one of the two back bars is laid out in a vine pattern, the background is removed by hand with engraving tools and files.

26 A section of the liners is done in a spiraling rope design; done first by hand with a file, and then hand finished with 2000 grit abrasive paper.

27 After the bolsters are carved and shaped, they are finished by hand with abrasive paper using specially designed sanding blocks.

28 The vise that Richard uses is mounted on a tripod stand fitted with a Timken roller bearing so that it will be able to spin on its own axis. This allows him to have a lot of flexibility while filing and engraving.

29 The final finish is done with 2000 grit silicon-carbide abrasive paper before being buffed.

30 The entire outside surface of the knife is hand rubbed to a mirror finish before being buffed by hand.

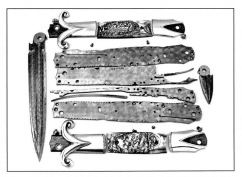

31 Everything finished and ready for etching and anodizing before final assembly.

Knife Related Arts and Crafts

Scrimshaw
Sharon Burger
Linda Karst Stone
Mirella Isnardi-Pachì

Engraving
Christian DeCamillis
Ronald P. Nott
Scott Pilkington
Darren P. Reeves
Andy Shinosky

Carving
André Andersson
David Broadwell
Vladimir Burkovski
Larry Fuegen
Dennis Greenbaum
William & Elizabeth Lloyd
Amayak Stepanyan

Mokume Gane
Boaz Shadmot

Damascus
Michael Andersson
Aldo Conto
Joel Davis
John Davis
Luciano Dorneles
Robert Eggerling
Tom Ferry
Ettore Gianferrari
Gary House
Jon Arthur Loose
Rodrigo M. Sfreddo
Boaz Shadmot

Sheaths
Alex Shamgar

Opposite:
Three Artists, One Knife, 2005
This one-of-a-kind art folding knife, resulted from the closely collaborated work of three Italian artists. The Mosaic Damascus maker Aldo Conto, the custom knifemaker Francesco Pachì and, his wife, scrimshaw artist Mirella Pachì.

Sharon Burger
"Scrimshaw", 2005

Born in 1969, in Bethlehem South Africa, Sharon has lived in and around Durban since the age of 12. In 1992 she finished her National Higher Diploma in Fine Arts, majoring in sculpture. In 1992, Sharon was introduced to scrimshaw by her father, a knifemaker, and became an Associate Member of the Knifemakers Guild of Southern Africa in 1997. The shift from constructing huge sculptures to Scrimshaw, in terms of scale, was a major conceptual adjustment. From 1997, Sharon has been doing scrimshaw on a full-time basis, finding this minute stippling process where the image is gradually revealed, totally transfixing. The majority of her work is done as commissions, primarily for knife collectors and knifemakers. "I do any subject that is requested of me but my favorites are portraits, figure studies, fantasy and intensely detailed subjects. As a personal preference I enjoy working in black only. For me this achieves a rather dramatic finished scrimshaw but I am open to working in color when the knife and subject lend themselves to it".

42A Sherwood Drive
Cluster Box 1625, Forest Hills/Kloof
3624 KZN, South Africa
email: scribble@iafrica.com
Site: www.kgsa.co.za/members/sharonburger
Phone: (+27) 31 7621349
Mobile: (+27) 83 7891675

"Tanto with Scrimshaw", 2005 Knife made by Theuns Prinsloo (South Africa), forged from his own Damascus. Given the large size of the elephant ivory handle, Sharon was able to do bold images in varying Japanese styles on both sides. Overall length 11 13/16" (300 mm).

1 In keeping with the Japanese style of the knife, Sharon decided to scrimshaw a Samurai on the front side and Japanese style prints/illustrations of Samurai worrier on its back.

3 Sharon uses a very sharp needle or a sharpened drill-bit or dentist's drill held in a pin-vice. A stippling scrimshaw machine, similar to a tattooing machine, can also be used. A Jeweler's visor (x4 magnification) is also used.

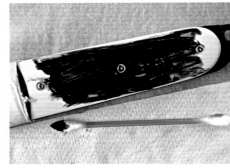

6 Every few minutes, Sharon wipes paint over the image to keep up with the stippling progress. The darker the area required, the more she stipples that area. The clearest way to see where she has worked is to regularly apply paint.

10 At her desk, Sharon prefers a slanted surface so as to elevate the work while working in such close proximity to it. She uses "cool" light as a warm light causes "dry eyes" and its heat can be harmful to the ivory.

2 Sharon uses artist's oil paints, preferring them to using ink. She finds oil paints to be richer in color intensity while some inks can stain the ivory if one is not careful. The black paint especially is much darker than black ink.

4 It is important to tape up the blade and bolster to protect them from getting damaged and from injuring one's self. Using the pin-vice held needle, she starts dotting to outline the basic proportions of the image.

5 Sharon alternates between using the x4 magnification jeweler's visor and the microscope. The microscope (x1 to x10 magnification) is ideal when working on really fine detail such as eyes. She always works from the original picture referring to it constantly. This microscope has three adjustable lights that illuminate the work wonderfully.

7 Once the area is covered in paint, she uses a soft tissue or cotton-wool to wipe the paint off again, avoiding any chance of scuffing the ivory surface. The stippled areas retain the paint and one is able to see the progress.

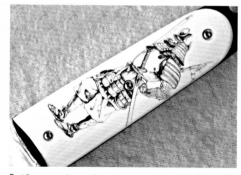

8 After many hours the scrimshaw will still look just like an outline, as one is still capturing detail and constantly working on proportions. Sharon is slowly stippling and constantly re-defining shape and detail.

9 Many, many hours later, the black is complete. The coloring can begin, always working from darkest to lightest color. Sharon works the black first to such a stage that it in itself when done, is a complete scrimshaw.

11 Starting on the second side of the knife, Sharon ensures that the side already finished is well protected by cutting a piece of paper and taping it over the finished art work.

12 A detail of side B. The image shown here is of the top figure on the handle. Sharon decided to go with full color on this side due to the nature of colored Japanese prints.

13 A detail of the finished scrim on side A. The image of the Samurai was kept in black adding color only to the background, relating as closely as possible to the knife and to the shades of the Damascus blade.

Linda Karst Stone
"Scrimshaw on Ivory", 2005

In 1976, as a high school art student Linda was introduced to scrimshaw when hired by a local business. The job only lasted long enough to teach the basic techniques and launch her long-lasting career. Linda pursued fine art training at the University of Toledo and the Toledo Museum of Art. She focused on anatomy, figure drawing and design and this is reflected in her work today.

Linda prefers ivory as her canvas; a material that can possess warmth and personality that often suggests a particular subject or composition. Her realistic style has depth and a sculptural quality that bring her subjects to life. Linda takes thousands of photographs to inspire her compositions. She enjoys bringing together the ideas, experiences and memories of her clients, with some of her own, to design a piece unique for them. Linda resides in the Texas Hill country and exhibits at select shows. She enjoys her collaborations with knife makers worldwide.

903 Tanglewood Lane
Kerrville, Texas 78028-2945, USA
Phone: (830) 896-4678
Email: karstone@ktc.com

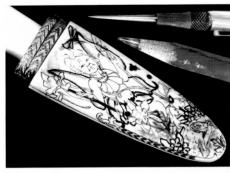

1 Linda's blank canvas is an ivory mini dagger by Dennis Friedly, 4" overall. Jim Sornberger did the engraving. A friend of hers, trusting her choice of subject matter, owns the knife.

5 Forget-me-nots and ferns are drawn adding to the design. The sheath is made of two ivory slabs; a version of Jim's engraving as a border up the side, helps cover the seam.

"Mini Dagger" by Dennis Friedly, 2005 This little Fairy is ready to play, if you can catch her! Scrimshaw by Linda Karst Stone. Overall length 4" (102 mm).

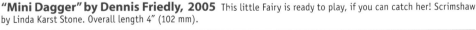

9 Starting with the darkest colors, the ivory is etched with the same scribe. The color is applied with a brush to the newly scratched area to fill it with ink. Light color will not cover darker ones.

11 The color starts to define the small details. Ivory is a porous material, polishing seals the surface. Anywhere you see color there are small "scratches" in the ivory holding the pigment.

2 Inspired by Cicely Mary Parker, a 19th century artist, Linda took several photos of children playing to serve as models for the fairy. Now the concept sketch is drawn on the ivory.

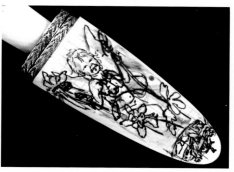

3 Details are redrawn in proportion with a #6B pencil and a rapidoliner ink pen. The ink sketch stays visible as she begins the etching process.

4 The design is lightly etch into the ivory with a hand held carbide steel rounded point scribe. Ivory burrs, carved out by the scribe, are wiped off and ink is rubbed into the fine lines.

6 All of the design is etched in place now. Some dragonflies and a ladybug for good luck add interest and are colored in, later in the process.

7 The handle is drawn, etched and inked in the same manner. Not too much, keeping the focus on the sheath. Renaissance wax rubbed over the lines protects the finished areas.

8 The black is finished, etched darker than it will appear on the finished piece. Linda lets this dry 2-3 days. Later, some ink will get lifted out of the grooves or scratched off when applying the color.

10 The depth of each new scratch affects how much pigment the mark will hold. Heavier and deeper for richer saturation, soft stippled dots for muted even tones.

12 On my work desk, templates, water, natural and light are all handy. Pelican waterproof India ink and high quality watercolor are my choices for pigment.

13 Linda's reference photos are close at hand. The knife is steadied with modeling clay, which forms around it, and a layer of thin plastic makes cleaning the finished piece easier. Some scrimshanders use oil paint as their choice of pigment and exacto knives to etch. Scrimshanders often learn on their own and come to the art with knowledge of other mediums to help them.

Mirella Isnardi-Pachì
"Scrimshaw", 2005

Mirella Isnardi was born in 1960, in a small village near Genoa. After receiving her diploma in graphic arts and advertising she began to work as a freelance art director for several of the best advertising companies in Genoa. This is when she met Francesco Pachì, a well-known photographer at the time. They got married in 1988, and started to work together. That was also when Francesco's started making knives. In constant contact with pictures of embellished custom knives from all over the world, Mirella was attracted to scrimshaw and tried her hand at it with her husband's knives. In 1995, while traveling in the United States, she

met Rick Fields and saw some of his scrimshaw art. Taking up Rick's suggestion, Mirella started to scrimshaw full-time, and almost exclusively on Francesco's knives. Preferring animal subjects for her scrimshaw, she lives in Sassello, in a house surrounded by woods and fields.

Via Pometta 1
17046 Sassello (SV), ITALY
Phone/fax: (+39) 19 720086
email: info@pachi-knives.com
Site: www.pachi-knives.com

1 To match the subject of Aldo Conto's Butterfly Mosaic Damascus, Mirella begins her search for suitable illustrations, looking through books, magazines and calendars.

5 Now black ink is applied for a few seconds.

"Butterfly Scrimshaw, 2005 The knife is a Folding Skinner by Francesco Pachì. Blade and bolsters are Mosaic Damascus made by Aldo Conto (Italy). Locking button with a citrine stone and the screws are solid gold. Fossil mammoth ivory handle slabs with scrimshaw by Mirella Pachì. Overall length 7 3/8" (187 mm).

7 Now it is time to add color, beginning with the dark shades and progressing to the lighter colors.

10 For the reverse side of the knife, Mirella chose a similar butterfly depicted in a different position.

2 Suitable subjects, when found, have to be adaptable in shape, position and size to fit the limited space dictated by the slabs of mammoth ivory.

3 After making her final choices, Mirella sketches the outlines of one of the chosen drawings onto the polished mammoth ivory, using a soft lead pencil.

4 Using a graver with a sharpened round point, she starts dotting the pencil outlines.

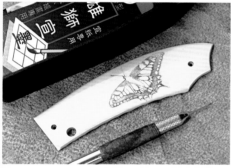

6 The excess ink is wiped off with alcohol. Repeating this several times, Mirella adds all the details and begins to create the stippled information of highlights and shadows.

8 Final detailing completes the art work for one side of the knife.

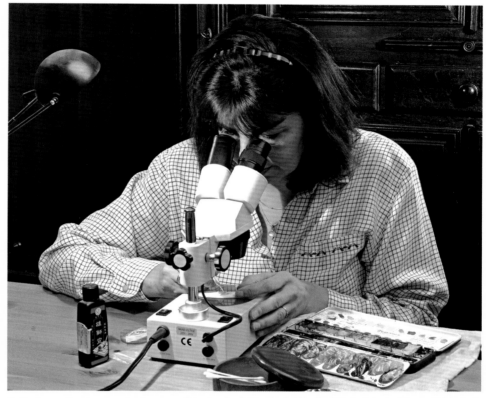

9 Mirella uses the stereoscopic microscope. This gives her full control while stippling the minute dots needed to create the smaller details in the picture.

11 After positioning the butterfly on the ivory, she traces its outline with a pencil. She goes on to stipple the outline with a graver, add black ink and proceed with the process untill the highlights and shadows are complete.

12 Now she adds color to the butterfly and the background.

13 When the scrimshaw on both slabs is done, Mirella compares between them and adds some details to give both sides of the knife a similar visual impact.

Christian DeCamillis
"Preditor and the Prey", 2005

Christian was born in Detroit, Michigan, in 1954. Starting at the age of 15, he pursued his love of art through jewelry-making for over 25 years. In 1995, he enrolled in basic and advanced engraving school, offered by GRS Corp. in Emporia, Kansas. In 2000, he traveled to a small valley in northern Italy, where some of the world's best engravers reside, to study Bulino, a specialized engraving technique perfected by the Italian master engravers. Attending the school of Cesare Giovanelli, he studied under the master engraver, Dario Cortini. Returning from Italy, he began engraving full-time on firearms, knives, and jewelry, specializing in game scenes and landscapes while using his newly acquired engraving skills. He also began to teach engraving and stone-setting at the GRS Training Center. He has traveled throughout the world for the GRS, attending trade shows and most recently, teaching engraving

at their European training center in Antwerp, Belgium. An avid hunter and fisherman, Christian often refers to his experiences when engraving wildlife scenes. His studio overlooks an inland lake and the beautiful wooded landscape of northern Michigan.

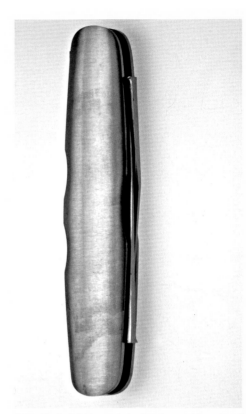

1 Double lock folder made by P.J. Tomes with scales of 416 stainless steel.

25 Lakeside Street, Traverse City
Michigan 49684, USA
Phone: (231) 943-7096
email: chrisdecamillis@hotmail.com

"Preditor and the Prey", 2005 The knife is engraved in the Italian Bulino style, which is performed by cutting a series of lines and small dots. The direction, depth and spacing of the cuts creates different shades of blacks, greys and white, producing the desired effects, without using ink or paint.

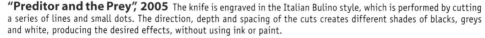

4 The surrounding landscape (sky, grass, etc.) is engraved before the main subject. Notice the outline of the pheasant hiding in the grass.

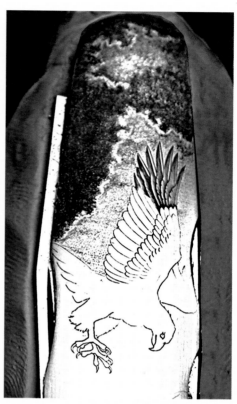

2 *"The first step in the engraving process is to pick a theme and make drawings of the subject matter. I never design the project fully in this initial step. Instead, I concentrate on the main subject matter (eagle pursuing pheasant) as I need it to stand out in the overall design. I later felt an overall need to enhance the drama, which led me to intensify the sky".*

3 Beginning with the outline of the eagle, very light cuts are made and the process of filling out the details begins.

5 The eagle's wings are complete and the body feathers are being filled in one-at-a-time, cutting them into the steel by using small lines.

6 The whole project has been completed. Christian sensed a need for more depth and added the mountain range, to create a distant background.

7 A closer look at the finished scene. One can see that all the details are done with a series of individually cut lines.

Ronald P. Nott
"Engraving a folder", 2005

Ronald P. Nott was born in Mt. Carmel, Pennsylvania, in 1941. There he spent most of his young adult life. After graduating from high-school, he went into the auto body repair business. 10 years later he went to work for Sherwin Williams Paint Company as a consultant. At that time he also became interested in firearms engraving. In 1970 Ron started to try his hand at engraving. He is self taught. In 1968 Ron moved to Harrisburg, PA, and after 10 years of service with Sherwin Williams went into the auto parts business for 13 years. At this time he became interested in making folding art-knives, and in 1995 went into full time engraving, and makes lock-back folding knives on the side.

105 Mountain Street
P.O. Box 281, Summer-dale
PA 17093, USA
Phone: (717) 732-2763
Cell phone: (717) 514-4976
email: neitznott@aol.com

1 The folder to be engraved, made by Steve Hoel. ATS-34 blade and 416 stainless steel frame. Inlays are desert iron wood.

3 The Steve Lindsay Classic AirGraver is used for his engraving. Ron also uses Lindsay's carbide-cobalt chisels that are very durable and will cut harder steels.

6 Sitting at his work station, he is making the first cuts in the steel and preparing the knife for gold inlay.

"Medium Coke Bottle folder," 2002 by Steve Hoel (USA), engraved in 2005 by Ronald P. Nott. Overall length 7 1/8" (181 mm).

8 Now the fine detailed shading is added after which the background is removed. The gold inlay is always added before begining the shading.

2 After deciding on the design Ron transfers it onto the steel with a lead pencil. The areas to be gold-inlaid are then marked off.

4 The knife is wrapped to avoid scratching damage while engraving. A special jig, milled to the knife's shape out of carian plastic and lined with leather, protects the frame while held in the vice.

7 After completing the gold inlay, the excess gold is finished-off and the bolster is polished.

9 Cutting outlines for the scroll design on the rear bolster. After the main scroll is cut, the leaves are added and shaded. Notice how the Airgraver is held in the palm of the hand.

5 This a general view of the work-bench with Ron's stereoscopic microscope, the Lindsay engraving system and a variety of tools and chisels used for engraving.

10 A view of Ron Nott at his work station with his vise and stereoscopic microscope set up for long engraving sessions.

Scott Pilkington
"Engraving Design", 1997-2005

Scott was born in 1964. As a teenager he took his talent in drawing and painting and began using the tip of a graver on the unforgiving canvases of steel and precious metals. As a full-time engraver for 25 years, he has done both technical and artistic engravings. Artistic engraving is creating the design based on the shape of the knife or material used, as opposed to simple scrollwork. When not thinking about and creating engraving designs in the mountains of Tennessee, Scott enjoys traveling around the world as a gunsmith and photojournalist for the US Olympic Shooting Team. He also teaches engraving for the GRS engraving school in Emporia, Kansas in between raising two children and managing a successful air-gun business catering to Olympic shooters.

Pilkington Competition, LLC
354 Little Trees Ramble Monteagle,
TN 37356, USA
Phone: (931) 924-3400
email: engraver@pilkguns.com
Site: http://www.pilkguns.com

"Design Determined By Knife Shape", 1997 This Joe Kious knife was originally intended for the King Tut layout shown opposite, but from design perspective, the sharp "spiky" points of the knife did not have an Egyptian feel. Instead the chosen medieval theme with flames, lighting bolts, and stars all blend and complement the sharp points of the knife. An excellent example of the knife shape being a determining factor in the layout and style of the engraving.

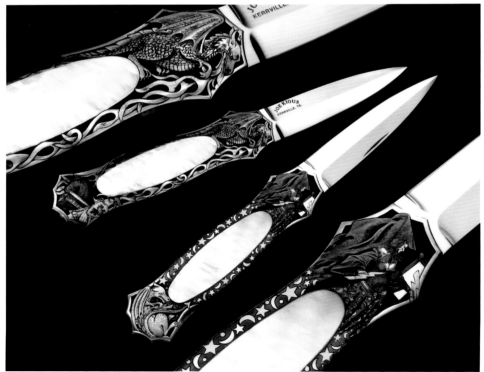

1 Using the hinge pin as the end ball of the scroll, the pattern is drawn on this bolster with a red micro-point marker. However this looks somewhat unbalanced because of the dark stag handle material above its origination point.

2 Scott would prefer to start the scroll at the front border of a rectangular bolster like this, and move it rearward with the flow of the knife as shown here. Because the hinge pin so visible in this case another design should be chosen.

3 Here the scroll originates from the hinge pin and the actual engraving process begins with the scroll's backbone. For a balanced look, the leaf and scroll areas should be roughly the same size as their adjacent background areas.

4 Here is the finished "technical" engraving (2005), with a single self-originating scroll with some leaves around the scroll. This is a fast and easy pattern to lay out and cut but even this had factors affecting its design.

5 The drawing process of an "artistic" engraving, by using the knife material to influence the design. Notice how Scott makes drawing corrections with a black micro-point marker over the original red design. Completed in 2004.

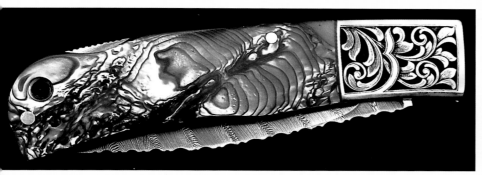

6 For the rectangular bolster of this knife Scott chose to extend the flow of the abalone onto the bolster, both by the vertical scroll placement and by the upward thrust of the lower border.

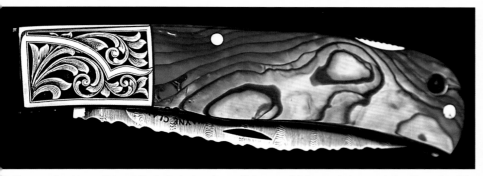

7 The opposite side scroll is not the typical mirror image. It is a completely new design, emulating the grain of the abalone by creating an interior border that the scrolls must cross over.

8 This is a technical scroll with a little artistic flair. The shape of this folding skinner is reflected in the re-defined borders, rather than just a simple square box for the scroll (2004).

9 This "Sgian dhu" by Jack Busfield was selected for the King Tut motif because of its inherent, almost perfect, sarcophagus shape. The engraving and inlay were finished in 1998.

Darren P. Reeves
Engraving Bob Crowder's "Aardvark", 2005

Born in New Jersey, in 1960, Darren is the second son of a career military man. Spending a good part of his youth living on military bases around the USA and Bermuda. During a four-year stay in Japan he was exposed to the wonderful art and culture of that country. Settling down in northern California, Darren excelled in sports and art during his high school years. He also had the opportunity to work part time as a buffer and sawyer for a small company that produced high-end trophy belt-buckles for the rodeo industry. This is where he was introduced to hand engraving. In 1979, Darren was offered the opportunity to learn the fine art of western style bright cut engraving. After moving to Montana in 1987, Darren

expanded his hand engraving skills to include such disciplines as lettering, sculptural game scenes, inlay and high relief ornamental scroll that he uses today to embellish fine custom knives. A full time hand engraver and part time knife maker, Darren is a member of the Montana knife makers Association. His hobbies include traditional archery and the martial arts.

1702 First Ave N.
Billings, Montana 59101, USA
Phone: (406) 656-4639
email: dpreeves@wtp.net
email: montanalongbow@hotmail.com

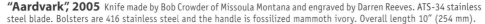

"Aardvark", 2005 Knife made by Bob Crowder of Missoula Montana and engraved by Darren Reeves. ATS-34 stainless steel blade. Bolsters are 416 stainless steel and the handle is fossilized mammoth ivory. Overall length 10" (254 mm).

1 The knife as received from its maker, Bob Crowder, is shown here with some of the engraving tools and 24k gold wire that will be used to embellish the bolsters.

3 The drawing of the engraving pattern is reduced to the original size and transferred onto the bolster. At this point, only the sections planned for gold inlay will be scribed onto the steel.

6 The square graver (single point graver) is used to engrave the main body and leaves of the scroll design. A properly sharpened graver is always very important.

9 The engraving block (vice) not only holds the knife but is the axis of rotation used by the engraver to create the smooth curved lines that make up the engraving pattern.

The engraving pattern is drawn 400% larger then actual size. This allows for a more accurate and detailed planning of the design.

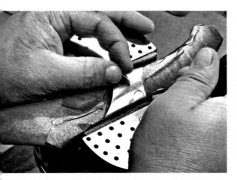

Taking into consideration the diameter of gold wire to be used, furrows are cut into the steel and then under cut (dove tailed) to create an anchor for the gold as it is hammered into place.

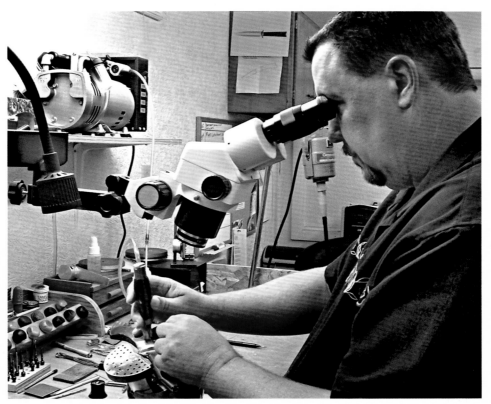

5 As the gold is gently hammered into the furrow-cut it will expand to fill the dove tailed under cuts, permanently anchoring itself into the steel. After the gold has been inlayed the bolster will be stoned flush and then polished with fine emery paper. The design will then be re-transferred and the remaining scroll pattern will be scribed onto the bolster.

7 A view from the engravers seat. A wide variety of push gravers and tools are always within easy reach to complete the task. The engraver must always be very careful to protect the un-engraved surfaces of the knife. Careful masking of the knife is very important. Notice the leather pads used on the jaws of the engraving block.

8 Relief engraving requires that the background be removed. The background is then stippled to provide texture and contrast for the smooth areas and shaded areas of the scroll work.

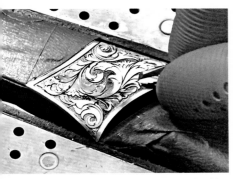

10 Finely engraved individual lines and cross hatching create the shading effect, giving depth and dimension to the finished engraving.

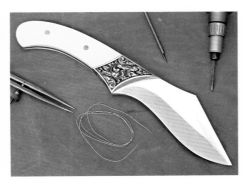

11 A final polish with emery paper, some black in the background and a thorough cleaning finish the job. The knife is now ready to be sent back to the maker.

12 The finished engraving enhances the beauty of the knife and upscales its value as an art piece.

Andy Shinosky
"Engraving a Single Action Automatic Dagger", 2005

Born in Warren, Ohio in 1959, Andy attributes his earliest attraction to knives to a day when, as a small child, a neighbor showed him a small pearl handled folder he kept in his pocket. Andy says he was mesmerized by that knife and never forgot that moment. Today if you should ask him what attracts him to knives he would tell you of his great love for tools in general, and for Andy there is no more personal tool than that of a folding knife. He feels that because of this personal nature that is attributed to knives, he choses to embellish and adorn them, making them even more unique and one of a kind. His favorite handle materials are various Mother-of-Pearls due to their inherent stability and natural beauty. Because Andy loves all aspects of the knifemaking craft he has taken time away to learn the art

of engraving so that he can further embellish his knives. It is Andy's knifemaking goal to produce knives that exemplify exceptional fit and finish. Because of the limited time he has to devote to his knifemaking Andy likes to choose every one of his knife projects very carefully.

3117 Meanderwood Drive
Canfield, Ohio 44406, USA
Phone: (330) 702-0299
email: andy@shinosky.com
Website: www.shinosky.com

"Single-Action Automatic Dagger", 2005 A folding dagger with a button-activated single-action automatic mechanism. The blade and lockbar are ATS-34. Handles are 416 stainless. Inlays are Black-Lip pearl. Fully engraved with 24k gold inlays. File worked on the inside edge of the handles. Closed length 4 3/8" (111 mm).

1   Finished knife ready for engraving. Normally when constructing a knife that is to be engraved Andy will only finish it to an 800 grit finish. The final finish will go on directly before the engraving shading process begins.

5   A fast drying transfer solution is applied to the area to be engraved. The design is printed in reverse on a sheet of film and then positioned over the knife. Once taped down, the design can be burnished onto the steel.

7   The areas to receive gold inlay are carefully cut away and the sides of the resulting pockets are then undercut. These undercuts will trap the gold and hold it in place.

10 Gold wire is chosen with a size slightly larger than that of the pocket which it is to be fit into. This insures that once the gold is hammered down, the pocket will be completely filled with no gaps and the excess then removed.

2 Doing a one to one trace of the knife. This will be scanned and then scaled up to 4 times size for use in the design layout. The computer is used extensively in the design layout process.

3 The knife is masked off to prevent contaminants entering into the mechanisms during the engraving process. To hold the knife in the vise it is first hot glued to a round bar of aluminum that has a flat machined onto it.

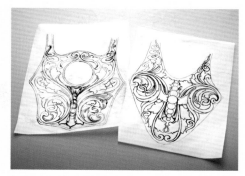

4 Once the design is worked out at 4x scale it is often scaled up to 8x scale and retraced to further refine the design. The final result is a dark fine line design that can be scaled back to full size with a great deal of fine detail.

8 The main lines and borders are the first step of actual cutting. The round aluminum bar allows the knife to be rotated slightly in the vise to align the rounded surfaces perpendicular to the microscopes field of view.

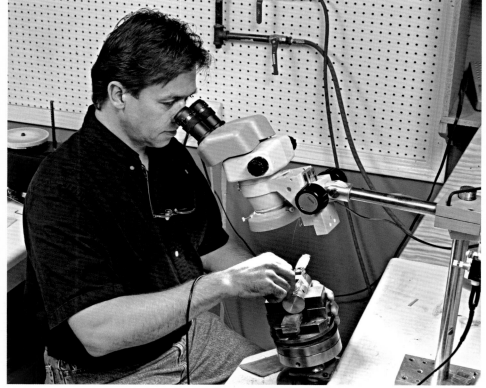

9 Andy uses a Nikon microscope mounted on a shop built boom stand. His engraving vise is also shop built as is much of his knifemaking equipment. Andy feels that his engraving took a giant leap after he purchased an AirChasing Graver handpiece built by Steve Lindsay in 2001. He also utilizes a number of other pieces of equipment made by the GRS Company such as the Power Hone & Sharpening system.

10 Various sizes of 24k gold wire are hammered into the sockets using a brass punch mounted in a Lindsay AirGraver handpiece. The very soft 24k gold is work-hardened by the hammering process.

11 A course sandpaper is used to remove the majority of the excess gold. Then a finer grade of sandpaper is used to bring the gold flush with the surface of the steel. Next comes cutting away the background material using different shaped gravers as well as micro carbide burrs. Later, the background surfaces will be given a dot punch treatment to even out the marks from the other tools. Shading will be begin after using a fine grade sandpaper to create a uniform finish.

12 Once all the engraving has been done, the pearl inlays will be cleaned of any scratches and then polished. The final step is an application of ink or paint to darken the background and to create the required contrast.

André Andersson
"Vanilla", 2005

André was born in the north of Sweden, in 1980. He always showed great interest in creating things with his hands, from medieval armor in his teens, to becoming a very dedicated drawing artist, later on. But when, at the age of 19, he discovered the great artistic potential in knife making, he really got hooked. He likes the many challenges facing him when starting on a new knife and the way he can express himself throughout the process. André loves working with fossil materials giving the knife not only visual depth but also a feeling of being connected to our world's history. Most of his knives are truly handmade, minimizing the use of machinery, but this does not prevent him to really enjoying the times when he needs to use advanced machinery. André wants the process of his knifemaking to be a challenge.

He constantly strives to create something new and is working not only on more advanced knives but also on blade weapons that are not considered knives. *"There is a huge world out there with endless possibilities, and I want to try out at least some of them".*

Forsnäsvägen 40
918 92 Bullmark, Sweden
Phone: (+46) 90 56216
email: northland@swipnet.se
Site: www.northland.nu

"Vanilla", 2005 A fully carved mammoth ivory and Damascus fighter. The blade is of a 3 bar Mosaic composition with an Explosion Damascus edge and spine. The steel used is Swedish tool steel, Uddeholm 20C and 15N20. Carved fossil walrus bolster, mammoth tooth middle section, mammoth ivory rear section and 2 steel spacers. Overall length 12 9/16" (320 mm).

1 The next step after the forging of the blade is grinding the edge. André does this with a 60 grit belt grinder. This is only a rough grind so he will get up to about 0.5 mm outside the marked design.

3 André carves the blade with hard-metal pins, rubber wheels and a dental machine. At this point the finish is not as important as carefully following the lines. Next it is time for the hardening and heat treating of the blade.

6 When André starts on the handle he prepares all the sections in advance. In this case, a fossil walrus bolster, mammoth tooth for the middle section, mammoth ivory for the rear section and 2 slices of steel for spacers.

10 When the main handle is finished, André makes one more steel plate for a rear spacer between the end piece and the rest of the handle. This plate is secured by 2 hole drilled into the handle.

2 During the grinding, it is important that the edge line follows the shape of the blade to create harmony. When André has completed the first grind, he uses a marker to draw outlines for the planned carving of the blade.

4 After the blade has been hardened, the edge is worked down to a fine stain finish and so is the carved section. When satisfied, André acid-etches the blade to bring out the pattern he welded into the steel.

5 André with a small selection of his abundant stock of materials used in the making of his knives. Among these is a large assortment of fossil ivory from various sources

7 The pieces are being fit together, attached with iron pins. When that is done, it is time for the final shaping of the handle.

8 After the handle is shaped André separates the finish sections held together by the iron pins. He begins the carving on each section separately.

9 The carving on the handle is made to match the carving on the blade. The only difference is that mammoth is very sensitive to heat so great care must be taken while it is being carved.

11 The end piece, roughly shaped, is fitted securely to the rear of the steel plate spacer.

12 When the end piece has been secured, lines are drawn on it marking the planned carving design. These lines will follow the carvings of the rest of the knife for a nice and harmonious look.

13 Finally the whole knife is finished off, polished and glued together with iron pins and Epoxy glue. The blade is attached to the handle in the same way.

David Broadwell
"The Base of the Mountain", 2005

Born in 1954, David Broadwell lives in North Texas. After studying Criminal Justice in college, he worked as a machinist. Picking up a worn shop file, his first attempt at grinding a knife in 1981, gave him a chill from head to toe and he thought, *"I have got to do this for a living!"* By 1989 Broadwell was making knives full-time. Large fighters, sub-hilts and bowies were followed by flowing daggers, elegant folders, more sculpting, texturing and patinas. By the mid-1990s his work was firmly focused on "art knives". Broadwell also makes one-of-a-kind fountain pens with the same level of artistic expression and many of the patterned metals and materials he uses in his art knives. The project for the book is a commissioned knife by an American of Japanese ancestry named Yamane. He requested that his name ("root of the mountain" in Japanese) be put into the blade forged by Tom Ferry. Other influences in this knife include Persian with the slightly upswept point, and the fittings that resemble a *habaki* and a *menuki*, all wrapped up in a sub hilt fighter.

4726 Kmart Drive, Wichita Falls,
TX 76308, USA
Phone: (940) 692-1727
email: david@broadwell.com
Site: http://www.david.broadwell.com

"The Base of the Mountain", 2005 Blade is a special order Mosaic from Tom Ferry with owner's name displayed in Japanese Kanji in the steel with blossoms surrounding it. Bronze guard and sub hilt with sterling silver habaki and pin. Handle is carved ebony. Overall length 15 1/4" (378 mm).

1 The rough forged blade is being laid out for the coordinated sculpting. At this stage, a black marker ink and a carbide scribe are the main tools. Note the hand drawn sketch under the blade.

3 The lay out of this area is roughed in with a rotary tool then precisely defined and shaped with files. This area is also finished to a fairly fine level with sandpaper as with the previous step.

6 The owner's family crest, or "mon", is carved into the face of the bronze guard using the smaller grinder and various burrs. This requires a steady hand and lots of patience.

8 The pin is hard brass with Sterling silver (in the shape of Mount Fuji) soldered in place. The handle has been cut so that the head of the pin is partially inlaid. Small blades have been specially shaped for this.

2 After filing, the choil area is finished with sandpaper. The upper and lower parts of the blade have been filed to fit the habaki.

4 Here Broadwell uses his micro grinder to cut in one area of sculpting. This is precise work and requires working close-up with a magnifier. Once finished and the bevels roughed in, the blade is ready for heat treatment.

7 Now that the mons have been finished, the background of the guard is relieved and textured. Different shaped burrs combined with cutting techniques determine the type of resulting texture.

9 Examining the fit of the pin head in the ebony. A magnifier is an essential tool for this level of work. Broadwell uses a 2X Optivisor to give enough magnification to see clearly.

5 Broadwell is working hard at soldering the silver components of the habaki, or blade sleeve. The rough parts were cut from Sterling plate and fitted to the blade, then held in place while silver soldered. After the assembly, the habaki is re-fitted to the blade (solder is cleaned from the inside), precisely laid out to flow with the blade, and carefully ground to shape.

10 Broadwell has placed the two piece handle with the "dummy" sub hilt spacer onto the blade without any other fittings and is sighting down the blade to insure that the handle has been shaped in line with the blade. This knife is of a complex design with components made separately from each other, not as an assembled knife. It would be all too easy to make one part off center without frequent and careful examination. Good lighting and an experienced eye are essential.

Vladimir Burkovski
"Mavka" The Forest Fairy, 2005

Born in 1970, in Nikolaev, Ukraine, Vladimir now resides in Haifa (Israel). A lover of nature and the human form, he used to, even as a child, fill notebooks with his sketches and drawings and used tree roots and branches for his carvings. With an artistic education acquired at the Odessa Theatrical and Artistic Technical School, he began making knives and various kinds of arms in 1990, for a film studio in Odessa. This opened for him a whole new world of creative opportunities, a form of plastic art that brought him close to his hidden passion for art knives. Completely captured by their beauty, he now creates his own art knives from beginning to end,

starting with detailed sketches that he draws again and again till fully satisfied. For his handles he uses natural materials, preferring to carve his intricate three-dimensional scenes on walrus ivory, fossilized mammoth ivory or pre-1966 sperm whale teeth from the Ukraine.

P.O. Box 4591 Haifa 31044, Israel
Phone: (+972) 544 993902
email: burkovskiart@yahoo.com
Site: www.knifearts.com

"Mavka" The Forest Fairy, 2005 Mavka is the forest fairy from a book by Leska Ukrainka's. Finding true love in a human being she soon realized the truth about mankind, but when trying to return to the forest she is refused entrance. The carved handle is made from an ancient sperm whale tooth, dug up near a historic Eskimo village in Siberia. Blade is Damasteel by Fallas Anders of Sweden. The guard was cast from silver. Overall length 7 1/2" (190 mm).

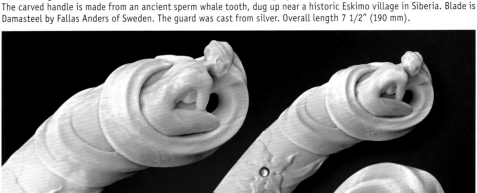

1 A medium-size sperm whale tooth for the handle, a blade made of Damasteel by Fallas Anders of Sweden, and the wax model for casting the silver guard.

5 Vladimir starts with detailed sketches from which he makes a life size model from Plasticine, while constantly checking for visual balance and ergonomics.

7 During the carving process, the work in progress is constantly compared to the Plasticine model. Vladimir self-makes tiny burrs for carving and finishing delicate features.

10 He usually uses Mother-of-Pearl inlays when working with ivory and tooth handles. These are carefully cut out using hollow diamond drill pieces, while constantly cooling the pearl with water during the process.

2 The whale tooth is cut to size by hand using a hack-saw and roughly shaped with sandpaper.

3 The guard is carefully fitted to the blade, then polished and stamped with Vladimir's personal marking. Seen here is the guard before and after the fitting and polishing process.

4 The knife is assembled and glued together using a powerful bonding Epoxy glue.

6 For his carving Vladimir uses two high power rotary carvers used by dentists. The smaller piece, which is also more comfortable in the hand, is used for carving the delicate features.

8 After completing the basic design, Vladimir uses fine chisels and a converted razor to continue the carving process.

9 The table on which Vladimir does most of his carving is the type used by jewelers in their workshops. Strong lighting, well directed at the job in progress, and good ventilation of the working area are most important. Vladimir does not use any magnifying aids while carving.

11 The Mother-of-Pearl inlays are glued into pockets accurately cut into the handle material.

12 Vladimir improves on the Plasticine model he created, changing small details to look better and more harmonious with the whole design.

13 After the carving process has been completed, polishing the handle begins with 400 grit sandpaper going all the way to 2,500 grit and diamond paste.

Larry Fuegen
Hand Carving Mother-of-Pearl and Steel, "Revival", 2005

Born in 1952, Larry has been creating with his hands since he was a child growing up on his parents' cattle ranch in Reliance, South Dakota. An early fascination with knives compelled him to take apart old knives then apply new handles and reshape the blades. He made his first knife in 1963, started forging blades in 1975 and became a full-time bladesmith in 1987. In 1989 he received his Master Smith rating from the American Bladesmith Society. Larry is also a member of the Art Knife Invitational group, representing 25 of the top makers.

Larry performs all of the work on each of his knives and sheaths and does not use any ready-made parts. A unique feature of every fixed-blade knife that

leaves his shop is the high-quality hand-sewn leather sheath, which is designed to complement the finished knife. His classic style and use of colors, textures and shapes continues to evolve as he masters a wider range of materials and techniques.

617 N. Coulter Circle
Prescott, AZ 86303-6270, USA
Phone/Fax: (928) 776-8777
email: fuegen@cableone.net

"Revival", 2005 Folder with hand carved Mother-of-Pearl and steel, gold overlay pins and 22k gold wire inlay, and a Damascus steel blade. Overall length 6 1/2" (165 mm).

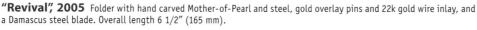

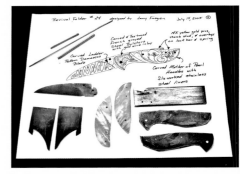

1 Each knife project begins with a basic sketch. The parts are rough cut and the main holes are drilled. Each knife is truly unique.

5 After the pearl slabs are shaped and contured, the carving design is transferred using small cut marks to establish the basic outline of the design.

7 The main lines are carved and each handle is checked against the other to keep the design even on both sides.

10 A flat punch is used to inlay 22k gold wire into the Damascus blade.

2 After the steel bolsters are soldered to the liners, the excess material is removed and the bevels are handfiled and smoothed prior to carving.

3 Using a paper pattern, the carving design in transferred to the bolster by making small cuts through the paper onto the bolster.

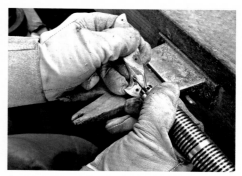

4 The bolser is carved with carbide burrs and engraving chisels. Final finishing is done by hand with sanding sticks and emery cloth.

6 When transferring the design is completed, the small cut marks are connected to create the main carving lines.

8 After the handles are carved, sanded and polished, the background is textured. This helps the carving stand out visually.

9 A flat graver is used to remove the background on the bolsters. While carving of the handles and bolsters is very time consuming, the most critical step is peening the domed heads on the gold pins. A missed hammer blow could crack the finished pearl or deeply mar the bolsters. This would create a major setback in time and materials.

11 The ricasso of the blade is carved with a flat graver chisel and textured.

12 A narrow stip of 18 guage gold is stamped using a handmade texturing stamp. This strip will be overlayed onto the top of the lockbar and spring.

13 After the bolsters are finished, the liners are fileworked and sanded to 1200 grit before polishing.

Dennis Greenbaum
"Topo Gigio #2", 2005

Born in Cleveland, Ohio, in 1951, Dennis is a marketing executive with 30 years of experience working in radio, TV, advertising, and related fields. He has spent the last 20 of those years as a brand consultant and recently co-founded a high-end firm specializing in graphic design and multimedia. Dennis has found that all those years working around leading-edge design have rubbed off and are evident in his work as a custom knifemaker. Most of his spare time is spent either in his well-equipped, home knifemaking workshop, or at his computer, where he can be found in any one of several online knife forums. Dennis is fascinated with embellishing and is particularly interested in carving metal, as well as "natural" materials such as ivory, Mother-

of-Pearl or wood. He finds that he is pushing himself to try new ideas and techniques as his own repertoire of skills continues to expand. Dennis and his lovely wife Michelle have been married since 1984. He feels that she and their daughter Piper are enthusiastically supportive of his knifemaking efforts, and are also his most honest critics.

2 Penny Lane, Baltimore
Maryland 21209, USA
Phone: (410) 960-1473
email: dgreenbaum@comcast.net
Site: www.greenbaumknives.com

"Topo Gigio #2", 2005   The 2nd in a series, the "mini-balisong" is 2 5/16" (62 mm) closed, with its Robert Eggerling carbon Damascus steel sculpted blade. The knife features carved ivory scales, fileworked and anodized (2-tone blue) titanium liners, nitre-blued alloy screws and inlaid sapphires that are revealed only when the blade is open. Overall length 3 31/32" (100 mm).

1   The blade profile and all the holes were carefully traced onto the steel. Design for ivory scales is selected from sketches. The ivory slabs and the titanium are cut to size.

2   After laying red carbon paper face down on the ivory, the sketch is placed over the carbon paper and the pattern is roughly traced onto the previously cut-to-size ivory slab.

4   The pattern is revealed! Due to spontaneous design revisions effected during carving, the first completed scale will also serve as a reference/template for the other three.

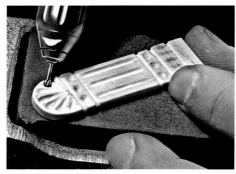

6   Scallops and fluting are detailed with the GRS high speed carver using various carbide, diamond, and stone round burs.

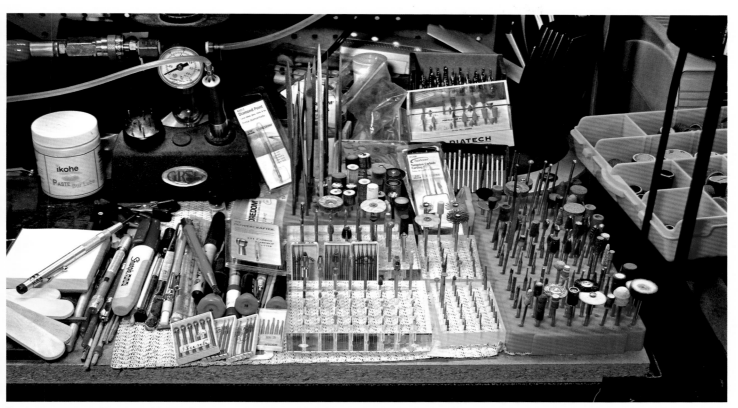

3 A huge assortment of burs is used for detailed carving, including carbide, diamond, and stone 1/16" friction burs (foreground) for use with the GRS 850 air turbine rotary carver (upper left corner), at speeds up to 320,000 rpm. The larger 3/32" and 1/8" burs are used with several different motor-driven and air-driven, flex shaft rotary tools. Needle files are among Dennis' primary tools for carving; a very small sampling is shown, here on his main work-bench (one of five benches).

5 Horizontal fluting is done using a very fine, small diameter, Swiss-cut, "parallel" (no taper), round file.

7 As work progresses, the carved ivory scales are constantly sight-fitted to one another to make sure they match.

8 The KMG grinder (which stands for Knifemaker's Grinder) is one of the best made and because of its versatility it is used for many different knifemaking functions. A large assortment of 72" abrasive belts are used with this type grinder, depending on the application. Here Dennis is profiling the blade out of a bar of Damascus steel made by Bob Eggerling. Note the always present safety equipment.

9 A Dremel rotary flex shaft equipped with abrasive sleeves is used to grind the blade, instead of using the KMG. This is due to to the blade's small size and its unusual shape.

10 Following the initial grind with abrasive sleeves (as well as hand files), the blade receives a finer finish using small, abrasive "flap" wheels. Final finish is hand-sanded.

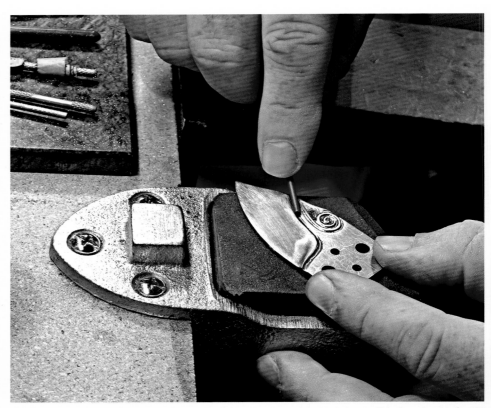

11 After the scroll pattern and the grooves are carved into both sides of the blade (accomplished mostly with the GRS carver using various diamond, carbide, and "green" stone burs), the somewhat rough grooves and "valleys" are scraped and sanded using miniature, ruby files.

12 The GRS Carver, equipped with "White Arkansas-stone" 1/16" friction burs, is used to further detail the grooves and the valleys in the blade.

13 Using a cylinder-shaped diamond bur with the Dremel rotary flex shaft to carve the decorative back of the blade.

14 Accurate drilling is a must skill for making small folding knives. The mini-mill/drill seen in this photo is very popular with knifemakers because of its accuracy, versatility, variable speed, and its small "footprint". After first drilling an undersize pivot hole through the liners, Dennis is preparing to ream the hole to size. To insure that the pivot hole is perfectly "square", he uses parallels to secure the liners in a small, high-precision vise.

15 With 4 different rotary tools within easy reach; a huge selection of burs of every size, shape, and material and over 100 hand files, needle files and miniature files, nearly all of Dennis' embellishing is done at his "main" workbench. The 5 halogen lamps he uses get so hot that he has a fan running at all times. Here he is wearing one of three different-strength "Opti-Visor" headband magnifiers as he fileworks the back of the blade.

16 Using a green silicon carbide file, Dennis shapes a very small diameter (2 mm) silicone polishing rod to the appropriate size and diameter for use in one of the grooves carved into the blade.

17 Using the pre-shaped silicone polishing rod mounted into a special mandrel that attaches to the miniature, 3-jaw chuck in the Dremel flex shaft, Dennis accesses the smallest grooves for a very fine finish.

18 The completed Topo Gigio #2. Such a cute little fellow; its simple function belies the subtle precision required of its mechanism to achieve proper function. It is the 2nd of a series; each one creatively different than its predecessor, and with the unique proportions presented by the short, side-by-side configuration of the handles, there is perhaps no limit to the possibilities.

William & Elizabeth Lloyd
"Ivory Dragon Damascus Friction Folder", 2005

William was born in 1962, in a small town in Utah, and was raised on farms and ranches in Idaho. He has been an artist his entire life. He first illustrated a book with black and white cartoon type sketches at the age of 16, which was his first paying job as an artist. William began carving antler, bone and ivory after he went to a Mountain Man Rendezvous and saw a carved eagle in an antler handled knife, he decided to try and carve one himself. After wearing his to the next Rendezvous, people asked to buy it and thus began his career as a carver. In 1994, Wiliam and Elizabeth met and by early 1995 they started a business together after renovating the basement of Elizabeth's home into an art studio. With William's carving talents and Elizabeth's skills at research, design, and business management they soon had a thriving art business, displaying at Fine Art Shows, Renaissance Festivals and

Blade Shows across the country. At their first Blade Show (Atlanta, 2004) they entered and won Best Sword of Show. Many of the swords and knives made by William & Elizabeth are historically accurate and based on actual relics.

510 East 17th Street #149
Idaho Falls, ID 83404 USA
Phone: (303) 378-0926
email: theartist@thechiselersart.com
Site: www.thechiselersart.com

"Ivory Dragon Damascus Friction Folder", 2005 A hand carved ivory folding knife based on a 7th century Norse relic. The blade is 1075 high carbon tool steel folded with 15N20. The handle is antique elephant ivory with emeralds inset for the eyes. Closed length 6" (152 mm).

1 Materials used to create this knife include the tip of a 100 year old African elephant tusk, two emerald cabachons, and a Norm Schenk Random Twist Damascus blade forged to design based on a 7th century Norse folding knife.

5 A medium flame tipped bit is used to create the wings and add more detail as the wings begin to take shape.

7 A round 1/4" wheel burr adds crispness and detail to the wings and muscle structure.

10 After cutting a precise bezel with an inverted cone burr, fine tipped stone setting tweezers are used to carefully place the emerald into the bezel with a drop of a thick acetate glue.

2 An assortment of Foredom handpieces pre-chucked with the carving bits used in the process of creating the ivory dragon handle on the folder.

3 After initial shaping on the belt sander, a large flame tipped bit is used for the initial roughing out of the dragon handle.

4 A large round tipped cylinder bit is used to create the facial form and musclature, and the dragon begins to emerge.

6 After marking and pre-cutting the blade slot with the bandsaw, an 1/8" spiral saw blade is used to refine the slot to the exact width of the blade.

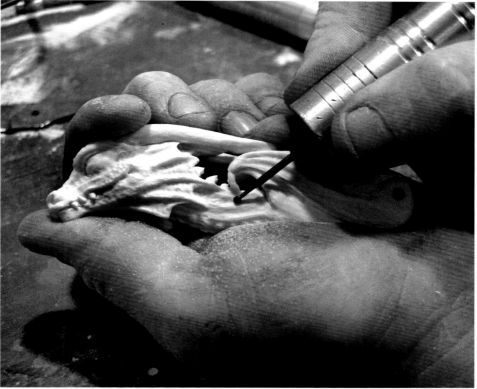

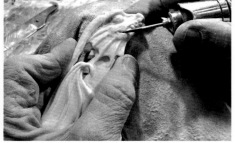

8 The fine point of a slim cone reamer burr outlines the teeth and adds lifegiving detail to the eyes and face of the dragon.

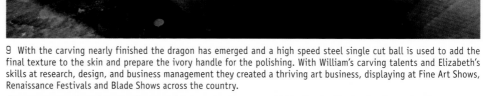

9 With the carving nearly finished the dragon has emerged and a high speed steel single cut ball is used to add the final texture to the skin and prepare the ivory handle for the polishing. With William's carving talents and Elizabeth's skills at research, design, and business management they created a thriving art business, displaying at Fine Art Shows, Renaissance Festivals and Blade Shows across the country.

11 The blade is placed in the handle and lined up with the pre-drilled holes. The iron rivet is placed through the holes with a steel washer on each side. A jeweler's hammer is used to peen the rivet to proper tightness and tension.

12 A tungsten carbide enlongated ball is used to dimple the rivet on both sides continuing the decorative detail into the functionality of the knife.

13 A golden oak antiquing stain is lightly brushed on the handle and then buffed off with a soft cloth bringing out the fine detail and increasing the visual depth of the Ivory Dragon Damascus folder.

Amayak Stepanyan
"High Relief Engraving of a folder", 2005

Born in 1949 in Yerevan, the capital of Armenia, Amayak lived in Russia from 1951 to 2000. He apprenticed as a watchmaker at the age of 17 and followed the profession for the next 11 years. Inspired by the engraving skills of a fellow watchmaker, Amayak taught himself to engrave in his spare time, first copying designs of famous artists, later creating designs of his own. Within a few years he was working as an engraver for the Russian Souvenir Company in Moscow. Over the years, he developed into a highly skilled, meticulous, technically accomplished artist and an inspired designer with a unique style of engraving. On the strength of this extraordinary ability and with the support of his American friends Bill Brinker, Lew Wackler and John Rohner he was permitted to immigrate to the USA in 2000.

Amayak and his wife, Svetlana, settled in Denver. In 2002, he was introduced to the custom knife world with its infinite creative possibilities. Through his successful collaboration with Owen Wood, Amayak fulfills his creative dreams engraving objects that had always fascinated him.

5620 West 80th Place # 57
Arvada, CO 80003, USA
Phone: (720) 540-4953
email: astepanyan@comcast.net

"High Relief Engraving of a folder", 2005 A collaboration between Owen Wood who made the folding dagger and Amayak who engraved the 18k rose gold front and rear bolsters with his favorite Art Deco themes. Blade length 3 5/32" (80 mm).

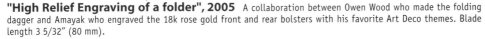

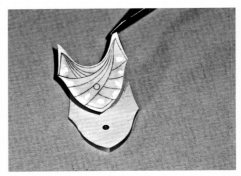

1 Laying the design down on the gold bolster coated with Chinese White.

2 With the design taped to the bolster Amayak traces the reverse side of the design on to the metal using a stylus with rounded and polished point. Next to it lies another bolster, with the design already transferred.

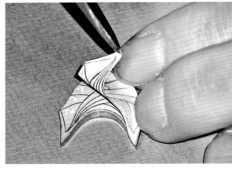

5 After going over the design with the stylus, Amayak removes the tape from one side of the bolster and checks the tracing, making sure it was transferred in every detail.

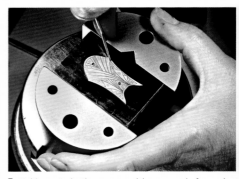

7 Making cuts in the corners with a graver before using chisel and hammer.

3 Another bolster being coated with Chinese White. This allows Amayak to correct the drawing using an eraser and pencil after transferring the design to the metal. Through his successful collaboration with Owen Wood, Amayak fulfills his creative dreams, engraving the objects he was always fascinated by ever since he held his first knife, a miniature folder he got when he was 5 years old.

4 Using a microscope, the design is carefully inspected, after finishing the drawing that was done directly onto the bolster.

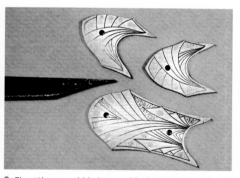

6 The 18k rose gold bolsters with the design transferred are now ready for cutting.

8 Cutting the design into the bolster using the traditional method, Amayak uses a chasing hammer and chisel.

9 Removing the burrs with sanding stick after the lines have been cut.

10 After the lines have been cut and burrs removed, Amayak begins to cut away the background using the flat chisel. Amayak taught himself to engrave in his spare time, first copying designs of famous artists, then creating designs of his own. In 2002, he was introduced to the custom knife world with its infinite creative possibilities. Through his successful collaboration with Owen Wood, Amayak fulfills his creative dreams engraving objects that had always fascinated him.

11 Giving the background a matte texture with a punch. The punch has an edge with several dots.

12 Creating a very fine matt texture on part of design.

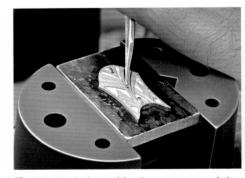

13 After the background has been cut away and then given a texture, it is time for sculpting. Amayak uses the flat chisel and chasing hammer to model each form of the design in a high relief.

14 The chiseled surfaces have to be worked using a variety of die sinker's riffler files, various stones, and sanding sticks to achieve a perfectly smooth finish.

15 After the stoning process, special wheels are used with a micro-motor for the final polishing.

16 The two 18k gold front bolsters are ready for the final polishing.

17 Finishing the sculptured relief on the rear gold bolster with a sanding stick.

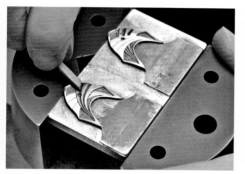

18 Finishing the sculptured relief on the other bolster.

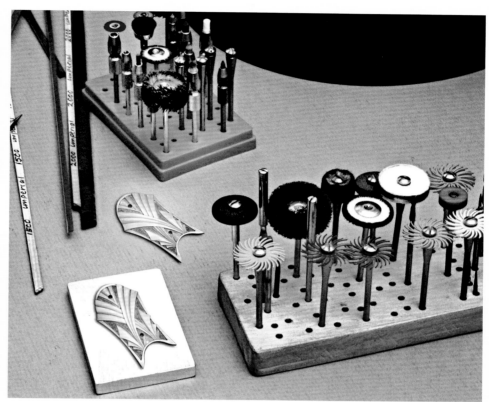

19 The front gold bolsters and a variety of tools, polishing wheels and sanding sticks that were used for the finishing stages.

20 All four 18k rose gold bolsters for Owen Wood's folding dagger are finally completed.

21 Front and rear 18k rose gold bolsters engraved in hugh relief on the finished folding dagger.

22 The finished parts of the folder ready for final assembly, front and rear bolsters, Damascus blade, spacer, liners, fasteners and the Black-lip scales, all lying on the original engraver's artwork.

Boaz Shadmot
"Mokume Gane Fittings", 2005

Boaz Shadmot was born in Petah Tikva, Israel, in 1949. As a small child, his attention was aroused when he saw a Turkish sword owned by one of the city's elders. This event was left nesting for many years in the back of his mind. Being a farmer and part time farrier released the blade-smithing bug out into the open when the time was right. Boaz owes special thanks to Jerry Fisk and Steven Schwarzer for the patience, support and assistance he received from them, despite  being thousands of miles away. Above all he wants to thank his wife, Ruti, for being there by his side all the way. Boaz prefers making pattern welded knives and swords, using recycled steels for the blades and organic materials for the handles.

Moshav Paran 71
DN Arava 86835, ISRAEL
Mobile phone: (+972) 523-666458
email: srb@arava.co.il

1 Flat pieces of fine silver and sheets of pure copper are selected to begin the process of making mokume gane. The materials are cleaned, sanded and "pickled" in a weak acid.

3 When the assembly is heated to the proper temperature, it is removed from the forge, placed carefully on the anvil, lightly tapped with a hammer and left to cool.

"Mokume Gane Fittings", 2005 The blade has a Turkish Ribbon pattern Damascus core and a Twisted Star Damascus cutting edge. Materials used were 4340, 1020, 5160 and 52100, bone handle and mokume gane fittings. Overall length 11" (280 mm).

6 The mokume gane billet is hot forged to reduce its thickness, providing for better bonding of all layers within the billet.

10 More grooves are cut in the billet to create the planned pattern for the mokume gane.

2 The silver and copper pieces are stacked alternately on a pressure-plate jig. The jig is then assembled, bolted tight and fired in the forge.

4 The bonded billet of the mokume gane is cleaned and the sides are sanded to check for flaws and de-lamination that might have occurred.

5 A close view of the pressure-plate jig. The bolts hold the heavy steel pressure plates. The newspaper pieces are placed on a refractory mortar in order to avoid contact between the pressure plates and the laminated pieces. Using a torque wrench, the bolts are tightened to provide equal pressure all around, keeping the billet level and assisting in accurate bonding. The jig is then fired in the forge, the same forge used to forge weld the steel billets to construct the blade.

7 Using a chisel, a groove is cut into the billet exposing the internal layers.

8 The exposed internal layers can be seen here, after the cut is done.

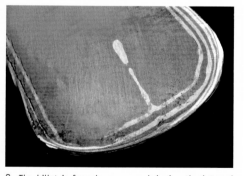

9 The billet is forged once more bringing the internal layers up to the surface.

11 The billet is forged again, cleaned and sanded to reveal the beauty of the final pattern.

12 All knife parts are shown before final assembly. The blade, the bone handle, the mokume guard, butt piece, nut and ferrule and two leather spacers.

13 Pattern welded steel, mokume gane and bone in harmony.

Michael Andersson
"Mimer", 2005

Michael Andersson, born in 1959, lives with his family in the idyllic village of Bullmark, near Umea in the north of Sweden. A man of many interests, with a love for hunting, long trips in the great outdoors on horseback or on his snowmobile, hand-gliding, windsurfing, karate and bodybuilding. For 20 years he owned a spray-painting shop with two friends doing various custom painting jobs. Knives were a great attraction since the days he was a little boy and hunting

showed him how important it was to own a good knife. In 2000 he was introduced to forging in a course on pattern welding held with Jano Knives, and demonstrated by Roger Bergh. Michael has the pleasure of working with his eldest son Andre, a talented knifemaker as well.

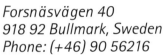

Forsnäsvägen 40
918 92 Bullmark, Sweden
Phone: (+46) 90 56216
email: Mickandersson@hotmail.com
Site: http://www.moosecountry.nu/

1 Material used for the sides of the blade are pure nickel strips in two sizes, 95x100mm and 10x100mm, and mild 10x10x100mm steel bars.

3 In the forge, the stacked billet is brought to a bonding temperature. The workshop was built in an old barn, dividing it into several sections, a smithy and a four room workshop with heated floors for the long and cold winters.

6 After forge welding the big billet together, it is now forged down to a 25x25mm (1"x1") sized bar, that will be cut into 3 pieces.

"Mimer", 2005 Named after the "Well of Knowledge" in the old Scandinavian mythology, Mimer's blade is made in a San Mai technique using Swedish tool steel for the cutting edge (15N20 and 20C), going through the whole blade, forged with a twist. Slices of Web Mosaic made from mild steel and pure Nickel are then forged on both sides of the cutting edge. Handle is ancient walrus ivory, Overall length is 11 3/8" (290 mm).

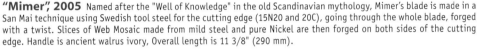

10 The hand forged blade.

2 Surrounding the mild steel bars with nickel on all sides, they are all welded together ending up with a rather heavy stacked billet.

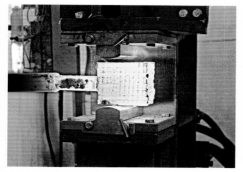

4 Forge welding the big billet together, using the hydraulic press, squeeze-bonds all the layers together.

5 *"I usually forge pattern welded blades with different patterns. One can never stop the fascination of looking at the beautiful patterns seen on the freshly etched blade as it emerges from the acid bath. We have a smithy supplied with all equipment needed to be able to make high quality custom knives and swords. For the handles we use natural materials, such as mammoth ivory and fossil walrus ivory".*

7 The three 25x25mm (1"x1") pieces are carefully ground, cleaned and then forged together.

8 The pieces used for the blade: In the center, the bar of Twist Damascus for the edge, made from Swedish tool steel, Uddeholm 15N20 and 20C. On each side is a nickel plate and the Web Mosaic Damascus bars.

9 The first stage of putting together the stacked material for making the blade.

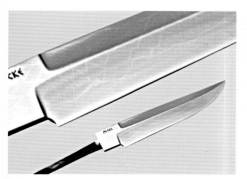

11 The blade after grinding and heat treating, ready for etching. The Anderssons have four different grinders set up in one of the four rooms of their workshop.

12 The blade after being etched in acid.

13 The materials and tools for the sheath. Stitching is done by hand, the old Scandinavian way, with the leather still wet. A piece of wood shaped like the blade is inserted into the wet sheath to keep its shape when dry.

Aldo Conto
"Butterfly Mosaic Damascus", 2005

Born in 1955, Aldo lives in a region in Italy were iron was put to work since the Roman times. His house is in the mountains, without central heating or a regular telephone line but with a nearby spring that supplies him with water. In 1995, Aldo started to forge Damascus learning the process completely by himself and becoming one of the best metalsmiths, even though he admits that he never stops learning. He refuses to use metallic powders in the making of his Damascus and works only with metal bars that he forges himself using a 50 years old hammer. Aldo shapes his steel on an anvil made in 1907 using a pair of blacksmith's thongs

over a hundred years old. Aldo has the wonderful capacity to understand the materials he is working with, and to visualize the whole process of forging any new Damascus pattern well in advance. Even though he is a man of few words, he teaches forging techniques and all his students have learnt to forge Damascus.

Frazione Piani
10010 Alice Superiore (TO), Italy
Phone: (+39) 349 184 2241

1 The basic components for creating the butterfly in steel are steel bars, iron and nickel.

5 The components are assembled in the required order. The spaces all around will be filled with iron and steel rods, not using any metal powder. It is now 2 1/2"x5 2/5" in size and it will be reduced to a 1"x3/4" bar.

7 The end grain of the bar shows the completed image of a butterfly but the process has not ended yet.

"Butterfly Mosaic Damascus", 2005 The bar of "Butterfly" Mosaic Damascus forged for the blade of the "Folding Skinner" to be made by Francesco Pachì and the Mosaic Damascus billet from which the the bolsters for the knife will be cut using the end grain Mosaic pattern.

10 The final stages of drawing and shaping operations are done manually. Aldo relies on his hand held hammer for the desired end result.

2 The components are arranged together in a steel box to make a solid billet. This is the first stage in the process of creating the butterfly's body and wings.

3 Aldo heats and forges the billet in a self-made carbon forge.

4 The billet has been hammered and reduced down in size. Now it is being manually arranged to put together the butterfly's wings.

6 The whole assembly is welded together.

9 A moment of concentration during the process of mechanical forging. The power hammer that Aldo is using is a very ancient but fully functioning piece of equipment.

8 Slices of the butterfly bar were assembled with various other pieces of Damascus, to make the final billet used for a blade.

11 getting close to the desired final shape. Aldo is holding the red hot steel with a pair of blacksmith's thongs that are more than a 100 years old.

12 Aldo forging and flattening the blade.

13 Aldo says that old forging tools produce the best results. The anvil he is working on was made in 1907.

Joel Davis
Forging "The Fire Within" Mosaic Damascus Pattern

Born in Minnesota, USA, in 1979, Joel crossed paths with the art of forging pattern-welded steel in 2001, at the age of 21. One of the first mosaic forming methods ever described to Joel, the "W" theory, caused an immediate brainstorm. "After acquiring the basic Damascus forging tools, the first few months of pattern experimentation were exhausting to say the least", notes Joel. He felt overwhelmingly compelled to jump head-first into the most complex of patterning techniques and made it a priority to exponentially accelerate his learning curve, leading him to where he is today. "At my forge, the volume and weight of a starting billet (20-30 pounds) depends not only upon the type and size of forging implements I have, but also how big a billet I can possibly handle. The ingredients I use the most, in order of relative proportions, are: 02, 1075, 15n20, 1095, 203E and pure nickel. When forging, grinding, heat-treating and surface finishing, each metal will behave differently, even when treated the same way. Each metal really has its own personality".

74538 165th ST
Albert Lea, MN 56007, USA
Phone: (507) 377-0808
email: joelknives@yahoo.com

The "W" Theory Manipulation of Steel, 2005 These are just a few sample pieces of Joel's high-grade mosaic Damascus patterns that implement the same "W" theory manipulations used in the creation of "The Fire Within" pattern.

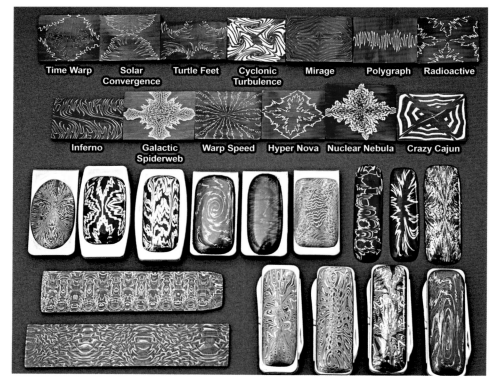

Time Warp · Solar Convergence · Turtle Feet · Cyclonic Turbulence · Mirage · Polygraph · Radioactive

Inferno · Galactic Spiderweb · Warp Speed · Hyper Nova · Nuclear Nebula · Crazy Cajun

1 The raw high-carbon bar stock is cut to length and surface ground clean & flat. The layers are then stacked in a strategic and specific order, clamped and arc-welded on the ends, to bind them tight.

5 The billet is then continually compressed, or drawn down and out, to strengthen the forge welded bonds, and to gain length for the "hot cutting" and folding steps.

2 At this point the tightly bound stack is submerged in a hydrocarbon (kerosene) to aid in the flux-less "dry welding" process Joel uses in all his Damascus. This yields very strong and clean forge welds and is also less wasteful.

3 The kerosene-saturated billet is then placed in the forge and brought to a solid-state diffusion bonding temperature of 2000° F. This can take up to 40 minutes for a large billet.

4 The yellow-hot billet is squeezed and welded under the 24-ton hydraulic forging press with large flat "welding" dies. This is repeated at least twice to ensure that all layers are intimately bonded to each other.

6 Joel developed a technique he calls "deliberate direction of 'c' layer collapse", where squaring dies are used to pre distort the layers in a specific way. The billet is brought to 2000° F and cut in the press with a special "hot cutting" die, that cuts only about 80% through, leaving a thin hinge of steel to help align and "book-match" the vertical layers on the end of the billet. The side of the billet that is to be folded back onto itself and welded is dome ground and completely cleaned (above) with a large angle grinder and a medium grit cup stone.

7 The cut and ground billet is now very quickly folded over with a hammer. The cutting and stacking (folding on edge) is the primary and most important key to any traditional "W" theory.

8 A linear pile of anhydrous borax is now applied to one side of the seam. The billet is placed back in the forge and the flux is allowed to melt.

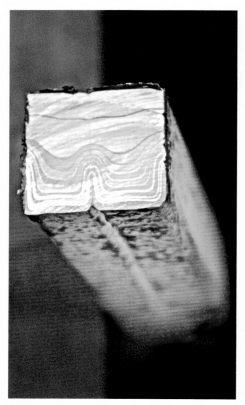

9 Again the billet is forge welded, but this time there are two partially compressed vertical layers on top of each other.

10 The consecutive cutting and folding of the billet will start to generate a "fiery" look in the mosaic end grain of the billet. The process was repeated three more times to reach this point.

11 A forging technique called re-squaring is now employed with the billet, to redirect the "fire" pattern in the end grain making it run diagonally. Done at 2000° F, great care must be taken to ensure uniform compression.

12 After re-squaring, the pattern on the end grain of the billet resembles fire flowing from corner to corner at a 45° angle. The billet is then hot cut, folded and forge welded in only one pattern-specific direction, creating a "phoenix of fire" look. At this point the billet could be a completed final product as bolster stock or could be further manipulated to create a more complex mosaic.

13 For the last operation of this particular pattern, the billet is cut again, folded and welded in a perpendicular direction to the last fold, to finally arrive at a pattern Joel Davis named "The Fire Within". "My techniques of successfully executing deliberately intended complex mosaic patterns are very carefully choreographed procedures, especially during the "pre-hot working" initial layer stacking. How long, wide and thick each and every layer is, will in turn, determine what the end pattern will look like. Staying one step ahead of each process, and anticipating what might happen after each process is critical in order to yield the specific 'look' I'm after".

John Davis
"The Vineyard", 2005

Born in 1951, in California, John Davis moved to Washington State in 1979, where he lives with his wife and two daughters. He has always been interested in hunting and fishing and as a result, fascinated with sharp, shiny objects. In 1985, John acquired a blade blank and, after much frustration, he finally completed his first knife. About 8 years later, he decided to try and create a knife with a 5" blade ending up with a 2" paring knife. In 1994, John met Ed Schempp who helped him with the knifemaking process and became his close friend and mentor. In 1996, John met knifemaker Randy Spanjer at a hammer-in and for the next three years, they forged Damascus almost every weekend and at least once a month they forged with Gary House and Ed, experimenting with different techniques and creating Mosaic Damascus. In 2000, John won Best Damascus at the Oregon Knife Collectors Show and received his Journeyman Smith stamp in the American Blade Society in 2002. It has become John's desire not only to create quality knives, but beautiful pieces of art that will last for generations to come.

235 Lampe Road,
Selah, WA 98942, USA
Phone: (509) 697-3845
email: jdwelds@charter.net

"The Vineyard", 2005 The abundance of grapes and vineyards in the Yakima Valley, inspired John to start a series of knives that pay tribute to the outstanding products of Washington vintners. The beginning of this series is the leaf and grape pattern shown here. Overall length 7 3/8" (187 mm).

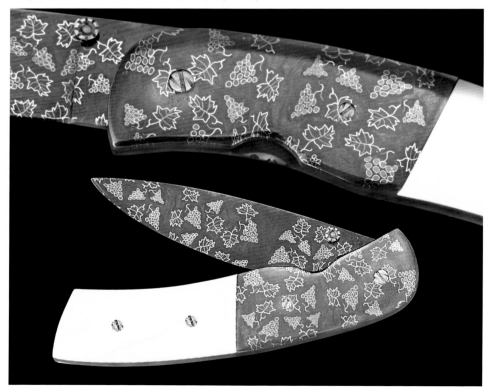

1 Assorted 1/2" and 7/16" drill rods are wrapped twice with .002" nickel foil, sealing one end, arranged as a grape cluster and glued upright on a piece of 4"x4" cardboard. A 1"x3" piece of .020" nickel, makes the stem.

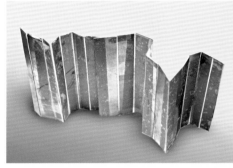

3 The leaf is made from various sized strips of 4" long .020" nickel. These are taped together, side-by-side until reaching a length of 8". Standing on its edge, the strip is bent into a leaf shape pattern.

6 The tubes of the second grape cluster are very carefully filled with 4600 powder, filling only the tubes and not the box. When all tubes are completely full and packed down, the box around cluster is filled with 1084 powder.

10 The 18" bar is cut into 4 pieces, stacked, wrapped all round with 1084 flat bars, forge welded down to a 1 3/4"x 4 1/2" loaf, normalized and annealed. A band saw is used to cut slab pieces off the loaf to the desired thickness.

2 Similar rods are wrapped twice with .004" nickel, sealed on one end then pushed out creating a nickel tube. The tubes, arranged into a grape cluster, and a .020" nickel stem are all glued onto a 4"x4" piece of cardboard.

4 Sheets of .004" nickel are slipped into the vine leaf pattern to create the veins. The whole setup is then glued upright onto a 4"x4" piece of cardboard.

5 Each grape cluster is placed in a 4"x4"x3" steel box, spraying a little WD 40 in the bottom of the box. Then the box containing the grape cluster with the 01-drill rods is halfway filled with 1084 powder. Tapping on the sides of the box while filling it, vibrates the box and packs the powder properly. This process is continued until the box is full.

7 After setting the leaf pattern in a 4"x4"x4" steel box, it is packed full with 1084 powder. Then the rest of the box is also filled with 1084 powder. Lids and handlebars are welded on all three boxes and they are forged separately.

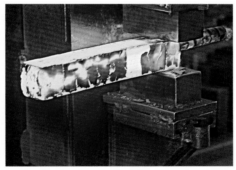

8 All three boxes are forged at 2250° F, down to 1" square and approximately 24" long. After all bars have cooled and the scale removed, they are cut into pieces 4" long.

9 After grinding away the metal from around the pattern on 4" pieces like these seen here, they are arranged in a 5"x5"x4" box. It is filled with 1084 powder, the lid and handle welded on and it is forged down into an 18" bar.

11 Laying the smaller pieces in the box, in a non-geometrical pattern, results in a free-form, flowing design. Re-forging four pieces, stacked side-by-side forms the loaf from which the blade and bolsters will be made.

12 The final result of the long process of putting together: 3" wide strips of .002" and .004" nickel, nickel strips of .020"x4", 16-17 pieces of 1/2" and 7/16" 01 steel drill rod cut into 3" lengths, 3 metal boxes 4"x4"x3" each, 1 metal box 4"x4"x4", 1 metal box 5"x5"x4", 1084 flat bar steel 5/16"x3", 1084 powdered metal, 4600 powder metal, WD 40 and cardboard cut into 4" squares.

Luciano Dorneles
"Tapê", 2005

Luciano was born in the city of Porto Alegre, capital city of Rio Grande do Sul. From a very early age he took to hunting and fishing, leading him in search of proper tools for the outdoors. Lacking the funds to buy good knives set his curious nature into making them. Soon he realized that there was a great deal involved in knifemaking, and being a perfectionist, he turned to public libraries and university libraries in search of metallurgical and technical knowledge. Luciano is self-taught, both in his knife making abilities and in the incredible machinery building skills he acquired. He built most of the power tools he uses in his workshop. Rodrigo Sfreddo, shared with him much knowledge and information and they became close friends. In 2001, Luciano attended the Jerry Fisk seminar held in Brazil, which was a breakthrough in his career. It helped him perfect his concepts of edge geometry and Damascus making, and supplied him with much information in other knifmaking fields. Luciano specializes in outdoor knives, hunters in particular, and the famous gaucho-style camp knives on which he formed his reputation.

Rua Pernanbuco, 554 - Centro
Nova Petrópolis / RS
Cep. 95150-000 Brazil
Phone: (+55) 54 3281 4512
email: thebufalo@hotmail.com
Site: www.brazilianbladesmiths.com.br/
dorneles.htm

"Tapê", 2005 Tapê, or "pathway", in Tupi-guarani indian language, is made of 15N20 and W1 Mosaic Damascus. The handle is giraffe bone with a Mother-of-Pearl escutcheon. Overall length 8 9/16" (217 mm).

1 Luciano starts out with four 150x15x5mm 15N20 bars, five W1 bars measuring 150x45x5mm and four more 150x30x5mm W1 bars. These will make the basic form that will be multiplied to create the final pattern.

3 Forge welding the billet he draws length, cutting it halfway to form two identical bars. Every time one does this, the grinder is used to flatten the sides and remove scale, to insure good welds.

6 Each new bar is forged to a triangular section. The grinder levels everything up and the bars are mounted to form a new four-bar diagonal-weld billet. The figures are arranged to form the planned pattern.

10 The bar is now drawn out rectangular and cut at a 45° angle, forming the final bars to be welded side by side. This is the Filicietti method for a strong weld and an undistorted pattern.

2 For the basic billet Luciano alternates the 45mm wide W1 with the 30mm wide W1 bars. This leaves a 15mm gap to be filled with the 15mm wide 15N20 bars. Everything is welded together, attaching a handle.

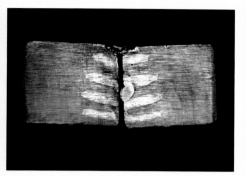

4 The result is revealed with a light acid etch and a new billet is forged from the two bars with the patterns facing each other. Forge welding and drawing length, the new bar is now cut into four.

5 Luciano uses the Steve Filicietti method to forge the final billet, avoiding deformation of the original figures. This is the key to any good Mosaic Damascus pattern. Here he prepares the bars to form the basic billet.

7 Forge welding the billet ends up as a square bar as seen here. his bar is cut into four, composing the pattern for the next billet.

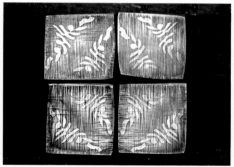

8 Careful forge welding results a radial square pattern. Repeating the previous procedures will result in a a clean and flawless weld.

9 This is the result of forging 32 bars of the basic billet.

11 After the previous step one gets a long and flat rectangular bar with the pattern showing on both sides, not on the end grain of the billet as before. From this Luciano forges the actual knife by hand.

12 Luciano grinds the blade using a 1" diameter roller, making it easier to grind the bolster's flowing curves as planned.

13 When the giraffe bone scales are ground to shape, Luciano uses his drill as a mill to cut the escutcheon's groove. Here the blade and scales are ready for final assembly.

Robert Eggerling
Forging "Crossroads" Mosaic Damascus, 2005

Robert (Bob) Eggerling was born in Beatrice, Nebraska in 1936 and his family moved to Kensington, Kansas in 1941, where he attended school. Kensington had a blacksmith shop where Robert got his first whiff of soft coal and a chance to watch farm equipment repairs done at the forge and power hammer. After high school he attended an engineering drafting school in Denver, Colorado, and then worked for several engineering companies. After 2 years in the Army he worked in sculptural design and residential construction. In 1991, a magazine introduced him to the world of knives and to a video by Don Ferdinand on making Damascus. In 1993 Robert made his first Damascus billet. In 1994 he received the Best

Damascus award at the Reading Custom Knife Show. That same year, meeting W.D. Pease encouraged his progress.

Robert's goal is to keep on creating. He has four children, one granddaughter and currently lives with his wife, 3 dogs and 3 cats in Pennsylvania.

29 Oak Road, Mertztown,
PA 19539, USA
Phone: (610) 682-6836

"Crossroad" Pattern Mosaic Damascus, 2005 Slices of Eggerling's "Crossroad" pattern Mosaic Damascus to be used as bolster material.

1 This is the original assembly of the billet. Five pieces of 3/4" square 02 steel and four pieces of 3/4" square pure iron, with .040" nickel 200 sheet in between.

5 The billet is removed from the forge and taken over to the fluxing station where approximately 1/4 cup of "20 Mule Team Borax" is poured over it.

9 All surfaces to be re-welded need to be ground down to shining metal.

11 Tack welding using Mig welder. At this point, the shaping process is repeated (steps 4 through 8).

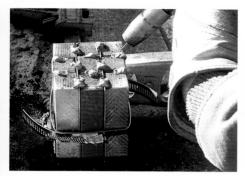

2 With a hose clamp to hold the parts in position it is tack welded on both ends with a Mig welder.

3 Home-made forge with squirrel cage blower, using propane gas. The forge is lined with fire brick and kaowool. The bricks in front are for accommodating different sized billets.

4 The billet is put into the forge and turned 180° every four or five minutes, until it reaches a bright red color.

6 After heating it to a bright yellow color, the billet is placed between the dies of the press and welded, turned 90° and welded again.

7 The billet is reheated and placed in the round dies of the press in order to give it a round shape.

8 The round bar is taken to the power-hammer, re-squared and drawn out.

10 After the billet has been ground and cut in four pieces with .032" nickel in between, it is ready to be tack welded with a Mig welder.

12 The finished billet with a slice cut off, then ground with a 400 grit sanding belt and etched with ferric chloride to bring out the pattern of the steel.

13 Summing up the sequence of events: 1 Original billet assembly. 2 Cross section of billet #1 made round. 3 Round billet is made square and reassembled. 4 Cross section of billet #3 made round. 5 Final billet made square from stage 4 ready to be sliced for bolster material.

Tom Ferry
"Complex Damascus Blade", 2005

Born in 1971, in Seattle, Washington, Tom's interest in knives was sparked when his father, an avid knife collector, forged a blade in their backyard out of a jackhammer bit. Tom started forging knives in 1995 and quickly became addicted to forging Damascus. In 1998 he proceeded to become a full time maker and in 1999 started attending knife shows and became good friends with many talented makers. Exchanging knowledge greatly improved his work, winning him numerous awards for his knives. Late in 2002 Ferry was the lead developer in a titanium based Damascus, now known as Timascus TM. He obtained his journeyman status with the ABS in 2004. His drive and obsession are complex Damascus and Timascus TM, with knives being the canvas for his art.

16005 SE 322nd St.
Auburn WA 98092, USA
Phone: (253) 939-4468
email: knfesmth71@aol.com

"Complex Damascus Blade", 2005 This is a collaboration project between knifemaker David Broadwell and Tom Ferry. The Damascus blade, created by Ferry, incorporates the collector's last name in Kanji (readable on both sides!), flower blossoms and a faux hamon along the edge. Tom incorporated 30 lbs of steel into 12 forge welds to create the blade. This blade, with all its complexity and characteristics, is truly the height of extreme Damascus patterning and progressive development.

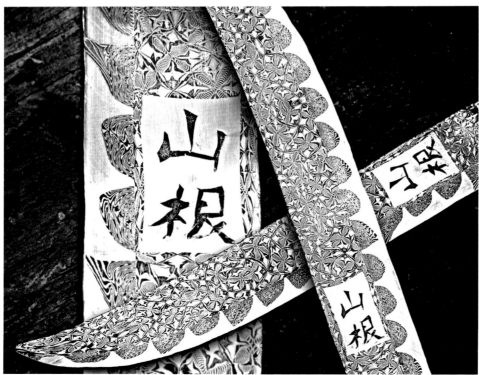

1 The first phase of making the Kanji consists of three free form molds for the powdered steels. These are made from 4" high and .008" thick 1018 shim stock bent to shape using various tools and shapes.

3 Machining of the billet will remove the fire scale, encapsulation canister as well as preparing a perfectly square bar for further bonding cycles.

6 Assembly of the Blossom Damascus for the blade consists of a unique initial layer stack, made up of 15n20 and 1084 high carbon steels. This will be tack welded together then forge welded at 2250° F.

8 The blossom billets are forge welded under the hydraulic press. Precision forging is not required as it was on the Kanji billets. The object here is to obtain a solid bond and reduce the billet for the next phase.

2 The Kanji forms are glued to the bottom of the canister and powder is poured into and around them. Outside powder is 4600E and inner powder is 1084 HC, giving dark letters on a bright background.

4 The two separate Kanji bars were machined, forge welded together, machined once more then the blossom pattern Damascus was forge welded around the perimeter.

5 Forge welding of the powdered Kanji billets under a 30 ton hydraulic press. The billets were assembled at the dimensions of 4"x4"x4" and they will be forged down to 1.5"x1.5"x12". This is a process that requires much patience and skill. If there is too much variation in forging from side to side you then run the risk of distorting the object inside, in this case the Kanji, into a non recognizable form.

7 The Blossom billets are heated in the forge and flux is applied to clean and create an oxygen free environment around the billet. The billets sizes are 3"x4"x6" and take approximately 45 minutes to reach welding heat.

9 Once the billets have been reduced close to the desired dimensions, the final forging will be accomplished with the use of height blocks between the press dies. This will produce a dimensionally uniform bar for the next step.

10 Phase two of forging the blossoms is to resquare the billets using squaring dies instead of flat dies in the hydraulic press. This will realign the corners of the billets where the flats once were. Manipulating the billet in this way allows the formation of blossoms on the next forge welding cycle. This is only one of an infinite number of ways to achieve this result. The possibilities and manipulations of Damascus are endless.

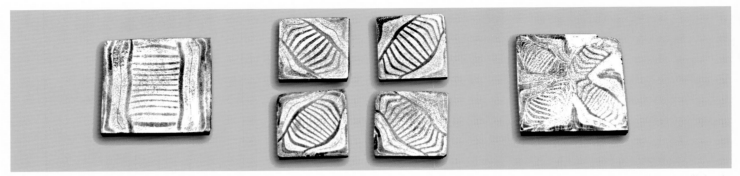

11 The formation of Blossom #1 created by the initial layer stack, the resquaring of the billet, then combining the billet to create a blossom. This simplistic blossom will then be recombined with blossom #2 to create yet another pattern altogether. This type of Damascus is termed progressive patterning, where two or more individual patterns are combined to create another larger pattern. The end result can be stunning as it demonstrates two or three patterns within a pattern.

12 Blossom #2 has been accomplished in the same manner as blossom #1. Although the initial layer stack has been altered. This particular layer stack is one of Tom's mainstay patterning techniques. Layering can be the greatest manipulation available to the artist and Damascus patterns can be significantly modified solely based on how the initial billet is layered. The random or precise stacking of layers as well as the whole Damascus process is only limited to the smith's imagination.

13 The combining of the blossoms consisted of 8 billets of each pattern, alternating throughout the billet. Once combined it is easy to see the progressive patterning that has appeared as well as the individual blossoms.

14 Notice the blossoms themselves are on the end of the billet instead of the flats where most Damascus patterns derive from. Being on the end can present challenges in displaying the pattern properly on a knife blade.

15 Cutting the blossom billet into 1" long pieces on a 30 degree angle in order to present the blossoms properly on the blade. Notice that the billet is no longer square, to account for future forging.

16 From left to right showing the blossom billet, the 1" pieces and the rotation of such pieces in order to bring the end pattern or the blossoms to the surface. These pieces, or tiles, will then be forge welded together. This is known as "tile welding" and when executed properly can demonstrate great patterns without a huge sacrifice of material. Pre-distortion of the billet to account for future forging operations is an absolute must at this step, if any of the original vision is to be present in the final blade.

17 The tiles are tack welded together along with a tile of the Kanji for forge welding. The 30 degree angle will allow the tiles to lap weld under flat dies in the hydraulic press.

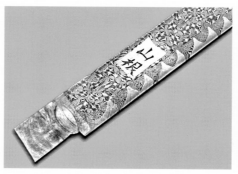

18 The final billet for the blade demonstrating how well the pre distortion allowed for future forging cycles. The faux hamon edge has also been combined into the billet at this step.

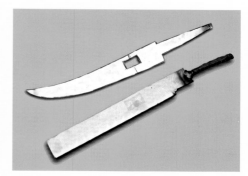

19 The forging template and billet for the knife with a cut out where the kanji is to be present in the final product. This will be the point of reference while forging the knife.

20 The complexity of this Damascus will require a higher forging temperature than normal. A proper and thorough normalizing cycle of the knife will compensate for this after forging.

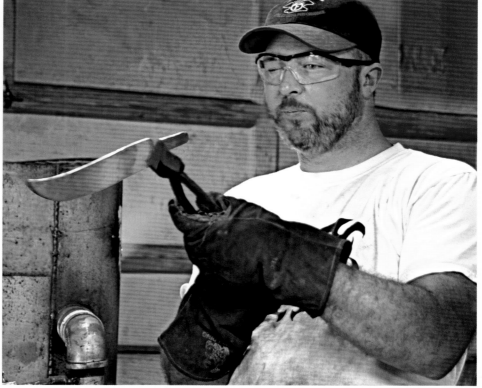

21 Forging the blade to shape is an art form in itself. Any errant hammer blows at this time can ruin the whole project, either by distortion of the pattern or delamination of the Damascus.

22 Precision forging of the blade is a requirement when Damascus of this complexity is employed. Every aspect of future knifemaking techniques must be considered, from the grinding of the bevels to the placement of the kanji in relation to the ricasso and plunge cuts. A precisely forged blade will result in a blade that is easier to clean up and grind, ending up with an equal Damascus pattern distribution from side to side.

23 The Kanji translates to "Root or Base of the Mountain" from top to bottom and will read with the tip of the knife pointed up. Notice how seamless and uniformed all the Damascus flows from one pattern to the next.

24 This blade shows the high level of complexity and control obtainable in making Damascus. The blossoms are bold yet there are delicate intricacies within them. The faux hamon edge is not a selectively etched variation, it is a solid steel edge within the Damascus. The Kanji script is very legible presented correctly on both sides of the blade. This project was a group vision that ended in a Damascus blade that demonstrates the current height of the art and the artist.

Ettore Gianferrari
Forging "Spirograph" Pattern Damascus, 2005

Born in 1945, in the little town of Bellinzona, Switzerland, Ettore completed his apprenticeship in cabinet making and decided to travel to Cape Town, South Africa, in search of new opportunities. There he met Elaine, and together they established a successful interior furnishing company. They have two daughters, Michelle and Dahlia. History often repeats itself and so it is with Ettore Gianferrari, as the words "gian" and "ferrar" in his surname imply, his family's origins lie in soldiering and metalworking. In 1986 he met Des Horn and established an immediate friendship which launched Ettore into knifemaking. By 1988 he was accepted into the Knifemakers Guild of Southern Africa, and ten years later he was made a "maestro"

of the Italian Knifemakers Guild. His quest for further skills led him to the forging of steel, and a return to the origins of his family name. Ettore has never sold any of his knives, but he sells Damascus, and enjoys working on projects with knifemakers and collectors.

13 Alphen Drive
Constantia, 7800, South Africa
Phone: (+27) 21 7946660
email: rettore@mweb.co.za
Site: www.kgsa.co.za/member/ettoregianferrari

"Fruits of the Forge and the Workshop" Ettore is also the creator of one-of-a-kind art daggers. In these he uses various combinations of his "Spirograph", "Twist", "Ladder" and "Laminate" Damascus patterns to form the blades and fittings. Seen here are three Gianferrari sole authorship daggers.

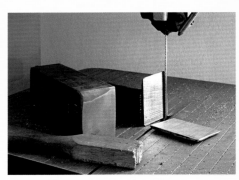

1 The beginning. Cut sheets of nickel, surface ground steel plates, and a section of mild steel tubing.

3 The first forge weld is complete, and the billet removed from the box tube (on the right). Note the clean removal thanks to the lining. The welded billet is then sectioned on a band-saw at a right angle to the layers.

6 The result is a uniform cross-hatched billet of steel and nickel. This is then forged down into a long, flat bar either in this position, or on edge, resulting in two very different types of Spirograph Damascus.

8 In the final stage, the bar of Spirograph Damascus being surface ground to the clients specifications.

2 The required combination of alternating nickel and steel plates are knocked into the tube and are ready for the first forge weld. A stainless steel lining sheet prevents the layers sticking to the box tube after forging.

4 The cut sections are then surface ground, cleaned, and packed into another box tube for the second stage. Liquid paraffin is used inside the box to create a vacuum at the moment of forging.

5 Ettore forging a billet down to a flat bar on his "Roberto Maccaferri" 60 kg air hammer (with the "Little Giant" mechanical hammer in the background). Ettore enjoys creating intricate patterns requiring multiple packing, forging, cutting and machining cycles in order to achieve the desired end billet. The outcome of the patterns is also affected by the ratio of different steel types, and quantities of nickel sheet, used.

7 The resultant bar then has 45 degree grooves machined across its length on both sides, giving it a wave shape in profile. Then it is back to the forge for the final stages of the process.

9 Two bars of Spirograph Damascus, two very different results. The bar on the right was knocked flat after photograph 6 stage, while the bar on the left was first rotated 45 degrees and then flattened out.

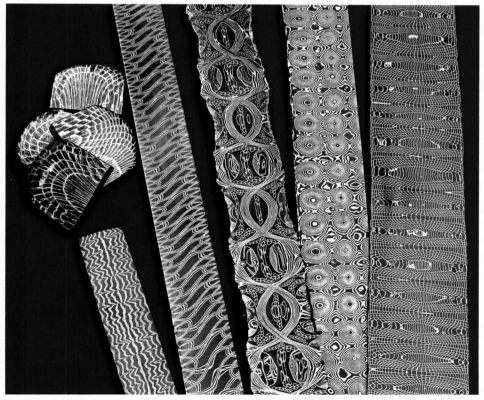

10 These pages demonstrate the process of forging one pattern of damascus steel, namely "Spirograph", but other variations are endless, limited only by the imagination of the bladesmith. From the left, off-cuts from the end of bars, a Mosaic bar, a Centipede pattern, a Mosaic Twist and butterflied bar, a Rose patterned bar, and a bar of Spirograph Damascus.

Gary House
"Mustache Project Mosaic Damascus", 2005

Gary was born in 1947, in Ephrata, Washington, where he still lives today. As a boy, Gary was never without a knife in his pocket. He discovered the wonderful world of custom knife making in the early 1990's. Becoming a serious collector he was fascinated by the Mosaic Damascus of the "Montana Mafia" Shane Taylor, Wade Colter and Rick Dunkerly. After attending a couple of Dunkerly's Hammer-Ins he got together with Ed Schempp and began forging Mosaic Damascus. He finished his own shop in 1998. In 2000 he attended the East Coast Custom Knife Show

and since then got to work with some of the top custom knife makers, supplying them with his unique Mosaic Damascus. In 2002 Gary received his Journeyman Smith stamp from the American Bladesmith Society. His goals are to continue forging Mosaic Damascus while working on his knife making skills, with the hopes of becoming a Mastersmith.

2851 Pierce Road
Ephrata, WA 98823, USA
Phone: (509) 754-3272
email: spindry101@aol.com

1 Pouring 1084 (high carbon) powdered steel. In this photo, Gary is demonstrating the process with a nickel star. After filling the can, a lid is welded on, and the forging process begins.

3 Drilling quarter inch holes along the centerline of billet. Gary uses a drill mill, but a drill press is sufficient.

"Mustache Project Mosaic Damascus", 2005 End grain view of the progression of pattern development. On the left is the progression of the "Mustache". On the right is the "Mustache" cut 4 times with radials added.

6 Grinding scale from the billet. This must be done between each forging step. Surfaces to be forge welded need to be clean to insure good welds.

8 Steel for a guard. Seen here are two triangles stacked back to back. These are forge welded to form the small billet for the guard. Forged back to back one ends up with the pattern on both sides of the small bar.

2 Forging the initial billet. A large mass is needed to begin with as there is a substantial loss of material in a project with this many forging steps.

4 The accordion cut. After drilling the holes along the center line of the billet, the pattern is drawn for an accordion cut. Triangles with X's will be removed from billet by cutting them out with a portable band saw.

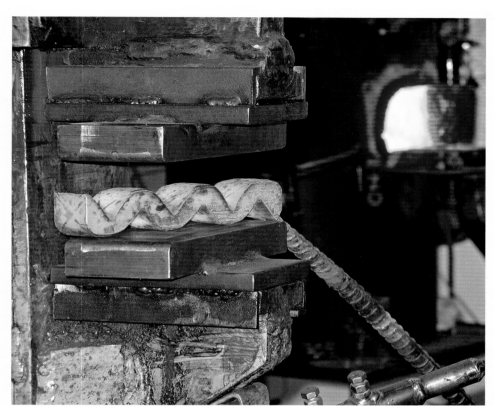

5 Forging the accordion cut billet. One can easily see how the billet is finished before forging. Every face of the angled cut will show the end grain of the mosaic billet on the surface of the flattened billet. The billet must be forged at a high temperature of above 2000° F. Gary uses a home made propane forge designed by Ed Schempp. His hydraulic press is an "Imagination Express" made by Jeff Carlisle in Great Falls, Montana.

7 The progression of pattern development. On the left is the progression of the "Mustache". In the middle is the "Mustache" cut 4 times with radials added. Billet on right is wrapped with W's pattern, ready for an accordion cut.

9 Forging the blade to shape. Gary uses a wooden stump to shape one side without distorting the profile of the other side.

10 The Finished accordion cut bar. One can see the "Mustache" pattern on the end grain of the billet. The stretched out areas on the surface of the flattened billet are the result of flattening the peaks and valleys of the wavy accordion bar.

Jon Arthur Loose
"Viking/Migration Era Pattern Welded Sax", 2005

Jon Arthur Loose was born in Albuquerque, New Mexico, in 1971. Inspired by his archaeologist parents he found an early love for history, and the tales told by artifacts of metal made long ago. A desire to leave his own legacy of precious objects led him to seek an education at Maine College of Art, where he made his first knife in 1990 and earned a BFA in Jewelry and Metalsmithing in 1993. After graduating, he travelled extensively and worked for several well-known

artist-jewelers until 1998, when he decided it was time to focus on his own work as a full-time professional. Loose is now inextricably rooted in the mountains of Vermont, where he makes jewelry and blades inspired by Antiquity.

P.O. Box 674 Moretown,
Vermont 05660, USA
Phone: (802) 583-1070
email: jonloose@jloose.com
Site: www.jloose.com

1 Two billets are welded together. One is 12 layers of 15N20 and 1070, the other is 10 layers of straight 1070. Traditionally, 12 layers would be a high count for a Migration/Viking Era Sax, with 7-10 being more common.

5 Each piece is carefully twisted with alternating spaces, to form the spine of the blade. The great difficulty lies in matching up the amount of twisting with the amount of straight sections.

7 The pieces have been bound tightly with binding wire, heated and lightly fluxed. After welding one side, the binding wire is clipped off and the rest of the billet returned to the forge and welded together.

"Viking/Migration Era Pattern Welded Sax", 2005 The pattern welded spine is made from 15N20/1070, with two interrupted and offset twists. The edge is a straight laminate of 1070 steel. Overall length 26" (660 mm).

10 The handle shape is forged in and the entire blade given a forward curve to offset the expansion that will be created by forging in the bevels. The blade will straighten out as a result.

2 Here the large billet is being drawn out on a reinforced treadle hammer before forging round and twisting.

3 The billet drawn out from an original 12"x1.5"x1" to a size of 20"x1"x1".

4 After forging round, the billet is cut in half. Each piece will form one section of the spine.

6 The billets have been forged back to square and numbered to keep track of order and alignment. The surfaces in between the pieces have been ground clean for welding.

8 The final billet has been ground clean and drawn out prior to being forged to shape.

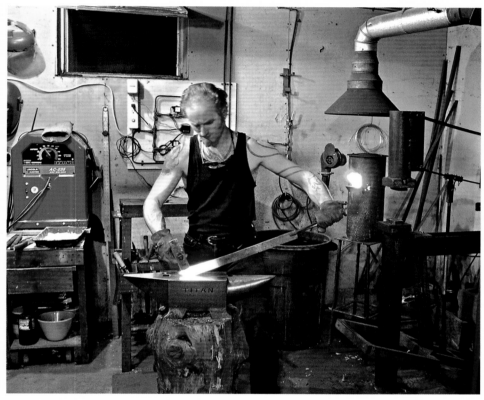

9 In order to make the edge material follow the tip of the blade, a portion of the spine is clipped off at a 45 degree angle. It is then forged up, forcing the edge material to flow upward. Care must now be taken at all steps of the forging process to shape the blade evenly, so that no part of the pattern is distorted. Migration patterns are deceptively simple, and must be very even to end up visually perfect.

11 The blade is ground to final shape. In the case of the Migration Era twist, it is beneficial to grind off at least 1/3 of the material to expose the "stars," underneath, meaning hours at the grinder.

12 The blade is being removed from a digitally controlled, propane-fired heat-treating salt tank at precisely 1475° F, about to be quenched in industrial quenching oil at 150° F.

13 The final blade just prior to etching, after it was removed from the quenching.

Rodrigo M. Sfreddo
"Perdiz", 2005

Rodrigo was born in 1974, in Santa Maria, a town with a strong knife related tradition, located in the heart of the southern state of Rio Grande do Sul. As a kid he started buying regular knives and modifying their shape and design to his taste. The growing passion for fine cutlery lead him to the stock removal method in by which he made knives for several years. Later on, when he began to forge his knives, he met Luciano Dorneles and the two helped each other throughout the years by sharing knowledge and experience. At first Rodrigo lived in an apartment and didn't have room to set up a proper workshop. His facilities were, at the time, located inside his wooden closet where he would lock himself while working in order to not disturb the neighbors. In November 2001, Rodrigo met Jerry Fisk at the famous Brazilian workshop. That day was a major landmark in his development as a bladesmith. Today, Rodrigo is an ABS member and is planning on taking his journeyman test in 2006. He is also the technical director of the Brazilian Knifemakers Society.

rua Sete de Setembro, 66-centro
Nova Petrópolis, RS
Cep. 95150-000 Brazil
Phone: (+55) 54 3033-0390
email: r.sfreddo@ig.com.br
Site: www.brazilianbladesmiths.com.br/sfreddo.htm

"Perdiz", 2005 Named after the Tinamou bird, the Integral blade and bolster of this knife are made of a 240 layer Ladder pattern Damascus. Wild olive wood handle has domed stainless steel pins. Overall length 10 1/2" (267 mm).

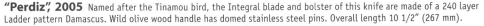

1 Rodrigo starts out with a seven layer billet. Four layers of 5160 steel and three of L10. He welds them together with the 5160 steel on the outside, and then welds on a good and strong handle.

3 The billet reaches welding temperature with flux bubbling all over the surface. Temperature should be even throughout the section, judging it by color. Precise hammer blows are more important then just using strength.

6 Before he folds and welds, the surfaces are cleaned with a steel brush, always applying flux to the billet before it goes back into the forge. It is brought to welding temperature and gently folded over before welding.

10 The billet is turned around and the other side is hot cut, proceeding to fold and weld the three pieces together.

2 The billet is heated up to a dark cherry color and then welding flux (borax) is generously applied.

4 After the welding process, the steel has to be drawn to twice the billets original length, before it is hot cut.

5 Working alone, Rodrigo hot cuts the billet by carefully holding the handle between his legs. This allows him to use both hands for the process and do a quick and accurate job.

7 Borax is applied throughout the process to prevent welding flaws. When drawing length, the bar is kept at welding temperature. This too prevents the occurrence of flaws.

8 The billet can also be cut and welded in three sections.

9 The first section is hot cut from the opposite side, relative to the handle, and folded back following previously described procedures.

11 Welding the three pieces together requires stronger blows, always keeping in mind that using more power also requires more control over the blows.

12 Once the welding of the three sections is completed, Rodrigo starts the process all over again, by drawing length, folding and welding until he has the desired number of layers in the final bar of steel.

13 The end product of this long process will be a quality steel bar, used to cut a pattern and forge the knife, ending up as a beautiful Ladder pattern Damascus blade.

Boaz Shadmot
"Composite Pattern Welded Hunter", 2005

Boaz Shadmot was born in Petah Tikva, Israel, in 1949. As a small child, his attention was aroused when he saw a Turkish sword owned by one of the city's elders. This event was left nesting for many years in the back of his mind. Being a farmer and part time farrier released the blade-smithing bug out into the open when the time was right. Boaz owes special thanks to Jerry Fisk and Steven Schwarzer for the patience, support and assistance he received from them, despite

being thousands of miles away. Above all he wants to thank his wife, Ruti, for being there by his side all the way. Boaz prefers making pattern welded knives and swords, using recycled steels for the blades and organic materials for the handles.

Moshav Paran 71
DN Arava 86835, ISRAEL
Mobile phone: (+972) 523-666458
email: srb@arava.co.il

1 The selected recycled materials for making the blade were, from the top, ball-bearing (52100 tool steel), tank chain pin (4340 tool steel) and an old car leaf spring (5160 spring steel).

3 The resulting billet is forge welded, cut into 4 pieces, re-stacked and re-welded several times until the desired amount of layers is achieved, in this case, about 90 layers.

"Composite Pattern Welded Hunter", 2005 The blade has a Turkish Ribbon pattern Damascus core and a Twisted Star Damascus cutting edge. Materials used were 4340, 1020, 5160 and 52100, bone handle and mokume gane fittings. Overall length 11" (280 mm).

6 Four twisted billets, forged to a square cross section, are placed together alternating one clockwise with one counterclockwise, to create the Turkish Ribbon pattern.

8 After completing the last welding process and the cutting edge is welded on, it is time to forge the blade to shape, grind, heat treat, polish and finish it.

2 Using his home-made power hammer, Boaz forges the steel into flat bars, surface grinds them to a clean metal surface and stacks them alternately.

4 Twisting is done at a welding temperature, using a simple twisting jig. The blade core is constructed of four billets. Two are twisted clockwise and two counterclockwise.

5 Forge welding is done at a welding temperature with light hammer blows. The billet is heated and fluxed with plain borax, reheated to a welding heat, placed on the anvil and welded, According to Jerry Fisk, the first weld is the most important one, so it is repeated to ensure clean future welding. After each welding cycle the billet is wire brushed, or ground clean, so that de-laminations and other faults can be detected and fixed.

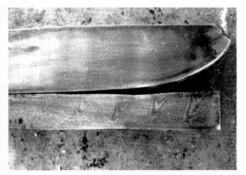

7 The core of 4 twisted billets forge welded and ground (bottom) and the cutting edge billet made of about 90 layers of 1070 steel and 52100 twisted bar (top), before being forge welded together to create the blade.

9 A close view of the blade after etching shows the Turkish Ribbon core and the Twisted Star cutting edge.

10 The first home-made air-hammer in Israel. This is a safe and simple power tool, made in 1994, following plans published by Ron Kinyon, and needs almost no maintenance at all. With its light blows, it helps with the forge welding process and mokume gane making. It easily draws billets and iron with a 3" square cross section, recycles steel scrap into flat bars and is a real time and energy saver in the shop.

Alex Shamgar
Making a Leather "Box Sheath", 2005

Born in 1945 in Russia, Alex immigrated to Israel in 1951, settling with his parents in a kibbutz on Mount Carmel near Haifa. He clearly remembers being attracted since childhood to knives, folders, guns and the leather works that came along with these articles. In 1963 he joined the Israeli Defense Forces serving as a paratrooper. During his military service, as a captain and later a major, he learned to appreciate the importance of having good quality weapons, especially guns and knives. He recalls one incident where in the course of a combat operation his knife, a Japanese imitation Kabar, snapped in half. Realizing that the army could not supply a knife of the quality he was looking for, he decided to make one himself: *"I acquired all the relevant knowledge in order to create my own knife together with a leather sheath. It was not long before I could proudly present my fellow officers with an impressive custom made knife and a respectable matching leather sheath which were both*

created by myself!" Over the years, Alex became a businessman and a collector of knives. He soon found out that quite often good quality knives lack custom made leather sheaths. So he began to create leather sheaths as well as fixed-blade knives of his own design.

5 Moria Street
Ramat Hasharon 47228, Israel
Phone: (+972) 3-5491538
email: Shamgar5@bezeqint.net
Site: http://www.alexshamgar.com

"Box Leather Sheath", 2005 The "Box" leather sheath and the classic Bowie it was created for, also made by Alex Shamgar.

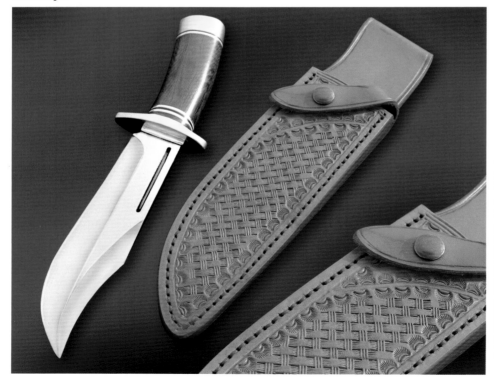

1 Seen on the working bench are parts of the cardboard model and the leather sections, cut from a solid sheet of natural cow skin and trimmed to fit the rough shape of the final sheath.

4 After cutting the leather parts, the exact fit and matching of all the parts is being carefully examined.

8 Punching holes with a table drill. A special needle replaces the drill and punches neat round holes all the way through several layers of leather.

12 After stitching, the bevels are carefully shaped and rounded off on a 2500 grain grinding wheel.

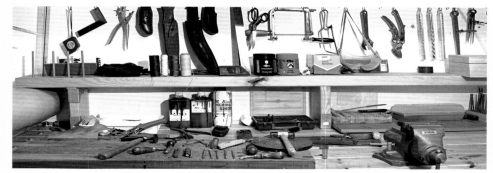

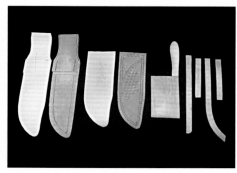

2 A general view of the working space made of a heavy wooden board, shows the various tools used in the process of making a sheath.

3 The 2 cardboard patterns of the sheath, representing the front and back parts are shown beside the matching leather front and back parts. The leather strips are fillers placed between the front and back parts.

5 Carving border lines and stamping a basket pattern within the lines. This process is done after moistening the leather.

6 Using the basket pattern leather stamper (# X-511). The tool is carefully placed on the leather and stamped onto it with a single tap of the hammer.

7 Using a shell pattern leather border-stamper (# D-436) along the interior borders of the design. The single tap ensures a clean-cut result.

9 A closer look at the needle penetrating the leather to create a clean round hole.

10 The sheath is being gripped in a special wooden vice and the stitching process is done with 2 needles on both ends of the thread.

11 A close look at the process Alex uses for stitching leather, working with two needles from both sides simultaneously. The result is very long-lasting no matter how much rough handling the sheath goes through.

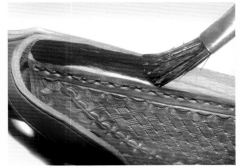

13 Dying the leather sheath all over with a brush using a special leather dye solution used by shoemakers.

14 The bevels are polished and dyed with thick paint to emphasize and seal the border lines of the sheath. The final stage is oiling the leather with a special saddle ointment.

15 A closer view of the finished sheath with the knife in place. The design for the knife, a classic Bowie hand made by Alex, was inspired by knives of the late John Nelson Cooper.

Alex Shamgar

(continued)

Making the "Purple Tongue Lizard Sheath", 2005

1 The workshop table and a massive 50x90 cm wooden board are used for the process of making leather sheaths. The flat stainless steel anvil is where Alex stamps patterns on the leather.

3 To give the leather work an exotic and fancy look, Alex used an old African lizard skin. Snake and baby crocodile skin can be used as well. Alternately, artificial imitations are also suitable.

"The Purple Tongue Lizard Sheath", 2005 Custom made cowhide sheath inlaid with African lizard skin, decorated with tooling. Made for a skinner knife by Rudi Zirlin with an African cider handle, silver guard and forged Damascus blade. Overall length of the knife 10 1/4"(260 mm).

6 The three main parts of the sheath are laid out before the gluing stage. These are the front, back and the belt loop. In this sheath model the belt loop and the safety strap are made of one flowing piece of leather.

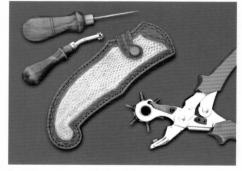

8 All three parts are glued and then sewn together. Having polished the sheath borders, Alex uses a dying agent to create the final patina. To protect against moisture and wear, saddle oil is recommended.

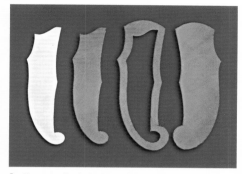

2 First step in designing a leather sheath is cutting a cardboard pattern to fit the knife. A custom made sheath will only fit the knife it is designed for. Here are the cardboard pattern and leather front and back pieces.

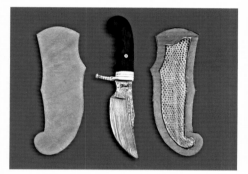

4 An inside look at the front and back pieces where the lizard skin is adhered using contact glue. Repetitive shapes and curves in the knife and in the leather sheath, create a visual harmony.

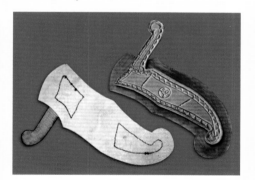

7 Now the rear part of the sheath and the belt loop are sewn together. They are seen here from both sides.

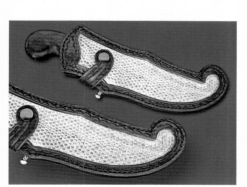

9 The finished sheath and some basic tools.

5 The crease around the leather shape is trimmed and marked on the board. This is done by an overstitch wheel that marks the holes for sewing the leather.

10 Alex uses a bench drill to make the sewing holes. He replaces the drill piece with a massive sharp needle. The needle is 10 cm long and at least 2 mm in diameter. It will make a hole suitable for 2 crossing threads to make a very strong and long lasting sheath.

Epilogue

Opposite:

Eliezer Weishoff, Israel

Eliezer Weishoff, a leading and outstanding Israeli artist and sculptor, was born in Jerusalem in 1938. He is today one of Israel's most prominent and exceptional artists to have attained international recognition. His unique personal style and the multi-faceted artistic media employed by him, have greatly contributed to his success in a wide range of diversified art fields. *http://www.weishoff.com*

Aftermarket Custom Adornment, 2005

Lost-wax casting and hand finished, this beautifully flowing designed silver handle-slab is attached to the flat surface of the handle of a Spyderco "Native" stainless steel knife (SP-C41PS). A Limited series signed by the artist. Blade, partly serrated, is 3 1/8" (79 mm) long AUS10 stainless steel. Overall length 7" (178 mm).

One more mega project has come to an end, and it is time to sit back and really take stock. When surveying the world of custom knifemaking as a whole, it is quite obvious that the work of one hundred custom knifemakers and knife-related artists is a mere drop in the ocean. On the other hand, it is worth considering that even a single drop from the ocean, when observed under a microscope, is an infinite world of wonder. It is also quite representative in many ways of the vast stretches of sea from which it came.

One thing that stands out about this wonderful group of people is their love for steel. This love is the heart and soul of their art. And it is what brings them all together. Few could say this better than Van Barnett - poet, artist and world-class art knifemaker extraordinaire.

How and Why

Van Barnett

Artistry from the mind with a breath of life from the soul,
a thousand thoughts and possibilities to make each
  creation whole.
The need to share what I felt when I gave the steel life,
for each piece is a feeling I never have twice.
I wish to share what I am so that all may understand
that they hold part of me within the palm of their hand.
For as those who have gone and those yet to be,
their creations will remain for all the world to see.
So I create what I feel whether in steel, canvas or clay,
and share what's within with each passing day.

Maker's Index

Opposite:

Edward Bradichansky, Israel

Born in 1948, in The Ukraine, Edward immigrated to Israel in 1978 and lived in Rehovot. He combined a rare artistic talent in everything he did, and was a technical designer, engineer, gunsmith, musician and custom knifemaker. Three of his designs were introduced to the cutlery world in conjunction with Spyderco. In 1999, while driving home from a visit to an artist's village in Israel, Edward was killed when he was ambushed by terrorists.

"Bat Push-dagger", 1990

An original design with a silver handle and ruby eyes set in gold. The knife comes inserted into a large bronze castle-like stand with the winged bat seeming to take off from the roof. The blade carries the maker's mark and his typical heart shaped cutout. Overall length 7 1/8" (181 mm).

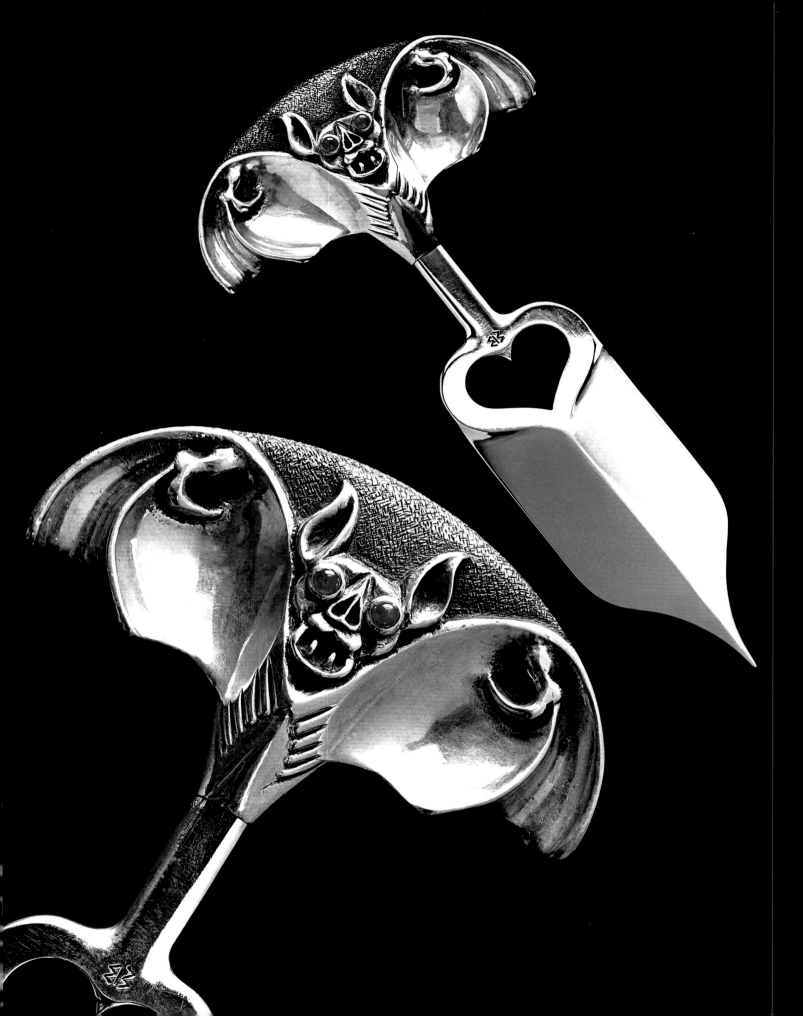

Related Books

Allara Roberto, **Hand-crafted Knives, Masterpieces of American Knifemakers**, Priuli & Verlucca, 1999

Allara Roberto, **The World of Custom Knives**, Tipografia Edizioni Saviolo, 2001

Darom David, Dr., **Art and Design in Modern Custom Folding Knives**, DDD and Tipografia Edizioni Saviolo, 2003

Darom David, Dr., **Art and Design in Modern Custom Fixed-Blade Knives**, DDD and Tipografia Edizioni Saviolo, 2005

Fowler Ed, **Knife Talk**, Krause Publications, 1998

Hughes B. R. and C. Houston Price, **Master of the Forge**, Knife World Books, 1996

Kapp Leon and Hiroko and Yoshindo Yoshihara, **Modern Japanese Swords and Swordsmiths**, Kodansha International, 2002

Kertzman Joe, 24th Annual **KNIVES 2004**, Krause Publications, 2003

Kertzman Joe, 25th Annual **KNIVES 2005**, Krause Publications, 2004

Kertzman Joe, editor, **Blade's Guide To Making Knives**, KP Books, 2005

Pascal Dominique, **Collectable Pocket Knives**, Flammarion Inc., 2001

Schroen Karl, **The Hand Forged Knife**, Knife World Publications, 1985

Terzuola Bob, **The Tactical Folding Knife**, Krause Publications, 2000

Weyer Jim, Knives: **Points of Interest**, Weyer International, Part I (1984), Part II (1987), Part III (1990), Part IV (1993), Part V (1999)

Opposite, from the top left:
Robert Eggerling, USA
Mosaic Damascus Patterns used for Making Bolsters, 2005
1. Windmill
2. Snake Belly
3. Cross Roads
4. Cross Roads (fine pattern)
5. Fish Skin
6. Ex Plus
7. Slanted Quilt
8. Basket Weave
9. Framed
10. Jelly Roll + Cross Roads
11. Nine Times Four
12. Flag
13. Leaf
14. Checkerboard
15. Barbed Wire
16. Snake Skin
17. Snake Skin
18. Turkish
19. Square in a Square
20. Diamond
21. Spider Web in a Box
22. Trellis

The boot knife is an original design by Robert Eggerling. Made from one piece of Ladder pattern Damascus, the knife is shown approximately in its actual size. The material is 1095, 15N20 and O2 (129 layers). The design of the handle (two wings, each folded in on itself from opposite directions) makes this knife unique.

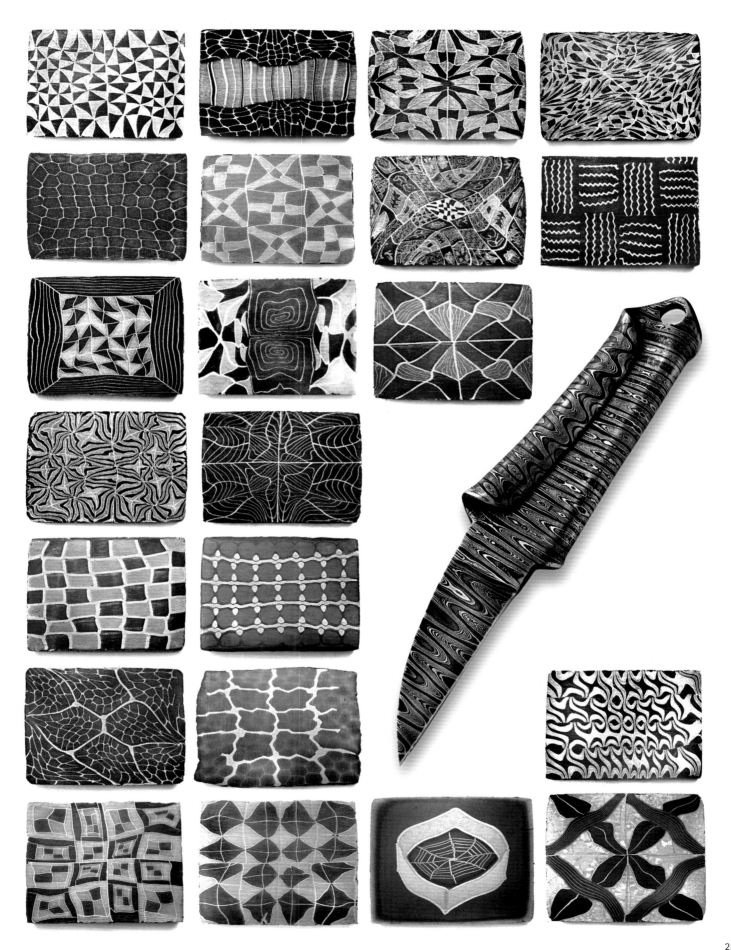

The Authors

Dr. David Darom, born in 1943, in Bombay (India), immigrated with his family to Israel, as a child, in 1949, settling down in Jerusalem. In 1972, his love for the sea led to a Ph.D. in Marine Biology, and he went on to become one of Israel's leading nature photographers. He seriously pursued his passion for documenting the wild life of the region on land and underwater, creating 21 books on these subjects. In 2003 he put together, **Art and Design in Modern Custom Folding Knives**, its success leading in 2005, to **Art and Design in Modern Custom Fixed-Blade Knives**.
Dr. Darom lives in Jerusalem with his family and is head of the Department of Scientific Illustration at the Hebrew University. **(+972)** 2-5665885, ddd@cc.huji.ac.il

Dennis Greenbaum was born in Cleveland, Ohio, in 1951. He is a marketing executive with 30 years of experience working in radio, TV, advertising, and related fields. He has spent the last 20 of those years as a brand consultant and recently co-founded a high-end firm specializing in graphic design and multimedia. Dennis has found that all those years working around leading-edge design have rubbed off and are evident in his work as a custom knifemaker. Most of his spare time is spent either in his well-equipped, home knifemaking workshop, or at his computer, where he can be found in any one of several online knife forums.
(410) 960-1473, dgreenbaum@comcast.net

The Publisher

Paolo Saviolo was born in Italy, in 1963. Climbing the entire corporate ladder for over 20 years, he became president of the Saviolo Publishing House in 1999. His publishing company has received many awards and constant international recognition for its exceptional printing quality and innovative page design. Ever attentive to his surroundings and ready to take on new challenges and projects, he will work where his ideas carry him. His operation is now based in Italy as well as in the United States. **(+39) 0161-391000**, paolo@tipografiaedizionisaviolo.191.it

The Photographers

Jim Cooper, SharpByCoop.com
9 Mathew Court, Norwalk, CT 06851, USA, Phone: (203) 838-8939
email: coop747@optonline.net Site: http://www.sharpbycoop.com

Eric Eggly, PointSeven Inc.
810 Seneca Street, Toledo, OH 43608, USA, Phone: (419) 243-8880
email: eric@pointsevenstudios.com Site: www.pointsevenstudios.com

Additional photography

Tomo Hasegawa, Francesco Pachì, Dr. Fred Carter, Dewald Reiners, Alain Miville-Deschêsnes, Chris Marchetti, Dennis Greenbaum, Mitch Lum, Oleg Yermolaiov, Mike Draper, Kim Aaron Green, Avi Mor, Johan Pretorius, Angela Ellard, Loretta Jakubiec, Hilton Purvis, Lynda Horn, Helmut Kempe, Brady Whitcomb, Owen Wood, Sue Broadwell, Phil Roach, Kim Davis, Dave Thurber, Nir Darom and Dr. David Darom.